Believe Me

Believe Me

*A Memoir of Love, Death
and Jazz Chickens*

EDDIE IZZARD

with Lauren Zigman

MICHAEL JOSEPH
an imprint of
PENGUIN BOOKS

Penguin
Random House
UK

Michael Joseph is part of the Penguin Random House group of companies
whose addresses can be found at global.penguinrandomhouse.com

First published in the United States of America by Blue Rider Press,
an imprint of Penguin Random House LLC 2017
First published in Great Britain by Michael Joseph 2017

001

Copyright © Eddie Izzard, 2017

The moral right of the author has been asserted

Set in 13.5/16pt Garamond MT Std
Typeset by Penguin Books
Printed in Great Britain by Clays Ltd, St Ives plc

A CIP catalogue record for this book is available from the British Library

HARDBACK ISBN: 978–0–718–18172–7
TRADE PAPERBACK ISBN: 978–1–405–92202–9

www.greenpenguin.co.uk

I dedicate this book to the Izzard family
Mum, Dad, and my brother, Mark.
I love you and thank you for all the help
and support along the way.

'How easily men could make things much better than they are – if they only all tried together!'

Winston Churchill, 1909

Contents

Introduction

I always thought I'd write a book about my life toward the end of my life, like Ulysses S. Grant did. Or Chaplin did. But I have noticed that a number of people (maybe lots of people) have done autobiographies in the middle of their lives, or even several autobiographies over different slices of their lives. I came to the conclusion that I don't really know what the rules are for this.

I think I'm a really boring person. I think I am naturally boring. Probably most of us are. Interesting people, too, probably decided at some point in life that they were boring and wanted to be more interesting. Like Che Guevara, who was a medical student, then threw on a beret, became a revolutionary, and became way more interesting. Billy Connolly, the great Scottish comedian, who really influenced my work, used to say in his stand-up material that he did certain things to make himself 'windswept and interesting.' I identify with that. It's bonkers that in this world some people are just trying to live and exist while I'm sitting here thinking, *Ooh! I've done some interesting things and now I'm going to write an autobiography!* But that is the situation I find myself in. I've done a certain number of things in my life and have now reached an age and a state of mind where I've come to reflect on those things. And some people want me to write them down.

It was at the end of the documentary *Believe: The Eddie Izzard Story* when Sarah Townsend, the director, who had been shooting interviews with me for some time, said that I never really 'say' anything.

I thought, *Well, I'm up for saying lots of things.*

But maybe I was being guarded, or trying to make everything very palatable, or funny, and therefore I never seemed to say anything that really cut through the mist of being a performer, an actor, and a personality of some sort.

Then, toward the end of the film, I started talking about my mother, who died when I was six. And that's when I said something revelatory:

'I know why I'm doing all this,' I said. 'Everything I do in life is trying to get her back. I think if I do enough things . . . that maybe she'll come back.'

I remember that when I said those words in the film it didn't feel like it was really me talking. Because it wasn't my conscious brain talking. It was my subconscious brain. And for some reason it was saying: *Here's what's really going on. Here's a note to yourself.* Something like that.

I think it's true. I think trying to bring my mother back is at the base of everything I'm doing, and everything I've ever done.

On top of that, of course, there is also ego and a love of adventure and trying to be, as Billy C. would say, 'windswept and interesting.' But it's quite a moment in the film. And it was quite a moment in my life.

So this book is intended to give you a chance to sit inside my head, behind my eyes, for a bit. I'm trying to share thoughts and feelings that I may not have covered in the documentary and that I don't normally talk about in my stand-up.

In a way, I've tried to live my life like a film. I'm trying to do interesting things so that somebody notices or so that maybe my mother notices, from beyond the mists of the living.

Real life is actually a lot of boring things with occasional spikes of interest. If you look at films of people's lives, they tend to focus on only one aspect of it because the whole life doesn't quite work as a story. We know how we like our stories, and they have to go down to the bottom at the end of the second act, and then come back up and win at the end of the third act. Stories don't really have to be like that, but that does get our motors going. Real life doesn't play that way, which is why I'd like to thank Sarah for making my life look interesting in the documentary, even though my life is lots of boring bits with occasional spikes of interestingness. She took all the boring bits out. Her film got an Emmy nomination for Best Documentary. Which means that my life story got a nomination for trying to be interesting, even though I know the truth.

So this is it – an autobiography – a walk through my life – in a nonlinear way. Belief or, more likely, self-belief, is central to what I have done, and that probably applies to anyone whose life could be deemed unusual. But I do also know self-belief can be used in a good or a bad way: some people with tremendous self-belief are complete psychotic mass murderers. So if you have a negative heart, then please don't read this book. But if you have a positive heart, then please do read this book. Because I have worked certain things out in life. I think there are certain patterns to the way human beings behave and I believe if you have analysis in one hand and instinct in the other hand, you can go a long way and live a life that is truly memorable.

Anyway.

Have a read.

Here we go.

PART ONE
The Early Years

March 4, 1968

It is the last day of my childhood. My brother, Mark, and I knock on the door of our mother's bedroom. Without waiting for an answer, we rush in and jump on her bed.

Because Mummy is ill, we have been told by Auntie Trudy that we have to knock on her door before entering. Which we do. We don't realize we are supposed to wait for an answer before rushing in and jumping on her bed.

Mummy is yellow. She is always yellow these days. I think she has some kind of yellow illness. Some kind of measles that makes you go yellow.

Not a problem.

I had measles before. I had spots all over. And then they went away.

Mummy is yellow. That colour is all over her skin. But then it will go away.

That's how it works.

So it's time for school. We kiss her good-bye (do we kiss her? I hope so). Then off we go. Satchels with books, crayons, and stuff. A uniform. A school cap. And then a car ride with Dad and we're at Oakleigh House School, Uplands, Swansea in Wales. The poet Dylan Thomas is from there. Is he? I'm six and I don't know about anything. What do I do at school? What the hell do six-year-olds do? I'm only just six – last month. My brother is seven, eight next month.

I got an Action Man toy and a windup watch on my birthday, or maybe I got the watch for Christmas. It's difficult to remember. Looking back, it's as if I'm not actually all there, at school.

But I am. I'm here, and so there are lessons – let's draw a picture of my house. Or maybe now I'm doing sums. Then there's a break and a run around in the playground. Football – not into that yet. Just run around, I think.

Then lunch. I hate lunch, as I don't like any food except sausage, eggs, and chips.

Then, I don't know, more stuff. Is this learning?

Now we're waiting after school for Dad to pick us up in the car. We're waiting with some other kids, too. It's what they call a carpool. Dad drives us all sometimes, someone else's dad or mum other times.

But today it's Dad – hang on. No, it's not Dad. It's someone else. Someone's mum. And new plans! We're going to someone else's house. For cake and pop (that's lemonade – we call it a glass of pop).

So we pull up in the car. Near our house but a bit around the corner. And everyone goes in. It's a party. An afternoon party. All the kids sit on one side and all the parents sit on the other side. All in one room. There's cake. Cake is made of sugar. I love sugar. I think it's fantastic. So I have cake and I have pop. And we munch. And all the kids have cake and pop and they munch. And the adults watch us and they don't have cake or pop.

And then we're finished eating, but there is more cake and pop there still.

'Can I have some more?' I'm Oliver Twist without the politeness.

'Yes,' say the parents (very un-Oliver Twisty).

So I have more cake and pop. The other kids have more cake and pop. My brother, Mark, doesn't have such a sweet tooth, so probably only has some pop. Or maybe a cup of tea, which I think is yucky.

And then we have some more and some more. Greed is good, says a man from a film in the future.

And then our dad is here. Mark and I are off into the car. Short drive home. And then into the house. A quiet house. It's always quiet now, as Mummy is yellow.

Dad (Daddy?) takes us into the lounge.

'Let's sit down on the sofa.'

Okeydokey. One of us on either side.

'Now, you know that Mummy has been ill. She wasn't well. Well, I'm afraid that she has got worse and now she's gone to sleep. And she's gone to sleep for a long time. And we won't be able to see her anymore. And she's gone up into the sky. But she will be okay – we just can't see her anymore.'

I don't understand.

'She's gone away. She had to go away.'

'Forever?'

'I'm sorry. I think we should all just have a cry now.'

So we do. Me, Mark, and Daddy just cry for between half an hour and a lifetime.

And then we ask to see her bedroom. We need to see.

Mummy is gone. The pillows are gone. The bedclothes are gone.

All is still. For Mark and me, our childhood is over.
I never said goodbye.

Goodbye, Mummy.

Our mum died on the fourth of March 1968.
Martin Luther King Jr. died on the fourth of April 1968.
Bobby Kennedy died on the sixth of June 1968.
But Apollo 8 orbited the moon on the twenty-fourth of December 1968.
So that was better.

Wonderland

My earliest childhood memories start when I was three, which I hear is quite unusual, but I think the reason I remember that early period so well is that it was the best time of my childhood:

My mum was alive. We were playing with kids in a gang. We were drawing pictures of houses with crayons.

It was great. No problems. What was not to like?

We lived in Northern Ireland,* then at 5 Ashford Drive, Bangor, County Down,† off Donaghadee Road. The gang, which was, as I remember it, fifteen to twenty kids, was probably only eight kids. Maybe just five. In any case, it included me and my older brother, Mark, and various and sundry other children from the neighbourhood. Age range: three to ten.

Writing now, as an adult, the idea of a 'gang' implies danger, criminality, drugs, mafia. Obviously these elements were not part of our gang. Our kids' gang was the kind of gang that wasn't trying to do bad things. All we were trying to do was muck about and do things that were slightly naughty.

There wasn't any trouble getting into this gang.

---

* I've kept up a distinct love and respect for Northern Ireland and for the island of Ireland as a whole. I really loved my time there, and I make sure to visit often: I always do gigs there, and I sometimes adopt a Northern Irish accent with other Northern Irish people, and they tend to say, 'Oh, that's okay. Yeah, you sound kind of right. It sounds like a Belfast accent.'
† Pronounced Bang-gor, Cowny Doi-n.

Later I realized with other gangs, cliques, and groups of kids at school that inclusion or exclusion could be very important. And very difficult. But this was easy. I was just in. We all were.[*]

In our gang you had to do stuff. It was rites-of-passage time. Which basically meant all doing whatever the bravest of us wanted to do. It was follow the leader.

I was a follower, as I was one of the youngest kids, and I was definitely eager to be part of this gang and do what the other kids did. I remember clambering over roofs of bungalows in the area where a housing estate was being constructed. The housing estate was half built and half not built. I was usually second to last in a line of kids. I remember walking along the top of a wall, like a cat would do, looking down at a whole load of stinging nettles on one side and a whole load of stinging nettles on the other side. Or maybe there were stinging nettles on one side and broken glass and concrete and spikes on the other side.

But stinging nettles: They just love existing, don't they? They're bastards. Stinging nettles are the Nazis of the weed world. If stinging nettles didn't sting, then they'd be fine, they'd just be stuff. But in fact, they sting and they sting children, and they make them cry, and then you can't get the sting away, and then you have to get a dock leaf, which is some other weed that grows near the stinging nettles, and

---

[*] Later on I found out that every kid in this gang was a child of a Protestant family. I had no clue about religion in Northern Ireland when I was there. This was 1964–1967, but The Troubles that were about to kick off in 1969, and had been around for four hundred years, just had no impact on me or my brother or probably any of the other kids we were playing with. But I do know that a Catholic family moved on to Ashford Drive and then later had to move out. I believe because they were ostracized. I learned this later. At the time we were all just kids.

then you rub it on the stinging bit on your body, and then nothing actually happens. The dock leaf doesn't work – but I was told that it did work – all kids were told this. So yes, stinging nettles. They were there. Death by stinging nettles was our fear.

At the housing estate building site there was a pile of earth at the top of the hill. The pile of earth was huge – in my mind it's about a mile high and touching the sky and mountaineers would climb it, but it was probably only about four or five feet high. When it rained, we slid down it on tea trays.* It was like sledging but in non-snowy times.

At some point we decided to throw mud balls at passing cars.†

But how do you throw mud balls? Just get mud and put it into your hand and make it into a thing like a snowball and then throw it at cars. This seemed to be the height of dangerous-kid activity. It could have ended very badly, but it was just something you had to do.

The bigger kids were doing it, so I had to, too. How I managed to throw a mud ball anywhere at the age of four or five – how it got any purchase! – I can't imagine, so whatever mud balls I threw probably didn't get close to cars‡.

---

*I don't know how we got hold of the tea trays, but it was probably planks of wood and things.

† This was a thing to do. Was it dangerous? Probably. But we didn't have a Health and Safety officer in our gang.

‡ 'That's my defense, Your Honour.' That's what I would say in court. 'I was only four. I didn't have the trajectory ability at the age of four.' Because if I had hit a car and a car had skidded off the road – then there'd be a crash and then terrible things would have happened. Then we would have run and scattered and been scarred for life and it would all be a film and you'd have to become a missionary and force people to take on Christianity even though they didn't want to. And then you'd have to become the inverse of a missionary to deal with that. And then you'd just explode. Forget this. Forget this whole train of thought.

The mud-balls day was a good one. I remember it.

Throwing mud balls and then trudging down the hill, and my mum found us. I've got an image of her at the gate, though she probably wasn't at the gate. She probably just answered the door when we -ding--donged. And she said, 'God, you're covered in mud! What's been going on?' So then there were baths and clothes in washing machines and then tea. And a good day was had by all.

Mum, who had been a nurse, was a very helpful and loving person. She would get up in the middle of the night and get me things if I asked for them. Sometimes I'd ask for a glass of pop (lemonade, remember?) or a mug of milky coffee. 'Can I have a milky coffee? Can I have a glass of pop?' I'd get out of bed and I'd go to my parents' bedroom door and just make this request through the door, not caring if anyone was awake or asleep. And Mum would always get up and get me a glass of pop or a mug of milky coffee. I couldn't do real coffee, so she'd have to boil up the milk in a saucepan on the stove, and then put the granules of instant coffee into a mug, and then she'd add the milk. She was obviously a very nice mother to be happy to do that at any time of the night.

There were also monsters under my bed. Apparently everyone thinks there are monsters under the bed, and I was certain there was one under mine. If a monster ever does manage to get under someone's bed for real, then that would be a bad day. I'm not sure exactly what monster I'm considering here but sort of a jellyfish/octopus/bear—type monster. Actually, that would be really freaky, so let's not try to 1) make one of these, or 2) put them under people's beds. An adult's bed, fine. Could adults actually deal with a weird monster under their bed? I think if the monsters started moving around, then – well, we'd get out of bed and we'd get a frying pan, and then we'd beat the crap out of the monster under the bed. Or we'd get a broom, and then we'd poke the monster out. No, we'd lock the door and set fire to the house. That's how we'd deal with a monster under the bed. If anyone disagrees with me, please write a letter on a postcard to the BBC.

I learned to ride a bicycle at the top of Ashford Drive when I was four or five. I had a little bike with big fat wheels and also training wheels, and Dad would take me up to the top of the hill and then, holding on to the back part of the bicycle so he could keep it vertical, let me go. You could get a bit of speed up that way. At some point Dad must have taken his hands off and then I was free.

Those were good days.

Once I'd learned to ride the bike, Mum and I would go shopping together. My older brother, Mark, was already at Ballyholme Primary School, so it was just Mum and me, and we'd go down to the shops. She'd put a little white basket with a clip – a pannier* – on the back of my bike, and Mum would put the shopping in – a pint of milk and a loaf of bread, basic things, not a hugely complex order, just from the local grocery shop. We'd go down a little walking path, then over a stream, and then back up. The shops were just a five-minute walk really, but it was quite an adventure, getting there and then putting all your shopping

---

* A French word that now seems like an English word.

15

into this little basket on the back of your bike. It was an adventure and I felt useful. Like I was helping my mum.

It was perfect. It makes me rather emotional thinking about it. I have found that, because my mother died when I was very young, I have instinctively locked the memories about her into my head. Maybe I've shaded some of those memories in with different-coloured crayons so that they look kind of brighter, but this adventure definitely happened.

There was also a department store a little farther away, on the main street in the town of Bangor, where Mum and my brother and I would go for tea. I didn't like tea at all, so I'd have a milky coffee or a glass of pop. There were other shops, too, I remember: a haircutting shop* and a sweet shop.

One time I asked Mum for sixpence for an orange iced lolly† – I was very addicted to orange lollies – and she gave me the money. With the sixpence in my hand, I started to run. I couldn't have been that far from the shop, since Mum wouldn't have let me go that far. But I took off and was running and running and running – and BOOM. I tripped, went down on the pavement, and knocked out one of my front rabbit teeth – the whole tooth, with the root attached, too.

Blood was streaming out of the front of my face, so much so that Mum had to knock on someone's door across the road and say, 'Do you have a bowl and could we possibly just dab this down until the bleeding stops?'

---

*You'd get a 'short back and sides.' That's all you could have – short back and sides. That was the only haircut available on the menu.
† 'Popsicles' for my American friends.

I'm sure there was a lot of wailing and crying going on, because I was pretty good at wailing and crying in those days.

So this very helpful woman gave us a bowl of water, and Mum spent the next twenty minutes dabbing at the bloody hole in my mouth. By then the bleeding had stopped, and we thanked the lady and continued on our walk home. But with the sixpence still in my hand, I still desperately wished to go and get an iced lolly.

Which I did.

Now, there are two things about this story:

One is my desperation to get sugar inside of myself. I just loved putting refined sugar inside of me, until the beginning of 2013 when I stopped trying to get this addictive substance into my body. It destroys all our taste buds and the sugar inside our system while we are teenagers means that Captain Acne comes to stay. I think the mathematical equation for acne is: hormonal changes + sugar = acne.[*]

And the second thing is the fact that I kept the tooth.

For what purpose?

Initially – no reason. Then, one Christmas, around 1973, we got a new toy called Plasticast. You'd pour this plastic liquid into a mould and then you could put something – anything – into the plastic liquid. You'd wait for it to set, but then you had an object set inside clear plastic and you could make a ring out of it, or a pendant or cufflinks or even a paperweight, using the little metal attachment bits that came with it.

So I put my tooth into the Plasticast to make one cuff

---

[*] I think there must be something there because very few wild animals get acne. You never go, 'Look at that spotty tiger. That young spotty tiger who's got a face full of acne.' It's just us.

link, and I put a broken toenail (my brother's) into the second cufflink to make a pair.

A toenail?

The story behind the toenail is this:

One term, a school bench had fallen on my brother's
right foot and smashed his big toe. The previous term, a
different school bench had fallen on *my* right foot and
smashed *my* big toe. Bizarre but true. If you can imagine a
school bench tumbling over and whacking your big toe, that
is not a good time for your big toe. Both of our big toenails
had come off. Mine was gone, lost, consigned to history,
but his was not. He kept his toenail and then I borrowed it
off him, and some years later put it into the Plasticast cufflink moulding set so that there was my front tooth and his
toenail in a pair of cufflinks, which I gave to him for
Christmas – probably in 1976.*

The tooth-and-toenail cufflinks are still somewhere in
the Izzard possessions, I think, maybe in my dad's attic,
maybe in my brother's, maybe they're nowhere, maybe in
the attic of the gods. But yes, that's the story of the toenail
and the tooth and the sugar and the running and the blood
and the gap-toothed photos from my childhood.

Live.

Run around with the gang.

Eat sugary things.

Die by stinging nettles.

---

* It's actually quite a punk thing to do, but I wasn't punk, so I couldn't claim that, but now I think
I could sell the cufflinks for a lot of money on eBay. We could raise money and build a rocket
with it.

These were the parameters of my early childhood. And then go home to Mum, drink pop, have a salad as the sun went down (yes, I remember eating salads as a child), and wave your dad off to work in the morning.

Which is something we liked to do – wave our dad off to work.

Harold John Michael Izzard – Dad – would get into his car, a cream-coloured VW Beetle, or sometimes he would get into his colleague John Taylor's car, a black Austin A30, and they would drive to work, at the BP[*] refinery in Belfast, together. We'd stand out in the street and wave to them as they went down the road.

Then they'd take a right and go down the Donaghadee Road into Bangor before taking a left toward Belfast. But we would run around to the back of the bungalow: in through the front door, out through the kitchen into the back garden, where you could see them drive down the Donaghadee Road into Bangor, the car flashing through the trees in the fields behind the back garden. It was all fields then – horses and moo cows and all that countryside stuff.[†] It was just as grandparents have described down the centuries: 'When I was young, all this was fields.'[‡] We'd wave furiously, which was pointless, because there was no way that Dad could have seen us, but we did it anyway.

---

[*] British Petroleum, which was once called the Anglo-Iranian Oil Company.
[†] I loved having fields or woods at the bottom of our garden. That's something I don't have now, but I do love that and I need to get that again.
[‡] And it was – great, fantastic fields. Fields with a tumbledown burned-out farmhouse that was scary and that had graffiti written on it. But fields with cows and sheep and occasionally horses in them, fields where we could pick blackberries and take them home to Mum and she'd put them in a pie. They were great fields. I'm sorry they're gone.

That's just what you do when you're that small. I'm not even sure if he knows now that we did it.

Apparently at this time my brother and I started speaking with a Northern Irish accent. I love that accent. Back then I would have had no sense of it being an accent. I do remember saying 'this wee thing' and 'that wee thing.'* Of course, you can't hear your own accent, so I don't know what I sounded like, but apparently my mum and probably my dad, too, were a bit thrown by the idea that my brother and I were going to be speaking with a Northern Irish accent. My parents were from Kent and East Sussex in the southeast of England, and we would have sounded totally different from them. I suppose that would be odd. But having the Northern Irish accent would have been fine by me.

We'd go swimming in the Irish Sea – or paddling, actually, because Mark and I didn't know how to swim, and I don't think Mum was a swimmer, either. We'd go down on to the beach at Bangor, which is a seaside town in the north of Northern Ireland. There it is always a little bit cold, so you have to be quite hardy to go for a swim, even in the summertime. We had two sets of swimming trunks: one had some kind of extra frilly bits, which were not good.†

We had a little blue plastic floating ship and one day we put it in the sea to play with it but it floated away. And we

---

*The word *wee* is standard Northern Irish, I think maybe Southern Irish as well, definitely Scottish. It means 'tiny,' 'little,' and I remember using the word when I lived in Bangor.

†My brother grew out of his and started wearing a new pair, which were just ordinary swimming trunks, without frilly bits. But I was still stuck with my lumpy, nappy-ish-style swimming trunks and I was not happy. At least they were my favourite colour – red – but eventually I got out of those bad frilly trunks and into better trunks, too. I may be transgender, but I don't like frilly things. I'm an action transvestite.

thought that was it. I remember watching the blue ship as it slowly floated out to sea, thinking it was going to be the end of that blue ship, but then some guy bravely swam out (probably walked out up to his knees), picked up the blue ship, and brought it back. What a great save.

Sometimes we'd take the Donaghadee Road to go all the way down to Donaghadee, a town to the east of Bangor, and there we'd run around in the sand dunes. We'd just run and run and run and jump about in them. I'm sure there is a lot more to Donaghadee, but in my memory it was just lots of sand dunes and we had a great time there.

Sometimes we'd go down to Dad's office in the BP refinery in Belfast, which was the big city, about five miles away. Dad was the chief accountant there. At the time I didn't know what he did. All I knew was that he worked at a refinery and that his office had electronic typewriters! For 1966, this was very advanced and I loved these machines.

The typewriters had a golf ball-like thing inside with all the letters of the alphabet on it, and you'd hit a key and the corresponding letter would go *fuhDONK*. You wouldn't have to use any force the way you did with a manual typewriter. You'd just touch a key and it would go *fuhDONK* and it would slap out a letter. I loved that sound, and I would hit lots of letters and make gobbledygook sentences and that was a fantastic thing. I liked being in the office because they had machines and early computers and technology and gadgety stuff, which has always appealed to me.

In my mind, I still imagine a fantasy life as an accountant. How crazy is that?

*

Some of the best parts of childhood involved Christmas. I loved Christmas. What child doesn't? Even Christ liked Christmas. I'm not sure of this, but I think he would've. Until he started asking questions . . .

Every Christmas we'd have presents and decorations and a tree. It was fantastic. Christmases were good then. They were all good, all through childhood. Even after Mum died, Dad kept the Christmases good. I particularly remember after Mum died, there were notes from Santa saying things like, *I'm sorry I couldn't get that toy, but I got this one instead.*

We'd have Christmas stockings filled with all sorts of smaller knickknacks, and then we'd have a number of main presents that would be around a tree that we'd open on Christmas morning.* Dad did all this himself after Mum died. There were seven years of just Dad and us two, and while I don't know when my brother and I caught on to the idea that there wasn't a Santa, and that it was actually Dad doing it, at some point we must have (I think I was forty).

But before all that, when she was with us, as the holidays were approaching, Mum would say, 'What do you want for Christmas?'

Then she'd make two lists for Santa – one for Mark and one for me – and when our lists were finished, she'd put the pieces of paper into the fire in the lounge at 5 Ashford Drive, and the lists would burn and go up the chimney to Santa. I couldn't quite work out how, but I still think of it as a wonderfully magical way of sending a message. Our fireplace was not an open fireplace but more the furnace

---

*In mainland Europe, it's all about Christmas Eve, but for the British people it's Christmas morning.

kind, with a little glass door that closed and kept the fire inside. And up the chimney it went to Santa Claus; we'd get messages back from Santa on Christmas Day.

Greed would kick in with me, as it does with most kids, I suppose, all around the world. I don't know why we didn't ever overreach and say, 'I'd like a Ferrari and another Ferrari and a rocket and two more Ferraris.' We didn't say that. I suppose we didn't because we couldn't drive Ferraris. But I didn't say, 'I'd like seventeen bottles of pop,' either, and that's what I wanted most.

Most of our requests were fairly reasonable and usually had something to do with the British television series *Thunderbirds*, a fantastic kids' series that was filmed using puppets.* One Christmas Mark got a plastic Thunderbird 2, which is the amazing transport flying craft with a pod in the middle of it that contains another amazing machine, and I got Thunderbird 1, which was a special rocket.

Several years later, somewhere around 1973, we got fruit in our stockings on Christmas morning because times were hard. I didn't know times could be hard, since Dad had always been climbing the ladder in his career. We were living at 74 Cranston Avenue, Bexhill-on-Sea, then, and I slept in a room with my brother: he was in the top bunk and I was in the bottom bunk. I woke up first because I was a greedier child and desperate for presents, presents, presents. Give me stuff! I have tried to calm down since

---

* *Thunderbirds* was loosely based around a rich American family, kind of like the Kennedys. It had a father with lots of sons who did amazing things but without the politics. Just imagine a family who had made a lot of money and they lived on an island where they ran an organization called International Rescue with amazing flying machines.

then. But back then, each Christmas morning I'd switch the little light on over the bed and then I'd pull the Christmas stocking down off the bunk bed ladder, where we had hung it, to see what I'd got: there were usually puzzles and toys and maybe a small book and a this and a that, and discovering it all would be fun.

But that year, leading up to Christmas, Dad had been telling us, 'This has been a tough year financially.' I suppose he was trying to manage – and lower – our expectations. So that Christmas, this is the series of noises that my brother would have heard on Christmas morning from up on the top bunk:

Click (the light goes on).

Struggling noises (out of bed).

Opening noises (the Christmas stocking).

A pause.

'Fruit? Oh, for fuck's sake.'

Struggling noises (back to bed).

Click (the light goes out).

When I finally got to go to Ballyholme Primary School, in 1966, I was very happy indeed. My brother had already been going for two years, and when I started Mum would walk us down to the school, both of us boys in our uniforms: shorts and a satchel for school things.

Primary school was great. You'd get to draw: 'Do a picture of your house.' And you'd think, *This is school? This is fantastic! All this school stuff is going to be easy!* Later on, when I was fifteen and they started adding in things like advanced maths, I started thinking, *Whoa! What happened to the pictures-of-your-house stuff? This stuff is really tricky.*

But still. Some hard stuff started right away: like spelling.

I remember being dyslexic, though I didn't understand what dyslexic was until much later, and I couldn't even spell *dyslexic* until even later than that. But back then, before I knew what it was, I was always spelling *cat* with a *k*.

We played the kids' game I Spy – usually on long drives or when there was nothing else to do. As you probably know, one person says, 'I spy with my little eye something beginning with *f*.' And then everyone says, 'Fish?! Fog?! Food?!' When it was my turn to pick the thing that people had to guess, it would take forever:

I'd say, 'I spy with my little eye something beginning with *s*.'

They'd guess lots of different *s* things – 'Sand?!' 'Sock?!' 'Sun?!' 'Solitude?!' 'Sobriety?!' and I'd keep saying no, until finally they'd give up.

'*S* for *ceiling*!' I'd exclaim as I high-fived a passing cat.

Everyone would look at me and moan.

I remember being in the first year at Ballyholme Primary School. Interestingly, these memories, visually, are of me. I can see myself sitting in the classroom, which is a bit weird because of course one wouldn't have had that memory. I see it like a camera shot, slightly above my head and to the left, whereas in fact the memories one should have are created by what comes straight into your eyes. So it should be a memory of what I saw from the desk up toward the teacher. But I don't have that memory.

And I remember the very small third of a pint of milk they would give you at break time.[*]

---

[*] Mrs Thatcher eventually got rid of those little third-pints of school milk because she hated children.

I remember running around in playgrounds.

We'd bring our sandwiches to school in Tupperware boxes and there was one kid who had this unusual smell. And this smell was not a good smell. I always said that he smelled of sandwiches, but if he did, these sandwiches were not happy sandwiches. In fact, he smelled like he just didn't know his way around a sink. I suppose every school has got to have one kid who doesn't smell good: 'You, sir, you will be the kid who does not smell good. You will smell of bad sandwiches.'

And there was a gymnasium where they performed plays, and even though I never got to perform there, I was always curious about the plays and the productions.

One day when I was in the first year (I was probably about five), some kid left the class above. A teacher came into our class and said, 'Anyone want to be in the next class up?'

Some kid put his hand up really quickly and he got moved up into the next class.

That made me think: *Is that how you get promoted, just by putting your hand up quickly?*

It was my first experience of someone getting promoted. Someone moving up the ladder of success (as it seemed to me). So I thought to myself, *I've got to learn to get my hand up quicker. If I learn to raise my hand really quickly and am ready for it at any time, I can do well in this world.* Under this logic I was thinking that you get to run a country just by putting your hand up. Someone would come in and say, 'Who wants to run a country?' And whoever put their hand up quickest would get to run the country. This is what this experience initially was teaching me with the lack of any other information: that if you just have one statistic . . .

And I remember that one day the Red Arrows[*] came and flew over Belfast. We were told we could all go outside and watch, so that's what we did. We all went up to the back of the school and hung off the railings and stared up at the sky. It was as if they'd come to do a flying display just for us.

But then one day, quite suddenly, we were leaving Northern Ireland and going to Wales. My brother and I didn't yet know why, but we were soon to find out.

---

[*] The Red Arrows are the United Kingdom's top flying display team, officially known as the Royal Air Force Aerobatic Team – bright red single-seater jet planes that do amazing stuff.

Upheaval

In 1965, when I was three and Mark was five, we went on holiday to Gothenburg, on the west coast of Sweden. This may be my first date-able memory. I do remember this holiday and it seems I was only three. It would turn out to be the second-to-last holiday we took together as a whole family. After that, Mum got sick, but of course we didn't know that at the time. All we knew was that we were going on holiday with Mum and Dad and that we were going to visit the Rydsund family: Tore Rydsund, who worked at BP and knew Dad; his wife, Stina Rydsund; and their children, one of whom I would meet up with again many years later when I went back to do a gig in Gothenburg. Because I always go back.*

The people in Gothenburg call their city 'Ye-ter-bor-i,' which seems wildly different from the word *Gothenburg*, especially since the Swedes call Stockholm 'Stockholm,' but that's what they call it, so there's nothing to be done about it.

Not surprisingly, the first thing I remember is the boat trip from Tilbury Docks (where the first Queen Elizabeth made a famous speech) to Gothenburg. Why do I remember this? Because it involves vomit. I think I succeeded

---

*I don't quite know why I always go back, but I do. I'm still trying to analyse this. Maybe I'll figure it out by the end of this book.

in throwing up a lot on this boat trip. Around this time – the age of three – I didn't know why that was, but I know now that I am a genius at vomit, that the bones in my inner ear don't do what they're supposed to do, or are hyperactive, or who knows what. But they don't serve me well.*

Back to Ye-ter-bor-i – the spelling, *and* the Swedish holiday destination.

On the crossing we stayed in bunk beds – a memorable detail, since this was probably our first time in bunk beds, before the ones we would have in 74 Cranston Avenue in Bexhill. Back then, waiting for the boat to Sweden, I was very excited to be sleeping in bunk beds. I don't know why bunk beds are so exciting to me, but they just are.†

What we actually did on that holiday in Gothenburg I can't remember exactly. We kids obviously went around and did things and drank pop, and the parents talked and smoked cigarettes and drank coffee and did stuff that parents do on holidays. We ran about. We probably went on boats on the boating lake. Stuff was done on that summer holiday and it was good. Then we went down to the south of Sweden where the Rydsund family had a summerhouse and we stayed there. We played in the sandpit and drank more pop. There must have been a ton of pop just following us around.

---

* I don't actually feel sick on so many things these days, but when I was learning to fly an airplane (yes, I can actually fly an airplane), and specifically when I was practising regaining control of the airplane while in a spiral dive, I really wanted to throw up quite a lot. After practising two or three of those spiral dives, I would say to the flying instructor that I had better fly straight and level for a little bit, otherwise my lunch and his lap were going to have an unrequested rendezvous.

† I'm now thinking as I write this about why they are exciting; I think because they are stacked beds and therefore it's a very simple rocket of people with no engine, but there is the potential for nighttime climbing.

I seem to remember more pop than anything else in my early childhood.[*]

At the Rydsunds' summerhouse in the south of Sweden I remember playing in the sandpit. I remember getting sand in my eyes. And then I did a lot of crying and then I got more pop. I think probably somewhere in here I thought, *Hey, if you cry, you get pop, and therefore, maybe do more crying.* I was always trying to work things like that out. Whenever something went wrong, I would cry in that 'Look at me! Look at me! See how loud I'm crying! Surely liquid sugar would be good right now!' type of way. My crying was quite loud. It usually involved the need to get a toy back, win a disagreement, or eat more sugar.

I loved that time – before Mum died. Everything after it was different, and not as good, as if it all happened in a different colour.

Unbeknownst to us, or perhaps we knew and had forgotten, Mr Rydsund had filmed our family holiday. Years later, their youngest daughter, Elisabeth, came up to me afterward at that gig I did in Sweden and said: 'My dad's got loads of 8mm film footage of you.'

The idea of it then, and later the reality when I actually watched the footage, was completely stunning to me. Because it reclaimed my family from my childhood. Mum had been gone, and suddenly she was back, quite bright and clear, in that faded 8mm footage.[†] There was Mum, alive again, holding our hands, mine and my brother's. There was

---

[*] Maybe that's what we should call my childhood: 'Pop: The Story of My Sugar-Laden Childhood.'

[†] It is all in the documentary – *Believe: The Eddie Izzard Story.*

Dad, smoking a slim cigar. There we were, all of us kids, in a park drinking endless glasses of pop.

Also unbeknownst to me is that this was when my father realized our mum was seriously ill. She had to come back from this holiday and have an operation in hospital in Bexhill once they worked out that cancer was happening.

Mum had cancer of the bowel.

And they had suspected something was wrong on that holiday in Sweden in 1965.

We came home, Mum had tests, and then she had to go into hospital for an operation, late in 1965, and then a stay in a nursing home to recuperate, while my brother and I stayed with our grandparents. I remember visiting the hospital and a nurse giving me a Barley Sugar boiled sweet. I loved the taste of it, but I never ate Barley Sugar again. I'm not sure why – maybe I linked it to that time. While it looked for a while like the operation had been successful, Dad would learn on his birthday in 1967 that it had not been successful, and that Mum was going to die.

Not a good birthday.

So, on the twenty-second of September 1967, Dad realized we had to move, fast, from Northern Ireland. He was already scheduled to move to South Wales anyway to work at the BP refinery in Llandarcy, in between Swansea and Neath, which are larger towns in the south of Wales. But the main reason they had to move quickly was because Mum, knowing her health was quickly fading, wished to be closer to her family, who mainly lived in Kent, in the southeast of England, and there was a direct road and direct railway line from London down to Swansea. She felt that would be easier for the family to get to see her, as she knew she was dying then.

My brother and I had been told that we were going to leave Bangor and that we were going to go to a house that had been newly built, which had a garage with an internal door so you could go straight from the garage into the kitchen in the house. I found this wildly exciting.* I thought this only happened in America.

But we weren't told anything else.

It was decided between Mum and Dad not to tell Mark and me that Mum was dying.

They felt it would make things easier for us and not make us feel really sad whilst Mum was living her last few months.

My brother and I have since discussed whether this was the best thing to do, the best plan to have. It's difficult to say. It's what happened, and because of it we did not live those last few months in sadness. But when she did die, we were not ready for the emotional loss.

We left 5 Ashford Drive, Bangor, in October 1967. It was a very quick move to a house that was owned by BP. Nowadays people in America go, 'BP, oh no, oil spillage, terrible things, Gulf of Mexico.' But for me growing up, it was just a company that Dad worked for, an oil company that was like a rich uncle. They did help Dad and us, particularly at this point in our lives. I don't remember thinking that there was anything weird about moving: we knew something was on the cards, but I didn't link it to any illness.

When we got to Wales, I ran into this new house, and

---

* Bunk-bed-architecture designs, certain features, new things, new builds, these sorts of things fascinated me.

into the kitchen to open the door to go into the garage. But when I got there the back door opened into a garden – which is nice – but it didn't open into the garage, this connecting door I'd been obsessively imagining and looking forward to. And in fact – there was no garage. Just a driveway. I was quite thrown by this, which just shows you how odd you are as a child. I didn't know about the illness, but I wanted to go to a house that was new and had that new-house smell.* And I wanted to have a door into the garage where the car was, I think because most American houses I saw on TV had doors from the house to the garage.

My obsession with America and Americana had already started to develop, but it wasn't yet an obsession. It was just a feeling of excitement. I was very into NASA, the space missions. And I was also very into getting free spacecraft in my breakfast cereal. This was late 1967, so NASA had already been doing missions for some time. Space missions were great and very exciting and toys came free in breakfast cereal. I remember the excitement of pouring out a bowl of cereal and hoping to get the free toy: whether it was a spacecraft or just a sock, the excitement was almost equal. Free things were brilliant.

I would pour out a bowl and usually the first bowl would not have a free thing in it. Often the second bowl the next day would not have a free thing in it. Third bowl, fourth bowl – nothing. Maybe the fifth or sixth or seventh bowl would give you the prize, the gold, the thing that Indiana Jones was looking for in a future film that didn't exist yet.

---

* Just like there is new-book smell, there is also new-house smell.

And then I would tear open the plastic wrapper and get the toy. This was a fantastic prize, better than a bought prize for some reason – probably because of the sugar in the cereal, and the milk, which helped the cereal get down your throat faster.

Kellogg's Ricicles cereal was my drug *du jour* – *de la semaine, du mois, de l'anneé.** Ricicles are like frosted Rice Krispies, with sugar built into them, in the same way that Frosted Flakes in America, which we Brits called Frosties, have sugar built into them. And then you could put sugar on top, too. Ricicles were bloody amazing. I could eat a bowl right now except that instead I would eat from two to twenty-three bowls, which is why I don't eat any breakfast cereal now. They did say on all the boxes of cereal that there was riboflavin, thiamine, and niacin in those breakfast cereals and I must have eaten enough riboflavin, thiamine, and niacin to save a planet, especially when I became a student and ate breakfast cereal by the box because I had no brakes on my sugar intake. But there is one thing I must say now and that is:

I have no idea what riboflavin, thiamine, and niacin do. Do they cure you of something? Do they help you do something? Did I run more marathons later in life because I put more riboflavin, thiamine, and niacin into my body than any other regular person? I have no idea.

Anyway, back to the free toy in the breakfast cereal. Which is yet another distraction, but bear with me.

All through my childhood, I would encourage Dad to

---

* Of the day – of the week, of the month, of the year.

buy cereal with free things in them. Then I'd have to wait for the fifth, sixth, seventh bowl to get the free thing that you usually played with for a bit before someone stepped on it and broke it (normally me). It wasn't until I was an adult that I realized you could buy a packet of cereal with a free gift and then just stick your hand in and root around in the packet until you found the free thing. It seems a much simpler way. But that took me about fifteen years to work out.

In my defence, I would say that it wasn't the central part of my life at that point – working out how to get free things out of boxes of cereal. But now I know. And, kids, if you're reading this, just stick your hand in and grab the thing, day one. Parents won't want you to do this, and probably it's bad for your anticipation/gratification sensibility, but that is the quickest way. If people are worried about hygiene and sticking your hand in a packet of cereal, you can buy one of these robotic arms that you get in a toy shop, and you could stick that in there. Or a fork. Or chopsticks. Or find a clean person and get them to stick their hand in and get the free gift. But don't ask the guy who smells of bad sandwiches.

One time I even got an oil rig as a gift! There was an offer on the cereal box that said – *Save up a number of tops from Corn Flakes* packets, and you can send them off with £4.50 and a stamped, addressed envelope to get an oil rig.* What a weird thing to give away for free in a packet of cereal, and what a weird thing that I just happened to be doing a geography project about oil rigs. I won the geography prize in the summer of 1977 with these packets of cereal.

---

*I think I was eating Kellogg's Corn Flakes by this time. I think I'd backed off the built-in sugar thing.

I don't think I deserved to. My dad had visited oil rigs, as he finished up group internal auditor for BP Worldwide (quite a long title, that), and by the end of his career he was going out on helicopters to oil rigs. So I said, 'Dad, can you get me any documentation on oil rigs?' And he said yes. And suddenly, a few days later, I got a whole brochure on oil rigs. There was a diagram of a drilling rig drawn on to several layers of clear plastic. It was one of those diagrams that, when you turned the first page, you still had the picture there, but it had removed the outer layer of the wall so you could see inside the oil rig. And then you turned the second layer of film and you could see farther inside. And so on and so on. So this was quite a diagram. And I pasted this on to my oil rig project, and then I sent away to Corn Flakes to get a plastic model of an oil rig. Then I built it with glue and painted it. And then all I wrote down, I think, was a couple of pages saying, *Oil rigs exist, they're in the sea and they drill down*, and I probably just wrote out what was written on the pamphlet. But it looked so amazing as a project, with blow-apart diagrams and an oil rig model. So I won first prize and I really shouldn't have.

But back to Wales.

The house was at 13 Cefn Park in Skewen (the address has changed since then) and it had no connecting door from the kitchen to the garage, and there was no garage. I was totally deflated. *No garage?* But luckily, there was an interesting thing at this house to distract me from my disappointment. Dad had these packing cases like you might see in *Raiders of the Lost Ark* when they put the Ark of the Covenant into a big wooden box and wheel it around to hide it somewhere in a warehouse in America. Dad had all these wooden packing cases because he and Mum had had to bring all our stuff back from 'Adan (which the British called and pronounced Aden – the 'A in Arabic means you should stress this letter and the A should sound like the *a* in *father*) in Yemen where he'd been for eight years with BP, where he'd married Mum, and where Mark and I had been born.

I don't know why we still had these packing cases – I don't know where we kept them when we were in Bangor in Northern Ireland – but we still had them. And so at the new house my brother and I decided to turn them into a hill-fort-James-Bond-headquarters-load-of-boxes-turned upside-down-in-the-garden thing. We arranged them so you could hide in them and run around and play Cowboys and Indians, Cops and Robbers, Venezuelans and Martians, whatever game we invented. I don't quite know how you play Venezuelans and Martians, but I think you spend most of your time arguing about socialism and the lack of oxygen.

The house also had an air-raid shelter, probably because this area, near the oil refinery and the industrial areas of Swansea and Neath, South Wales, was heavily bombed during World War II by Nazi long-range bombers.

Neither of these things completely made up for the lack of a garage with a connecting door to the house, but they both kept my imagination occupied.

Moving to a new house meant changing schools, and our new school was Oakleigh House in Uplands, Swansea. We must've joined the school late in the Christmas term. I seem to remember that when we got there, things weren't quite standard procedure.

Christmas was coming and everyone was in a school play – I was appointed a role as a raven. Mum was still well enough to be involved with us, and having been given a raven pattern by the school, she cut black cloth into a costume for me, with an orange beak.

There is a photo. I think my expression in the photo says it all. My expression says: 'Where's the connecting door to the garage?'

I was, I think, intrigued by being a raven, or maybe curious about being a raven. I think I was just curious, not intrigued. And there must have been rehearsals. And I had to say one line. Which I said with another kid. It's standard practice in kids' dramas for multiple kids to say single lines. This doesn't happen in normal life. Me and one other raven – I'll call him 2nd Raven, as I surely would have fought for the 1st Raven billing – we had to say, 'Pardon me, Your Majesty . . .' I'm not sure exactly what I said after that, but I do remember 'Pardon me, Your Majesty.'*

At the performance of this play, when the lines came up, instead of saying, 'Pardon me, Your Majesty . . .' I said, 'I beg your pardon, Your Majesty . . .'

That's as far as I got before the crowd burst out laughing.

It was my first laugh. I didn't think it was my laugh, and

---

* It could have been a story about ravens in a pie. I think there were more than two of us, but our special effects department was not up to a) us flying out of a pie or b) even putting us into a pie. So I think us two ravens just commented on the pie (of potential ravens). We might have said something like, 'Pardon me, Your Majesty, but this pie is rubbish,' or 'This pie is not up to snuff.' Or 'This pie defies the Trade Descriptions Act. You've got too many ravens in it. Why aren't we in there?'

I wasn't joyful at the noise of it. It just happened. I'd made a mistake. And in retrospect, not a very funny mistake. This was a very easy audience. I've had much tougher audiences since then.

I think they laughed because the show was interminably boring. I think most kids' shows are.*

There was probably a lot of silence onstage when I said the wrong line because I think the other raven (my co-raven) was dead or had exploded or had resigned like Nixon, and into that silence I repeated, 'I beg your pardon, Your Majesty.' And I guess it sounded like an affront, and they laughed, and so a career was born, except it wasn't, because I didn't think I'd done anything.

But that was it. My first raven gig and my last raven gig.

I do remember that my older brother, Mark, was due to have an event, too. Maybe it was his school play, or maybe it was something else, but whatever it was, it was Christmassy. I think I stopped him from going by moaning and wailing to my mother that I would be sad or lonely if he went. I think Mum was in bed at this point. It was as if I made a plea to the head office. But it was wrong of me. It was just a selfish way of stopping something happening that would have been fun for my brother. I can't quite remember the full details, but it was not right. So, sorry for that, Mark.

*

* I should say here I'm not trying to denigrate the Oakleigh House young kids' production qualities. I just don't think all five-year-olds are doing unbelievably brilliant theatrical work. Parents are always being very supportive, and that's great, but shows can't be that fantastic, otherwise we'd all be putting kids' shows on in the West End and on Broadway, shelling out hundreds of pounds and dollars and euros and buckets of gold bullion to go and see these five-year-olds do shows. And we don't, so their shows can't be that good.

When Christmas came, I got an Action Man doll, something for boys like me who liked human toys that wore uniforms and had fighting equipment and had adventures. That's what I was into.

Now, this is interesting for students of sexuality: given my early (and lifelong) wish to express the feminine side of myself, I was not into girly dolls.*

But the Action Man doll (in America the G.I. Joe), he's got a dagger and a gun and a fishing line and spare underpants and a hat and shoes. That I thought was great, because I am an action transvestite and that appealed to the action part of me.

There were other presents, too, and I suppose Mum knew this would be her last Christmas.

We didn't know this. We were oblivious.

But clearly this was very much on her mind, because despite her being so ill she had gone out with Dad to the shops in Swansea and bought Omega Constellation watches for me and my brother, for each of us to receive on our eighteenth birthdays. Which we now have.

It was the last thing she bought for us.

The Omega Constellation is quite a beautiful classic Omega watch. It's self-winding – as you move your hand, the mechanism winds itself due to some pendulum system. And on the back of the watch there is a gold image of an observatory and a night sky. Dad has one, too. Mum had already bought it for him.

---

*I bought one fairly recently – a Barbie or something like a Barbie – but I still don't know what's so interesting with Barbie. The endless clothes-changing thing doesn't grab me. The brushing of the hair doesn't grab me. Barbie just doesn't really work for me.

And that is how Christmas 1967 passed. For me, it was a good Christmas. For me, it was a fun Christmas. I don't think Mark and I had any worries.

Dad told me recently that Mum had made the Christmas meal, but after that she went to bed and didn't ever get out again.

That next term at Oakleigh House, I'm sure we did more things, painted more pictures of houses, did slightly more complicated algebra, and started on quantum physics (probably not) – just the stuff five-year-olds do at school. We played with the kids in the area. We were trying to re-create the kid-gang thing that we'd had in Northern Ireland. I remember cycling around on my little bike with no gears and fat wheels: I had to pedal like crazy to keep up with everyone else because the bigger kids had three gears, which was unbelievable. Some even had Raleigh Choppers, the bicycle that god* would have ridden when he was a child, before he became a twit.†

So. Early 1968.

March 4 is the hellish day.

Before that, we had a January and a February, and I had a birthday.

My sixth birthday was on February 7, 1968. I got a windup watch. It was my first watch. Not a self-winding watch but the kind you had to remember to wind every day. And if you didn't, the watch wouldn't work. And if you overwound it,

---

* Since I don't believe in god, I will spell god throughout this book with a lower case *g* instead of a godlike uppercase *G*.

† A Raleigh Chopper had a central gear stick so you could change gears as if you were in a car or on a motorbike. It was madness. It was quite beautiful.

you'd break it. I definitely liked the watch at this point, though I don't remember who bought it for me.

I don't think I can remember any more things about what happened between Christmas and the fourth of March.

I wasn't playing football at this point.

I wasn't doing school plays at this point.

I wasn't making people laugh at this point.

I wasn't flying many airplanes at this point.

Then Mum died, and that was the emotional equivalent to someone hitting us in the stomach with a baseball bat.

Maybe it was god hitting us in the stomach with a baseball bat.

But I don't believe in a god.

People say, 'God moves in mysterious ways, his wonders to perform.'

Well, I think if there is a god, then god needs to have a plan. If the god does not have a plan for us, and the god just lets random shit happen, then what is the point of him, or her, or it, or the flying sandwich they may be?

If there is a god they need to come down to Earth and explain WWII, Hitler, bowel cancer, and Croc shoes. But no god has ever come to Earth.

But let's go back to Tore Rydsund's film footage from that 1965 holiday in Gothenburg.

A few years ago, when I told Dad that I'd met Elisabeth Rydsund (now Elisabeth Johansen) at my gig in Gothenburg and that she'd mentioned the film footage her father had taken, he got very excited about making contact with the Rydsund family again.

'I want to come to Gothenburg with you when you next play there,' Dad said, which was very unusual for him. He wouldn't normally do such a thing, but we made the trip together and we went to visit the Rydsund family. Once there, after Stina had taken our coats, she said to me, 'Would you like to sit down, Edward?'

She called me Edward.

I thought to myself, *No one calls me Edward.* And then I thought, *Stina and Mum were very close.* So I turned and asked Dad, 'Did Mum call me Edward?'

Indeed she had. I had been an Edward, not an Eddie, to my mother. 'Eddie' must have been my invention.

And I realized this was some sort of amazing link, a journey into the past, because Stina had been there with Mum to hear her calling me Edward when I was three years old on that holiday, and when they'd visited us in Belfast. I would have been Edward all the time back then.

It might seem like a small thing, but it was quite an incredible thing to me – to find out what she'd called me when I was a child. It's knowledge that most people take for granted, because it's something that most people know about themselves – what their mother called them – but it's a piece of the puzzle of my fractured childhood that I'd never had.

So thank you, the Rydsunds. And no thank you, god.

A year after Mum died, we went on a sad but memorable holiday. We had a Sprite caravan trailer-thingy that attached to the back of the car, and Dad said, 'We're going to hitch the caravan on to the car and we're going to go on holiday around Ireland.'

We were all happy about this because we'd had a good holiday in Ireland with Mum when she was still with us. So we were off on holiday going all the way around the island of Ireland.

Mark and I grew up in cream-coloured VWs – Dad had two for more than thirteen years until the early 70s. The classic old VW Beetles from the late 50s, early 60s, the kinds he owned, had two front seats and a back seat for probably three kids or two adults, but only two front doors. Behind the back seat, there was a long bucket-shaped space in front of the rear window. On long trips Mark would sleep on the back seat, and I would sleep in the very back, beneath the rear window, in the long bucket-shaped bit, while Mum and Dad sat in the front.

My brother and I developed a certain bit of car behaviour when we were in the car. When Dad was reversing, we would drop our heads down so he could see out the back window. Dad would reverse, like many people in those days, by wrapping one arm around the back of the front seat and turning right around so he could look through the back window of the car. Nowadays, most people use side mirrors to reverse, or some weird televisual screen that appears and shows you how to reverse backwards. But back then, it was a definite turning of the body around, getting your arm over the other side of the seat, pulling yourself up a bit, and reversing, taking your eyes entirely off the road in front of you. So we would instinctively duck down – even when someone else was driving their car.

When we were driving around as a four-person family, I would be sitting in the back, where I couldn't see the road.

I didn't know exactly what made me carsick, but I would always end up throwing up when sitting in the back.

In my life, I have thrown up in cars, buses, coaches, airplanes, taxis, and once on a train over an old lady on the way to Penrith. I haven't yet thrown up on a bicycle, but there's always time. Sometimes I'd throw up in the car, sometimes just outside the car. You get embarrassed about getting sick, so you tended not to tell anyone until it was too late. This was not good news.

On the trip around Ireland, I sat in the front seat, on the passenger side, and I could, for once, have the window open. For the first time, I could actually see the road, see the horizon, and I started feeling less ill. We gradually worked out that this back seat/ front seat thing could have had something to do with it all along. My brother now had the whole backseat, and hopefully he was okay with that. Being able to look at the traffic and see the horizon really helped me throw up less often.

What I remember most about this journey around Ireland, though, had nothing to do with whether to vomit or not to vomit – that wasn't the question. It had to do with the fact that I sang a song over and over and over: the theme song from a German/Yugoslavian TV series called *The White Horses.** The lyrics, which I didn't notice at the time, are very soft and fuzzy – *On white horses let me ride away / To my world of dreams so far away.* They're not aggressive. They're not punk. They're about living in a world of dreams.

---

*The UK theme song became a top ten hit in the UK in 1968. You can actually download the song now, by Jackie Lee, and while I'm not sure if it's the original version or not, it's quite close to the original.

Which is what I needed back then. I didn't listen to the lyrics. I didn't repeat the lyrics. I just sang the melody quietly to myself. I always used to do this, just listen to the music of a song and not the words. But I must have sung it so many times, over and over – probably not so loud that it would annoy Mark and Dad, because they would have shouted at me. But I did sing it over and over. And it was a comforting sound, and a comforting melody, and that's what I needed right then.

But immediately after Mum died, Dad didn't have time to set up a proper holiday. And he had to travel to Rotterdam to do work at the BP refinery there. So he decided to take us with him so we could be together. Auntie Trudy also came out to visit us. I'm not sure how long it was for, but it was a few weeks.

We became latchkey kids, staying in a high-rise apartment block and having the front door key hanging on a string behind the letterbox in the door. The trick was to stick your hand through the letterbox, grab the string, pull the key through, and unlock the door. In Rotterdam I became fascinated by all the canals and wanted to find a rubber dinghy and paddle it around. On this break from school, we found out that Dad and Mum had made plans for Mark and me to go to a boarding school. That way, Dad would be able to work and keep everything going, and we would survive as a family unit. He told me that they'd picked St John's School in Porthcawl because it was the only school that would be near enough for him to keep in close touch with us. Again, it's tricky to work these things out, but our family situation was about to go from four of us in the house to

46

just one of us in the house – Dad – with us two kids being away from home for thirty-two weeks of the year.

We got school uniforms for St John's School that were brown with red trim! With caps and everything. I was going off to somewhere new, and I think I felt some positive excitement about that. But I should have known that life in this new place would be a much different and less happy existence to the one we had known with Mum and Dad, back in Northern Ireland. Unlike the *White Horses* song of my future, I was not riding off to the world of my dreams. In ways I would eventually come to understand and in other ways that I don't think I ever will, our new life would change my brother and me forever.

Exile

Mark and I started at St John's School, in Porthcawl, in the summer term of 1968. Starting a new school during the last term of the year is incredibly weird, but that was the least of it. The worst of it was finding out we were actually going to boarding school.

'Boarding school? You mean, you don't go home at all?'

Not much.

I was six and my brother was only just eight, so it was quite miserable and it meant a lot of crying and wailing for me.

I was a crier up until the age of eleven. At which point I stopped crying because I realized it would lose you the argument. I was fighting Andrew Isherwood, a good footballer, and something went wrong. I don't remember what the fight was about – chocolate, fish, who was best at Scrabble – probably some stupid disagreement. The details of this do not come back to me, but the key points do, which are:

We got in a scuffle. He hit/hurt me just a bit better than I was trying to hit/hurt him. I started crying.

And I suddenly realized:

I've lost the battle.

Which led me to rethink and do a complete reversal on the whole crying thing. I realized: *Crying is bad. Remove crying from your emotional colour palette. Don't ever cry again.*

And I didn't ever cry again until I was nineteen, when I

48

discovered I had become emotionally dead.

I think a lot of kids who go to boarding school end up like that: In order to survive, they become unemotional. It's a coping strategy. Until they figure out they're dead inside and that they better start crying again as soon as possible. I don't know how many boarding school kids actually realize this, but I'd guess it's only 10 or 20 per cent.

Going to boarding school wasn't just miserable for Mark and me; it was crap for our father as well. Because while we'd lost our mother entirely and now would see Dad only about a third of the year after that – Dad had lost everyone. She wasn't there, and we weren't there. That's when he started leaving the radio on all night and falling asleep to it.

Being at St John's School felt like being on a deserted island.

Porthcawl is a Welsh seaside resort, and I'm sure it's a very pleasant place to visit when you're on holiday and the weather is nice and you're having a good family time. But from our point of view, Porthcawl was right on the sea, next to huge expanses of sandy beaches, and we would often go on walks down to these beaches, and the school would give us sandwiches. These sandwiches were made out of things that shouldn't have been in sandwiches and we were given lemonade that had had all the lemonade removed from it and had had the stuff that shouldn't have been in sand- wiches put into it. St John's School also had a holiday caravan park right next to it, with an amusement arcade at the centre of it. We would walk past the amusement park to get to the endless sandy beaches that went on for miles and where we never saw anyone – the kind of place where

49

you'd expect a few dead bodies to wash up occasionally.

But no – no such luck.

There was a little playground in the nearby town of Newton, right next to the church, and I remember walking from the school, past the church to where the swings and slides were, which we were allowed to play on. And there was a spooky old well, too, a little old stone hut of a building with steps that went down and down into the depths of hell. It had a door with a metal grate in it, and I was pretty sure that the devil lived down there. I also remember the Jolly Sailor Inn, which we weren't allowed to enter, because when you're six you're not allowed to go into the pub. That's just the way it is. There were no six-year-olds drinking lots of alcohol and driving cars.

Dad had given an old radio from his days in 'Adan to me and Mark, and I remember listening to two songs in particular on this. One was Mary Hopkin's 'Those Were the Days.' And the other was 'Delilah' by Tom Jones, who is from Wales and may have actually driven past Porthcawl while I was listening to his song on the radio.

The combination of listening to the radio, which sounded like contact with the outside world, then walking through the empty caravan park during term time, when no one was on holiday, when no one was ever there, past an amusement arcade that was always closed, to get to endless stretches of deserted beaches where strange caterpillars danced a weird dance on weeds that grew on the sand dunes always made the area around the school feel very desolate.

Especially to a six-year-old and an eight-year-old with no mum.

And living in dormitories didn't help. British dormitories seem very different from the kinds of dormitories that American kids move into when they go to university. They have two beds to a room.* Our dormitories were like hospital wards – a hospital ward where you have twenty very old Victorian metal beds with twenty little boys in them. Not the most cozy or private environment for a boy who would sing himself to sleep every night.

I would sing 'Jingle Bells' over and over, to myself, to get myself to sleep.

I would rock my body from side to side. I would cry. And I would suck my fingers – just the first two fingers of my right hand – instead of just sucking my thumb, god knows why.†

Speaking of god, St John's is where we started going to church for the first time. That's where we met with god. Apparently god comes and lives in a cold building every Sunday – I don't know why they do that, but they never tell us anything anyway. So we would troop down from the school, walking all the way down the school entrance driveway on to the road. 'Keep together,' teachers would shout. And then we'd troop down the road to the little church in Newton, and we'd all go in and sing songs praising god and building him up in an enormous way – as if he had such a weak character that he really needed the encouragement. I didn't analyse it quite like that at the time. But we were there, and we were singing songs. And it was compulsory.

---

* Our dormitories were named after British heroes: Drake, Nelson – British naval heroes, all. Or maybe it was just military heroes. Maybe there was a Wellington dormitory as well.
† Except there isn't a god.

And speaking of singing, I was in the school choir for five minutes.

I was in, I think, the form three class, and they said, 'If you can sing, stand on this side of the room; if you can't sing, stand on the other side.' Which was the right side. I normally sat on the left side of the classroom and there was an aisle between the desks up the centre. So on the left you couldn't sing. On the right, you could sing.

So I moved to the right because I could sing. Or, I thought I could sing.

I don't know why I thought I could sing, except for the fact that my mother was a singer, but by that time she had already passed away and even before that I don't remember her ever singing to me or my brother, which is curious because she did sing. She sang with a choir at the Albert Hall once. Anyway, I was in the choir for one lesson. We probably sang really complicated songs like 'Snug as a Bug in a Rug,' which is an actual song,* or 'Frère Jacques,' until at some point some kid said to me:

'You can't be in the choir. That's too girly. That's not a tough-boy thing.'

So I thought, *Oh. Okay. I'd better not be in the choir anymore.* I had no sense of self at this age. I wasn't really in touch with my feminine side at this point, and I instantly thought I needed to be on the fighting, rough-and-tough 'pirate' side of the classroom. So halfway through the lesson I moved back to the other side.

And that was the end of my singing career.

---

*Who the hell would write a song called that?

Peer pressure at this time was quite intense, and even though I already had a vague notion that I had something in me that I needed to express that was more on the girl side than the boy side, I also knew that I had a lot of boy stuff as well, and I instinctively felt that expressing the girl side of me was going to be tricky to argue on the playground.

I find it tricky to articulate these feelings as an adult, so how in the hell was I supposed to articulate them at the age of six going on seven?

That's still how it works at school. Survival of the fittest. The playground is still the only place where pure fascism exists. Big kids stomp on little kids.*

Aside from allowing myself to be emotionally bullied into believing that being in the choir was too girly, I was not really picked on at school – because I would argue.

I would argue and argue and argue and argue.

If you picked on me it was like picking on a rock. An argumentative rock. After a while, arguing with me just didn't seem worth the energy expended.

I was stubborn, and pigheaded, and scared, but I was trying not to show the fear.

We'd suddenly arrived at this desolate, deserted island of a place in the summer term where there were sand dunes, bad sandwiches, and empty caravan parks. This was after growing up in a gang and going out and having adventures all day and then Mum making us tea when we came home and then to bed and next day up and off to primary school.

---

*Maybe that's where all our problems come from. Maybe if we could ever get fair and equitable playgrounds to grow up in, we wouldn't have Hitlers, and Stalins, and Saddam Husseins, and Miloševićes.

53

Suddenly we'd started sleeping in large dormitories and we had headmasters and teachers and matrons and kids we didn't know.

All that good stuff had just disappeared forever.

And that whole other life that we once had had stopped.

Sometimes I wonder about that other life – the one that would have continued for my brother and my father and me, the one that my mother would have been alive to see and be a part of – and I do believe I started performing and doing all sorts of big, crazy, ambitious things because on some level, on some childlike magical-thinking level, I thought doing those things might bring her back. Might make her come back.

But she never has come back. I keep trying, though, just in case.

St John's School also had compulsory judo, so at the age of six, I learned judo. Everyone put on big white pyjama-like things and then lined up to do forward rolls on the gym mat. It was really easy to do because when you're a kid, you're close to the ground and quite bendy and that all works.

Now, as an adult, if you try to forward roll, you will die. We know this. We don't have to test it. We just think, *I'll tuck my head in, I'll start a forward roll, and then I'll just die.*

But back then, everyone put on these big white pyjamas when they told us to, and we lined up and we did the forward rolls. They're interesting, these forward rolls. You have to tuck your right arm in so you don't go straight forwards and over. You go sideways, forwards, and over. Which is a lot easier.

I liked judo. I liked fighting other kids in white pyjamas. If there was a big kid, you would pull at his white pyjamas, but he wouldn't move at all. You'd try to *hoik* him over your outstretched leg – that's a typical judo throw – but he still wouldn't move, because he was a big kid. So judo with big kids seemed a little bit pointless for us smaller kids.

If you did things right, though, you'd get coloured belts. I liked belts. There was the plain belt you started with, and then you moved up to an orange belt, and then there were red belts and green belts and different colours, but no one got anywhere near a black belt. I was into that. I remember all the white pyjamas and coloured belts were kept in a big basket. The problem with that was if you had passed the test and become an orange belt but couldn't find an orange belt in the basket, you'd just put on a green belt or a brown belt. It seemed you could get promoted in judo if you just picked up the wrong belt. I don't think we were obeying the rules.

But that was the last time I did judo, which I eventually decided was mainly about fighting people in big pyjamas. Before you had a fight in the real world, you would have to say, 'Excuse me, sir, I must first put on some white pyjamas and then you can try to beat the crap out of me.' And that's quite difficult because your pyjamas always come undone. For me, it was always about the pyjamas.

At the end of the summer term they had a sports day, as most schools do, and on that day I won a blue football by winning the sack race. There's a photo of this, I believe. A photo of me crossing the line in the sack race.

Now, the sack race, if you don't have one in your country, goes like this:

You get in a sack and then you race. It's that simple.

Essentially you're supposed to do a two-legged, jumpy-uppy-downy, rabbit-kangaroo-style hop as fast as you can to cross the finish line first. But the sacks are large and I was only six. I was not very big. My dad, who had come to watch, saw an opportunity as I lined up with other kids to try and win the sack race. He leaned over to me and said, 'Put your feet in the corners of the sack and then don't hop – just run!'

That seemed like a good idea. So I gathered the bag up, I put my feet in the corners, and when they said 'Go!' I just ran like crazy.

I tore down the track. In the photo I think you can see the person coming in second and they are a long way behind. I think the kid coming second had also started to do the feet-in-the-corners-of-the-sack-style sack race. I don't think there are any United Nations rules on sack races. So I was deemed the winner and given the Nobel Prize for sack races – with one blue football.

UN rules not withstanding, I, with help from my dad, won the blue football, which was unfortunately lost in some bramble hedges on Bexhill Down in about 1970. I actually remember which bramble hedge it was lost in. It should still be there. I sometimes wonder about getting electric cutting equipment and cutting into that impenetrable bush to find it.*

They also had the Investiture of the Prince of Wales for

---

* Maybe in the middle of the night. But that would be crazy because I wouldn't be able to see anything, so I would just make a lot of noise and cut up bushes, someone would probably report me, and then the police would come and find me dressed in protective gear, tearing up bushes in the middle of the night. I don't know what they could charge me with, but it would become a cause célèbre in the Bexhill-on-Sea *Observer* and I'd never hear the end of it.

Prince Charles in 1969, his twentieth year, while we were there. The Prince of Wales investiture is an old custom and one that requires a bit of explanation, which goes like this:

King Edward I was a bastard. He liked killing people. He killed a lot of Welsh people and Scottish people. England is very close geographically to Wales, so Edward I attacked and killed and reattacked and then built castles and did a whole heap of crap stuff to the Welsh.

I now apologize for all that on behalf of humanity.

At some point the Welsh people said something like, 'We will only be ruled by a prince who is born in Wales.'

So Edward I ran off and got his pregnant wife over to Wales just in time to have her baby there. So his kid, the future Edward II, was born in Wales, and was therefore technically a Prince of Wales. Since then, the oldest son of the reigning British monarch has to have his investiture in Carmarthen, at Caernarfon Castle, on the coming of his twentieth birthday.

Back in 1969, my brother had mumps. No one gets mumps anymore. Mumps sounded like bumps, but with an *m* in the front. Anyway, it was contagious, and when my brother got mumps he had to sit away from me because I didn't have mumps. Which was surprising, since I'd begun collecting most diseases in earnest. I'd had measles. I'd had chicken pox. I had shingles in my teenage years, which is normally terribly painful. It wasn't painful for me for some unknown reason. They just sprayed my body with plastic skin. Which is weird. Apparently all my nerve endings had become hypersensitive. I basically just had lots of spots again. I spent quite a lot of my childhood either throwing up or having spots.

57

When this Prince of Wales investiture took place, Dad was away working somewhere else in the world. He didn't realize, and we didn't realize, that everyone got a day off on the Prince of Wales Investiture Day. So all the kids who were boarders at the school were allowed to – and in fact had to – go home for a long weekend. But our dad wasn't available. In fact, he hadn't been told; as he later said, he would have come back and picked us up.

Since Mark had mumps and I didn't have mumps and we couldn't go away together, Mark was assigned to spend the weekend with a boy who'd already had mumps, and I was assigned to some other boy. I went to stay with this kid and his family on their farm – in a real house, in a non-dormitory bedroom, with real Mum-cooked food instead of terrible school food. The sun was shining, I remember, and it turned out to be a magical weekend. I remember it like a scene from a film. I think I want to live on a farm like that – somewhere in the countryside with endless fields.

After that whole other life stopped, we lived essentially in old manor houses. Not stately manor houses where the gentry live (maybe that's what they were before they became schools) but big, old country houses with tons of rooms and a refectory or dining room.

Now, the dining room was a problem for me as well.

Apparently I was very 'fussy' with food. That's what people said to me. But I don't believe I was 'fussy' with food. I believe I was 'choosy' with food. I believe I had a problem with certain foodstuffs. I believe I couldn't keep certain foodstuffs inside my body – they would just come back up. Unfortunately they would come back up as vomit. Because of this vomit issue, which, as I've already said, was a big problem, I had a sort of deal going with some of the teachers:

'I'll eat anything you want, as long as you will welcome my vomit gladly. Are you a fan of vomit? Because if you force me to eat that liver, I *will* vomit on the plate.'*

Back at St John's they must have had a chat with the devil and asked, 'What do you think is a completely disgusting meal we could serve to children that would haunt them forever?'

And the devil must have said, 'Well, you know, you could always try macaroni in warm milk.'

'Yes,' said the caterers at St John's. 'Yes. That sounds brilliant. Macaroni in warm milk. We will add it to our à la carte menu – where the boys can choose anything they wish from the menu, but there's only one choice. And if they don't eat it, we will just have to insist.'

So one day, they served this stuff up: macaroni in warm milk. I tried it and I thought, 'Please, sir, can I have some less?'

'*Less?* What are you, a reverse Oliver Twist?'

'Yes, sir. I think if Oliver Twist was eating this crap, he would have asked for less, too, and would have preferred to die on a rubbish dump than eat macaroni in warm milk, which I have on good authority has been suggested to you by the devil. I read it in a biography.'

---

* This I did twice with liver. That was later, at St Bede's School in Eastbourne. St Bede's School was a decent school, but they chose to serve liver. I have eaten liver since then, and if cooked well it can taste all right. But when cooked at school, the words *liver* and *leather* are not far from each other – either in the dictionary or in the lexicon of taste. I just couldn't keep liver down.

Maybe not the first time we had it, but the second time, it was served as an evening meal. Macaroni in warm milk seemed to be a one-size-fits-all stopgap meal. 'Would you like it for breakfast? Lunch? Dinner?' Maybe some guy in the kitchen just said, 'Look, I've got a lot of spare macaroni, and these cows have got way too much milk.'

Now, the milk on its own I loved. Cold milk, yes – yum. But hot milk? No. Warm, tepid milk? Ooh, no. No, no, no, no. All wrong. Add that to macaroni, and it's very wrong. Extremely wrong.

So they served it up as an evening meal, this macaroni and warm milk. And we barely touched ours. Mark and I – is the word *demurred*? We decided not to partake. Or we partook a little bit, moved it around, and then left it.

A digression.

Making food seem to disappear from your plate without actually eating any was a useful trick. I first learned it when I was four, living at home in Bangor.

I got a hernia and had to have an operation, just above the nether regions, where something that had become unattached was then reattached. Whatever a child hernia is, I got it. Family legend has it that I tried to pick up a Mini Cooper and ruptured myself. I asked Dad about this, and he said, 'No, no, it wasn't that. You just got a child hernia.' I think this story sounds more fun, so in the film version we can use that. So in fact, I tried to pick up a Mini Cooper, maybe two Mini Coopers, and juggle a cat at the same time.

Because of this hernia thing, they sent me to Ards

Hospital in Newtownards down the road, where there was a head nurse with whom I got on very well. It was the first time I'd been away from home, and I don't remember much, but I do remember I was given fun toothpaste with cartoon characters on the tube. But back to the head nurse: she was attractive and probably in her late twenties and I was four. But – we had a connection. At some point, as a deal, she let me clean her car. Which seems like a bit of an inverse deal. It seems like she got the better part of that deal, since she got a clean car out if it. Except, with the way a four-year-old cleans a car, I don't know. But I do remember doing this, so I must have been helping her with cleaning her car, and in return she let me bend the rules a bit. She let me eat less soup.

Now let me tell you about soup.

Soup, for me, in those days, was well-presented vomit. If you ate soup and it came back out of you, there seemed to be no difference. I did not like soup. The consistency I did not like. The taste also disagreed with me. (And I do now realize that having refined sugar in my body, because I was a sugar junkie most of my life, was actually screwing up my taste buds. Otherwise I could have liked all these foods I'm talking about.)

Normally I never touched soup, but I was in hospital: I had a hernia. I had tried to lift up an aircraft carrier or a bear, and so now I had to have soup. Soup makes you better, apparently. Nowadays I realize soup is good for you and it has decent stuff in it, and actually tastes okay (because I've since given up refined sugar and have better use of my taste buds), but back then I just looked at it and refused to eat it.

The head nurse came up to me and said, 'You've got to

eat some of your soup. It will put hairs on your chest.'

Why was everyone trying to be a gorilla back in those days?

And I said, 'But it's horrible. I don't like it at all. I'd prefer not to. I think if we're going to remain friends, if you really want me to clean your car, you shouldn't force this thing on me.'

Now, soup and soap are spelled very similarly. Have you noticed? This doesn't help my argument, I know. But who is to say that a dyslexic chef has not put some soap into the soup just because it was a bad day at the office and they thought, *Is this soap or soup that they want?*

'Just try some of it,' the head nurse said. 'If you just have some of it, then you won't have to have all of it.'

That was the deal. That's what I negotiated. Through hard bargaining, all I had to do was have *some* soup.

So I plonked my spoon in and got the soup loaded up on the spoon. Then I lifted the spoon up, but then I decided to pour it back into the bowl. That's almost like eating soup, but it just didn't quite make it to my mouth. So I had bits of the eating-soup ritual going on, just my mouth was not involved in it. But I discovered that by lifting the soup up from the bowl in a spoon and then pouring it back in, it created a soupy tsunami, a tiny soupy tsunami that washed up on the edges of the bowl. And this overwash, I realized, made the soup level look like it had gone down. By just picking some soup up and pouring it back over and over again, I created tiny tidal waves that made it look like I'd eaten the whole top level of soup.

So this is what I did. When the head nurse came back, I said, 'Look!'

And she said, 'Well, good! You've had a bit of a go at that. All right. You don't have to eat the rest.'

And I thought, *What a great result!*

Unfortunately I haven't been able to use this in any other circumstances, because you would think, *Ah, now that I've invented this, I will be a millionaire. I will sell it. I will make cars out of it.* No, it's just a method for how to not eat soup when you don't like soup.

But back to Mark and me not finishing – not partaking – of our macaroni in warm milk.

Once, after dinner, everyone went off to bed. But as we were getting ready in the dormitories, someone senior came up and said, 'You two haven't eaten your macaroni and warm milk. Put your dressing gowns on over your pyjamas, put your slippers on, and go back down to the dining room and finish it all up.'

We were ordered to go back down and sit in a darkened dining hall in our pyjamas and dressing gowns. We were told to finish eating our macaroni and our warm milk – milk that surely, by now, would have been colder milk but on no account would make the food taste any better. We sat side by side on a bench at a long dinner table in the darkened dining room where there were only a few lights on. The whole place had a Dickensian air to it, though this was 1968, not 1868.

And then my older brother had an idea:

'Why don't we tip this down the toilet?'

It was a radical thought. To take any food that you do not like and flush it down a toilet is a wonderfully simple idea.

Why couldn't I do this every time I had food that was seemingly disgusting?

The problem was, of course, normally there'd be masters and head teachers and matrons and gun emplacements and attack dogs there waiting to take your legs off and shout, 'No, don't pour that down the toilet.'

But that night there were no guards on duty, no attack dogs, and the gun emplacements were unmanned at this late, late hour, which I remember as being somewhere between midnight and one in the morning, but of course was probably seven p.m., or maybe even six thirty p.m.[*]

Mark went first. He took his bowl of macaroni and warm milk with him and went to the downstairs toilet that was part of the school complex, and he threw it in. Then he flushed the loo.

Job done, all gone, no evidence. To get evidence, you'd have to dive down the U-bend of the toilet and swim through with some sort of net, with which you could collect all the bits of macaroni and then drag them back through the U-bend, and come out. And you'd have to be the size of a small frog to do this. This was impossible so it was perfect.

I went second.

But because I'd forgotten that the school had downstairs toilets, I went upstairs to where all the kids were getting ready for bed. I don't know why I did this. I guess toilet geography was not at the top of my abilities in those days.[†]

---

[*] Times that you're sent to bed when you're six are just ridiculous.

[†] Now when I get to a building, I like to map out all the toilets and note them down on Google Maps with stars.

So I went up the stairs, past the matron's room,* and then on to the first toilet I found.

Let me explain the thing about matrons. A matron would look after the boys (or girls) in the sense that she (it was always a she) would give us medicine if we were ill, and be in charge of our laundry, washing, and bedtime. Those, I think, were the basic duties of a matron. There were probably more duties, but I wasn't paying enough attention to notice them. The only other thing I noticed was that matrons were usually fairly officious women, single women who didn't appear to have much of a life elsewhere.†

This toilet was slightly separate from the other toilets of the dormitory system. I don't know exactly why. I can't remember why. It just was 'slightly' separate. So it wasn't an awful idea to do this; no one was about to go in there immediately, but someone could have gone in there. It was also close enough to the rest of the dormitory complex.‡

This toilet was only occasionally used, probably by kids

---

*There was a matron in every boarding school, usually a single lady somewhere between thirty-five and seven hundred years old.

†Later, at my next school, St Bede's School, which I went to from the age of seven to thirteen, there was a matron called Miss Hatter. Definitely a 'Miss.' Miss Hatter was not a woman whom I hugely liked or disliked, but later I would find out that she died in her bed at the school. I know this because I went back to the school and was shown around and at one point my old headmaster pointed to a part of a room and said, 'That's where Miss Hatter was found dead.' I saw her room only a few times, when she would open the door to get something and I would see a room that was a master's room, an adult's room, a room that I was not allowed into. I found the news very alarming because the idea that you could live your full life in one little room for maybe twenty or thirty years and then die in it one night is just a little sad. There was one matron that I did like: a Mrs Bonnell, who had one or two kids at the school. She was the assistant matron, and she was very friendly and personable and almost like a surrogate mother to me. She didn't offer that, but she would have got my vote if it were offered.

‡This is now beginning to sound like the escape from Stalag Luft III in World War II – on which *The Great Escape* is based. Which I suppose isn't a bad thing.

who had been to see the matron because they had a sore thumb, and then, on returning to their dormitory, they decided they just couldn't make it and had to run and unload things in the loo. It was a way station loo. It was a loo for people who just couldn't hold it another twenty meters. So I poured the macaroni and warm milk into the welcoming toilet that was saying, 'Feed me, feed me, put stuff in me. That's all I want. That's the way I like it.'

And I said to the toilet, 'This is macaroni; this is not actually poo.'

The toilet said, 'No, I think it is poo. I think you've just saved a whole journey of going through the body, because this doesn't look good, kid. This stuff is synonymous with poo.'

And I said, 'Synonymous?'

'Abso-bloody-lutely.'

'I agree with you, toilet,' I said. 'I think macaroni and warm milk is synonymous with poo and should be made carefully by cooks in boarding schools and then poured straight into toilets to cut out the middleman.'

The toilet agreed heartily with me and we high-fived each other in a way that wouldn't be standard practice for another twenty or thirty years. How you high-five a toilet I leave to your imagination.

I realized at that point that if I flushed the toilet, people would hear the toilet – one not often used, only in emergencies when seeing the matron. The flush of the toilet could incriminate me in a way that Richard Nixon would have understood. So I left the macaroni and warm milk sitting in the bowl of the toilet and went back downstairs, hoping that no one would go to the toilet to use it in an emergency and see macaroni, put two and two together, add five, divide by nine, and say, 'The Izzard boys, they're probably throwing macaroni and warm milk down the toilet!' Even though not everyone would know that actually there were two Izzards down in the dining room throwing macaroni down different toilets.

But there was still a chance.

My heart was pounding.* If I'd had an Apple Watch back then, I'd have been able to tell that my heart rate had gone from my standard seventy beats per minute, which it always unfailingly is, to somewhere around three thousand beats per minute.

The macaroni was out of the bowl and into another bowl, and it just needed a courtesy flush a little bit later. But I knew the delay made it tricky. So I nipped back downstairs as fast as I could.

I had to go back downstairs to wash the plate and spoon in the school dining room kitchen sink, which was a year's march away in six-year-old-leg terms. In reality it wasn't far. An adult could get there in three or four minutes. But when you're only six, it's a long way with legs that are short. So there I was, creeping quickly around the place trying not to make any noise so that no one would say, 'Hey, there's someone creeping on the stairs – he must have shoved macaroni down the toilet. Quick, let's kill him with sticks.'

So I furiously tiptoed downstairs. (Try doing that.) When

---

* I'm trying to build the excitement in this event to the equivalent of some great heist story.

I told my brother what I'd done, he said I was a foolish fool because we still had to go and wash the bowls and the spoons. When we were finally finished, we put them back so they'd be ready for tomorrow's torture and then we headed upstairs, where I discovered to my great relief that no one had yet found the macaroni in the bowl. So I flushed the toilet proudly and high-fived the toilet once again, who couldn't remember the last time I'd high-fived it, because he was a toilet and had a memory shorter than a goldfish.

Later, my brother and I petitioned our father to get him to say to the headmaster, 'Boys of human parents don't eat macaroni in warm milk. So we request not to eat it.'

I didn't know that Dad could actually tell a school, 'Don't give them macaroni in warm milk.' And I don't think they did actually listen. They just sort of made *harrumph* noises. But we did get less macaroni in warm milk (or maybe it was that I became more and more expert at pushing it around the plate). I can't remember what – I've cut this from my memory files.

But I do remember one day it was served again, and that day some kid loved his macaroni in warm milk. He was not human, this child. He just wasn't right. He ate many bowls of macaroni in warm milk and then, interestingly, on the way back to lessons after lunch, he threw it all up. I have no idea how you go from 'Yum, yum, this is great, I'll have several bowls' to throwing it up in such a short period of time. Normally you'd have to get into a tumble dryer to get that kind of inner-ear action going on in order to screw yourself up like that. But no, this kid was a genius in the

68

ways of vomit. He could take food in and throw it up in under twenty minutes.

There was one meal at St John's School that was decent. They must have sat down and said, 'Let's have one meal that actually is vaguely tasty. Should we try this? Yes. Okay, what will it be? It will be sausages and chips – what the Americans call french fries but were actually invented in Belgium.'*

Sausages and chips!

Every Thursday we would be taken to a swimming pool in Swansea or Neath. I still remember the smell of chlorine and the chill in the air. It was always too cold out of the pool in the old days. We'd all be running around freezing outside the pool, and then jumping in and drowning. Because all I could do was drown at that point. So the drill was:

Get in the water.

Do a bit of drowning.

Get out of the water.

Watch some other kids who are good at swimming swim.

Get cold.

Get changed.

Go back to school.

Eat sausage and chips.

And it was godlike. God would have been happy to have

---

* I should say that the people who ran St John's School in the later days seemed very nice, and they probably didn't do anything like this. But in the olden days, it was not good. It's all to do with who's head of the administration.

that meal.* I never wanted that meal to end. I can still taste that meal in my mind.

But we were also served porridge every morning. Which – surprise, surprise – I really didn't like. Porridge was wrong. I like porridge now, so it must have been the lack of sugar. Back then I couldn't work out what was going on with porridge. I'd taste a bit of it and I'd think, *Urgh, no this, too, is not for me.* They did serve treacle – treacle is a kind of sweet-honey-liquid-maple-syrup thing. Bees would eat it if they could be bothered to. So you could put as much of that as you wanted into the porridge.

I didn't really have a bowl of porridge with a bit of syrup. I probably had a bowl of syrup with a bit of porridge. And that kind of worked.

At boarding school there were no sweets. No bonbons. No candy. Kids were not allowed to eat sugary things at St John's. But one day I did see somebody chewing gum and this looked very cool. This looked very American.

I thought, *I'd like to chew gum.*

Unfortunately, I had no money and nowhere to shop, so there was no gum to be had. It was incredibly lucky that I found some chewing gum in a hedge.

Now, I didn't just take it home and eat it. I washed it first.

I washed the gum very thoroughly (I ran it under the tap) and then I bit into it and got a good head of steam going and then it was gum again.

So I started chewing this pre-chewed gum – and despite

---

* If only god existed.

the disgusting-ness and the germy-ness of that fact, I'm still alive today.* Which is surprising because you would think I would die from this Gum-found-in-hedge Disease.

'Mr Izzard, I'm afraid your son is suffering from Gum-found-in-hedge Disease. It's a typical thing for a six-year-old. They find the gum. They chew the gum. Their head falls off. We're very sorry to tell you this. And that there is no known cure.'

I felt very cool. And I only had one bit of gum. That was it. That was my entire gum inventory.

I had a school locker. And since I could not chew the gum all through the night, I'd put the gum in the locker. The next morning I'd come down, open the locker, and I would have gum again. Sure, it needed a little bit of action to get going – you had to start it up like a traction engine – so after breakfast, in would go the gum, and I'd get it going again. I had this gum for somewhere between two weeks and a year. I think it was a few weeks. A few weeks of: got the gum; I'm chewing the gum; I'm cool; only a few other people got the gum.

I felt chewing gum gave me a certain coolness, which is something that is a very aspirational thing in life. The 'cool' thing is a very interesting aspect of child and teenage-hood. And maybe chewing that gum there as a six-year-old, with my socks falling down, short trousers, probably with one

---

* There is a theory that you should always eat a piece of dirt with your food. The wonderful Joanna Lumley from *Absolutely Fabulous* told me that. We worked together on the film *The Cat's Meow*, directed by Peter Bogdanovich, and when we were filming in Greece she told me that her mother or grandmother had always told her this. And all wild animals eat a load of dirt with their food. So me eating that chewing gum was probably a good idea. At the time people would have screamed if they knew, but now I can retro claim that it was always good for my health.

tooth still missing so I looked like Bugs Bunny after a fight, made me look just a little bit cool.

Or maybe it didn't make me cool at all. But I had gum.

So what, you might ask, besides secret gum chewing and tipping macaroni and warm milk down the toilet, was there to do at St John's School?

Not much.

Before we went to the school we were sent the brochure showing all the activities and things we would be doing there, one of which appeared to be canoeing. I say 'appeared' because the brochure had a picture of a canoe, implying that canoeing-a-go-go would be happening there, and when we got there they did have a canoe – one canoe – and that was it. They never put this canoe in any water, as far as I knew. They just kept it in the attic of the school.

They had a horse as well.*

And they had gooseberries. Gooseberries I was suspicious of. You could pick gooseberries from the gooseberry fields at the back of the school. They grew gooseberries at the school? Why? Probably just to scare children. If they'd grown strawberries, we would have eaten the strawberries. We would have been happy children. We would have sung the praises of the teachers and the headmaster, shouting, 'Kaloo, kalay – it's strawberry day.' But no, they decided to grow bloody gooseberries.

Maybe it was prime gooseberry ground. Like grapevines have to be grown in the right soil. Maybe Porthcawl, South

---

*Now, this was a long time ago, so I could be adding the horse, but I do remember it and being surprised that it was there.

Wales, is the gooseberries soil capital of the world. Maybe there was a government scheme like in World War II where they just said, 'We're going to grow gooseberries. Some-one's gotta do it. Someone's gotta grow gooseberries so that we can have gooseberries, and then we can offer them to children, and then they will eat them and throw up.'[*]

I must say I did like the idea that St John's School grew gooseberries. I think it was the idea that they grew anything. Giving life to things seemed good. The fact that the goose-berries were green was okay. The fact that they were hairy and green was not okay. I don't know if they are really hairy or if they're just fuzzy (which is better). But if there is a god, and as I've said before there isn't, but if there is – they must have sat there smoking a joint when they created gooseberries, saying, 'I want one fruit that's kind of fuzzy.'

So for the year and one term that we were at St John's School, games were played and football was played, and I suppose cricket, too, but I don't remember that. There was some snow, and we were in Wales, and we were on a des-erted island.

And that's most of what I remember about the year or so after Mum died, when I was still a child but not really a child anymore. When life as I'd always known it changed in ways that didn't feel fair and often made me cry.

Mum was in heaven, whatever that meant, without us, and we were still on Earth, a lesser and lonelier place in her absence. No more baths after playing outside and Mum tucking us into our beds. No more Mum making warm

---

[*] Actually, gooseberries didn't make me throw up. Fruit didn't make me throw up. I don't think it makes anyone throw up. I'm just on a bit of a throw-up roll here.

milky coffee when I woke in the middle of the night to help me go back to sleep. We were motherless boys now, boarding school boys, boys without the comfort of home, for most of the year. Sometimes it didn't feel real. Sometimes it still doesn't feel real – another world lost, never to be seen again, except in dreams and memories. A brief, happy childhood. Gone forever.

The Adventurers

Both our parents separately decided to leave England and go and work in an Arabic land, at the corner of the Red Sea. This is how they met.

Dad, who was born Harold John Michael Izzard, grew up as John Izzard, using the second name in his endless list of names. I think his mother just started calling him John. Therefore he was John Izzard growing up. Then, when he went to work at BP (British Petroleum), someone (everyone?) there called him Harold – the first in his list of names. Therefore, as he didn't want to start a new job with an argument, he was Harold from then on, even though he was still married to his first wife, whose name was Joy, whom he had met in Bexhill, where he was known as John. All this can lead to confusion.

After being in the navy, and doing a few years at BP, he got a posting to go to 'Adan. He had visited what was then British-controlled Aden in Yemen while he was in the navy, and so he felt a certain connection with it. His posting had been offered first to someone else whose wife didn't want to go.

Dad was happy to take it as he had visited 'Adan in the navy. Joy said it was okay and so off he went (just him initially).

This was in 1955, and for two years Dad worked away at

his job in the accounting department as assistant cost accountant and then financial accountant. Joy lived for six months, out of those two years in 'Adan, but in 1957 this personal relationship went southward, and Joy ended up disappearing with someone else. She and this other guy were transferred out of 'Adan. Divorced, Dad moved into a bachelor apartment. He was obviously not happy about his situation, and so he started to drink more than was sensible.[*]

Luckily, sometime in 1958, a new batch of nurses turned up for the BP hospital in Al Ghadir,[†] which is still there today, probably very similar to how it was back then in the late 50s. You can find it on Google Maps.[‡]

That's where Mum turned up to work in July of 1958.

In October, there was a party thrown for the new nurses, fresh nurses who'd just arrived, and the residents of the bachelor apartments – Somerset Court – where Dad now lived. He says he saw Mum, they got chatting and immediately hit it off, and then he told everyone else, maybe later that night, to back off, as he felt that this was potentially going to be a relationship.

And it did turn into a relationship. They had a six-month courtship that started that night, from the very moment Dad interrupted Mum dancing with one of his colleagues. He said he saw her every day from then on.

Mum – Dorothy Ella Chacksfield – was into amateur

---

[*] He said it was a pint of gin a day – with some lime cordial, I think (I'm not sure what the mix was).

[†] The Arabic name for Little Aden, which was the British name for where the refinery was.

[‡] If you search on Google Maps for *Aden refinery* and then look to the south of that, down a little winding road toward the peninsula, you will see a series of buildings with green roofs. That is the refinery hospital where my mum worked and where my brother and I were born.

dramatics. She performed with the Little Aden Dramatic Society (LADS). This was an amateur company comprised of people who worked at the refinery, and they did a number of productions that were all set up by the man who was the dentist for the refinery. That Christmas of '58, she played the role of Princess Yasmin in the Little Aden Dramatic Society's production of *Aladdin*. She was the performer and Dad had the sense of humour. Mum's sense of humour was more like the musical comedy act Flanders and Swann,[*] so my full-blown, surreal, off-the-wall comedy stuff must have come from my father.

When Mum met Dad she'd had a previous relationship that did not end up in marriage back in Britain, Dad had had one marriage that ended up in divorce, and so I suppose both of them were thinking:

Should we get married and could this be a relationship that would last?

Dad had a four-month leave coming up, which meant he could go back to Britain and have a holiday for four months. But Mum's leave was not in sync with Dad's leave, as she had only been at the refinery for a short period of time. So she said to Dad, 'If you go off now, then I'm not going to just put our relationship on hold for four months, waiting for you to come back.'

By which she meant, she might see other people.

Dad talked to Freddie Scrivens, the ex-RAF chief accountant at the refinery who had been very positive and encouraging to Dad in his career in 'Adan. Dad asked him

---

[*] They were a musical double act who sang witty comedic songs.

if their leave periods could go together at the same time. This was allowed.

They then decided to get married. Dad asked Mum (while writing this, I just ran downstairs and asked Dad who asked who, and he said yes, he did pop the question – as I would have expected). With this plan, they could get married, go on leave for four months, and then come back and move into married quarters – which turned out to be at 10 Surrey Street.*

They got married on May 2, 1959, at the Crater courthouse in 'Adan by a Mr J.A.C.W. Gillet who was the acting chief magistrate and who arrived dressed in polo gear. Apparently he officiated over their brief wedding ceremony in a spirit of 'Okay, get on with it. I have a polo match to go to.'

I later found out who he was, this official, because I acted with his son in the film *Shadow of the Vampire*. Aden Gillett is the actor, a very nice bloke, and as we were acting away, I said to him, 'It's interesting that your first name is Aden, because that's where I was born.'

And he said, 'That's where I was born as well. My real name is John, but I use Aden because of equity rules. Someone else has the name John Gillett.'

He must have said something about his dad officiating at weddings, because I told him that the guy officiating at my parents' wedding was not in formal dress but wearing his polo gear.

'Well, Dad played a lot of polo,' he said.

I asked him to check with his father to see if he remem-

___
*The roads had very British names then. Now they have Arabic names (understandably).

bered marrying a couple in May of 1959 and having to leave quickly to go to a polo match. And his dad did remember this.

This story proves something, only I have no idea what it is.

So they got married, they had a reception, photos were taken, and then they flew off for their honeymoon, the first stop of which was in Beirut. Beirut at the time was known as the Paris of the Middle East. So they flew to the Paris of the Middle East, checked into their hotel, and then they sat in a café having a drink with an American guy named Dick Fish (great name). He was an electrical engineer from Seattle who worked for Westinghouse and had been contracted to work at the refinery in 'Adan and just happened to be on the same plane as Mum and Dad on their way to Beirut. While they were chatting, a photographer guy turned up – as they do – saying, 'Photograph? Photograph?' to anyone and everyone sitting in the café.

I think Mum and Dad didn't respond, didn't go for it. But this guy took photographs of them anyway. He just shot away, black-and-white film footage, which he then, it seems, took home and developed in his own darkroom in quite a short time, because he quickly came back to the café with an actual print and left it for my mum and dad.

The implication was, and he probably said this at the time: 'If you want more photographs I have more photographs. Here is a free sample.' But they decided just to stick with the free sample, which Dad sent home to his mother, my grandmother.

She kept that photo all her life.

And when she passed away it came back to Dad, but it was rather beaten up by then. Dad showed it to me and I thought it was actually a wonderful photograph, but it *was* quite beaten up. So I gave it to a designer friend of mine, Lewis Macleod, and asked him to scan it and remove the imperfections from the creases and the battering it had taken over several decades. Which he did. He worked on it and made a wonderful finished print, which my ex, Sarah Townsend, got copied and framed. And I presented one to my father and one to my brother.

Look at the way my mum is looking at my dad, and how intensely my dad is chatting to Dick Fish (who is just out of the photograph) and how Mum's and Dad's hands are together.

It is a great photograph and one I treasure the most of my parents.

I've always admired how necessary Dad made himself to his job.

He had joined BP in 1951 when it was still called the Anglo-Iranian Oil Company (set up in a deal with Iran by Winston Churchill). He'd left school at seventeen, in October 1945, just after WWII, to join the navy. After a couple of years in the navy, he set up two job interviews. After doing his first job interview, he was offered a job and he decided he would take that and not bother doing the second job interview.* Dad was young-looking for his age, so in his

---

* Which is what I did when I got my first job at the Rock Garden restaurant in Covent Garden: one interview, one job offer. There are things that my dad did that I do as well – it's as if we have very similar genetic propensities. We didn't discuss doing this – I just worked this out later.

first years at BP he was treated like an office junior even though he was older than that.

So not too long after he started, he decided to change the entire filing system in the office.

After that, no one knew where anything was except him, and that's when he became 'very necessary' there.

I don't think he did it specifically for that result. He just found that the filing system was no good, so he changed it. Later on, when the Iranian government pushed the British and BP out of Iran and away from the Abadan refinery,* BP had to set up other refineries around the world to deal with the lack of capacity to refine oil.

The key thing that got Dad's career going in 'Adan in the refinery – over the eight-year period when he divorced his first wife, met and married my mum, and my brother and I were born – was that he changed the way refinery account-ing was done. He was, by 1958, when he met Mum, the financial accountant for the refinery, and he'd noticed that every month the refinery was producing accounting figures that didn't make any sense. When he told his colleagues that every month they were coming up with whole loads of figures that were useless because the figures gave them lots of information but not useful information, the other people in the accounting department, a number of whom had come over from Abadan, said, 'Well, this is how we've al-ways done it.'

So that's when Dad decided to redesign the accounting system for the refinery in 'Adan. He didn't implement it at

---

*Which was a huge refinery, one of the biggest in the world, refining twenty-four million barrels of oil a year. The one in 'Adan refined only five million barrels of oil a year.

every BP refinery right away, just for the one in 'Adan at this point. His boss, Freddie Scrivens, was maybe the first person who actively encouraged my dad and said, 'If it makes sense to you, go do it.' And so he did. This was a big deal because it eventually changed all the figures coming through for the company's refineries: they moved to quarterly reporting instead of monthly reporting and the figures now actually meant something. The monthly reporting meant that they were coming up with figures and more figures, but no one was looking at any of this, and apparently people would put these figures straight in the bin. By moving it to quarterly reporting and making the figures more useful to the different departments, he made it so the refinery in 'Adan actually had some accounting numbers that were useful.

When he went back to London, he was called in to the head office and asked why he did this. 'Because the previous figures were rubbish,' he said.

'You can't say that,' people said.

And he said, 'Well, I've said it. And I'll back it up.'

It seems there's only a small number of people in life, religion, sports, and other areas who look at the systems in place and say, 'Can we make these better?' This is what Dad did his entire working life, until he retired at age fifty-six on a really decent pension.

He is a big success in what he did. He may not have ended up as a director or the CEO, but in the way that he approached life as a single parent, keeping his job going forwards because he needed to provide for his family. So he made it all work. And his life moved from his working-class roots to a middle-income middle-class life.

And he made it possible for me to do what I have done.
I've told him this. He gave me a solid concrete base of confidence from which I could drop out of university and go
for my dreams. Though I would have to go through my
'wilderness years' first.[*]

---

[*] The Wilderness Years are what historians called the decade in the 1930s when nothing was
working right for Winston Churchill.

Teddy Bear Show Business

I always wanted to get really good acting roles – once I decided I wanted to act. Which is why I began creating my own 'shows' when I was very young.

The first one was with my teddy bears.

It's rather difficult to get a good acting role in a teddy bear show, but you've got to start somewhere. So I was an impresario from the age of about nine or ten.

One day at boarding school, I was in my dormitory, playing around with my dressing gown/bathrobe-thingy, which I'd just draped over the metal headboard of my bed. Looking at it, I noticed something interesting:

If I played around with the cord of the dressing gown, I could attach it in such a way that when I pulled the cord the dressing gown would lift up, like the front curtain of a theatre.

This looked fantastic to me. And in a very back-to-front way, it suddenly hit me:

I have to create a show to fit around my dressing gown.

This is not the way productions should be done. This is not necessarily the way creativity should be done.

But up to the age of twenty-five, this is how my creativity was fuelled. Instead of trying to create a really good show, I would hire a venue and *then* try to put a show inside it. I became good at making the show happen, producing the show, publicizing the show. But I realized, at the age of twenty-four and a half, that I was *not* so good at focusing on the content of the show.

That's when I realized that story is everything. Content is everything. The product is everything.* Which is probably why they say in film that with a good script, anyone can make it work. But with a bad script, even god cannot get it to work (probably because he doesn't exist). And when I understood that, my career really started.

But back in that dormitory, I just had a venue and the curtains of my show. The bed was my stage. And I had a few teddy bears that I'd brought with me from home that were going to be the 'stars' of the show.

I put out chairs, and the headmaster remembers me in-viting the matron, Miss Hatter.† He happened to be wandering around, so I was obviously just grabbing everyone and pulling them in. I'd forced a show upon people, which was quite a brazen thing to do at the age of ten.

Then the teddy bears were on the bed. We reenacted this scene in the *Believe* documentary. And if you've ever seen a standard B movie, you know they always end up in a chase. I think I began with a chase and finished with a chase, which meant that the show was mainly bears chasing each other – there could have been shooting and treasure involved. It was me doing *Raiders of the Lost Ark: The Bear Version*, without even doing a first draft of the script (and without having an ark).

---

* As Steve Jobs said in *The Lost Interview*.

† When the *Believe* documentary was made, my headmaster from St Bede's School, Peter Pyemont, was asked if he remembered seeing the show, which he suddenly realized he did. He didn't re-member the story, though, and neither did I, because the story was nonexistent. This means: Good impresario. Bad storyteller.

The show was not great, but at least it was only about five minutes long.* But my first show was inspired by a dressing gown and I kind of like that.†

Having played a raven in the winter school play of 1967, the next time I got the chance at performing a role was in the winter of 1969. I was at St John's School in Porthcawl from the summer of 1968 to the summer of 1969, but I don't remember ever playing a theatrical role there. That is odd, but when I got to St Bede's School (now just Bede's School) in Eastbourne, in the south of England, in the winter of 1969, I did get to play a street urchin and a shepherd.

The winter of '69 was tough for kids in the UK (and

---

*I think I issued tickets for the show. My brother had already done something like this, I think. He had done a small play in a senior dormitory, so I was probably just copying him.

†Americans call dressing gowns 'bathrobes' or 'robes.' This slight confusion once led to even more confusion when I was in Luxembourg filming *Shadow of the Vampire*. There was no dressing gown/bathrobe in my room at the hotel, so I called down to reception. Speaking a fairly good conversational French, I thought I would ask – in French – about the missing-item situation:

'*Monsieur, il n'y a pas de robe ici.*' (There is no 'robe' here.)

He said, '*Oui.*' (Yes.)

'*Mais, je voudrais une robe.*' (But I would like a 'robe.')

'*C'est impossible.*' (It's impossible.)

I was confused.

'*Vous n'avez pas de robes dans cet hôtel?*' (You don't have any 'robes' in this hotel?)

'*Non.*' (No.)

'*C'est bizarre.*' (That's weird.)

So then I put the phone down.

The problem was, I was using the word *robe* here because I'd been working in America, and in America the word *robe* means 'dressing gown.' So when reaching for the French word for *dressing gown*, I landed on the word *robe*.

But in French, *une robe* means 'a dress.' So I'd been urgently requesting a dress in my hotel room: 'Do you not provide a dress?' 'Can you not bring me a dress?'

And the receptionist had been refusing to bring me a dress.

He was not going to help *any* transgender person to find a dress in *his* hotel at this late hour.

Finally I realized that the French for *dressing gown/bathrobe* is *un peignoir*. So I felt slightly foolish.

maybe around the world) – there had been a number of flu epidemics over the years, but in this particular winter term, school attendance was cut almost in half. Everyone was sick, it seemed – except for a few of us for some reason.

Every Christmas, like most schools, we'd do a bunch of shows before the holidays. Mostly nativity plays. This was a standard Church of England school thing. My form, the A-form, was supposed to perform *Beauty and the Beast.** Some beauty was given the role of Beauty, some thuggish kid was given the role of Beast, and some tall kid got the role of Beauty's dad – all decent speaking roles. After that, there must have been a few other roles, like Bloke at the Castle and 1st and 2nd Henchman.

But I was not given any role. No decent speaking role.

The rest of the kids like me, who were obviously no good at talking words, were told to play street urchins – a group of useless kids playing a group of useless kids. We had one collective line, which we of course did in that weird singsongy way that children do. The line was:

'Oh, Beauty, don't go.'

The way we said it in rehearsals was:

'Ohhhhh, Beauty, don't go . . .' in a long, drawn-out, straggly way with zero commitment, as if we were being prodded with an electric cattle prod.

Still desperate for a speaking role, I realized that while

---

*That winter term, due to the flu epidemic and the temporary shortage of student actors, I was seconded into the nativity play by the B-form to play one of the shepherds. But I don't remember being able to grab any of the good lines. Or get in on any of the action. I didn't get Joseph. Didn't get Gabriel. I was just one of the three shepherds, washing their socks by night (the Christmas hymn is actually 'While Shepherds Watched Their Flocks by Night,' but we would sing, 'While Shepherds Washed Their Socks by Night').

everyone was trying to draw in breath to say in unison, *'Ohhhhh, Beauty, don't go . . .'* I could just nip in there and say the line first, in a clear and quite fast voice before the other kids had actually got a syllable out.

'Oh, Beauty, don't go!'

So that's what I did. On the night of the performance, when I heard the cue line, I stepped forward and shouted out quickly and loudly – *'Oh, Beauty, don't go!'* – and then some other main character picked up their next cue and the play went on.

It became my first solo line.

This was, I realized later, called upstaging. But I was only upstaging all the other kids who probably weren't paying attention, probably didn't even notice I'd said it, and probably were still in the changing room trying to put socks on their heads.

That was my first performance success for some time. All these successes to this point and beyond this point were small and few and far between.

I remember we all went to see a few plays in which kids from our school played the child roles – including *The Sound of Music* – performed at the Congress Theatre, the main theatre in Eastbourne. Not only did they get out of lessons to do school plays, they got out of lessons to do professional plays in town. I don't know exactly what colour 'green with envy' actually is, but that's what I was.

And I thought: *Can I do that? Because I'd really, really, really like to do that.*

Asking myself that question was something I did quite often.

I remember going to the cinema in Bexhill on Western Road and watching *Bugsy Malone* in 1976, and there were all these kids playing gangsters and shooting custard pies out of guns. I thought it was beyond fantastic. If I'd been able to, I'd have watched it over and over and again and again – like I did with *Blade Runner* (eight times) when it was playing at the Anvil cinema in Sheffield for £1 a ticket and like we can now do on Netflix. But I do remember thinking, even then: *I want to be in this film,* Bugsy Malone. *Who do I talk to about doing this?*

But the film was already made wonderfully by Alan Parker. So I was not only *not* going to be in that film – I *couldn't* be in that film because I didn't know it was being made when it was being shot, and the winding back of time to get in that film wasn't going to happen. So then I thought: *Can I be in the next film?*

I think watching *Bugsy Malone* in the cinema led me to the idea of breaking into Pinewood Studios, one of the best-known film studios in the UK.

I realized that I should watch films all the way to the end of the credits, and to learn as much as I could about the business, I should copy things down. The names of actors. Crew. Cinematographers. Cameramen. Gaffers. Best boys. I saw these titles and scribbled things down even though I didn't really know what to do with this information. Then one day I was watching the film *The Battle of Britain.* This is a film and historical story that had a big effect upon me – above all, for the historical significance of it. But right at the end of the film, there is this big full-screen credit that says:

Filmed entirely on location at Pinewood Studios, Iver Heath, Bucks.*

This I wrote down, too: *Pinewood Studios, Iver Heath, Bucks.* I'd seen other films where it said *Filmed at Pinewood Studios.* Every time I'd see this I'd think, *That's where films happen. I have to go there. How do I get there?*

So I got a map that also had an alphabetical list of every town and village in the whole of the UK, because at this time (the late '70s) there was no Internet. After slogging through all the letters (remember: no small task for a dyslexic like me), I found Iver Heath near Windsor, Buckinghamshire, about twenty miles west of London.

I was in the southeast of England, which meant to get there I had to take a train to London, take the Underground train to Uxbridge, and then take a bus to Iver Heath.

I got off the bus and said, 'Is Pinewood Studios around here?'

'About a mile down the road, mate.'

I walked a mile down a big country road until I got there. At the entrance of Pinewood Studios, I went up to the main gabled entrance where all the stars had driven in over many years and said:

'Hello. I'm going to work in films. Can I come in?'

And they said words to the effect of 'Fuck off, kid.'

And I said, 'But you don't understand – I'm going to be in the film industry.'

And they said, 'What part of *fuck off* did you not understand?'

---

* A British film and television studio to the west of London where things like *Oliver Twist, The Persuaders!,* four *James Bond* movies *(Dr No, For Your Eyes Only, Octopussy, A View to a Kill), Superman,* and three *Star Wars* sequels were shot.

And I said, 'The word *off.*'

But that seemed to be it. I couldn't think of any other argument to use to get in, which meant I'd gone all that way – on the train and the Underground and then a bus and then a long walk down a long country road – and now I would be leaving with nothing.

Failure was not an option – they said that in *Apollo 13* – and although my situation was not life threatening and not on a spacecraft, and completely different, still, failure was not an option. It's something that came into my mind just now, not at the time. I wasn't going to give up. Not yet.

I headed away from the gabled entrance where all the big stars would come in* and walked a little farther up the road. There I saw another entrance – for workers – which had a drawbridge-barrier thing that would go up and down to let vehicles in and out. Watching people walk in, I noticed that most of them were carrying things – like clipboards and big envelopes and folders – and that some of them would stop and talk to the guards, but others would just walk straight in.

I deduced: *If you look like you know where you're going, and if you're carrying something, you can just walk right in.*

So even though I had nothing to carry, I put on the air of knowing what I was doing and just walked right up past the guardhouse and straight into Pinewood Studios.

The minute I was inside, I instantly became the 'creeping kid' creeping around Pinewood Studios, hoping that someone would see me and go, 'Hey, a creeping kid! We're

---

*They don't use it anymore, but you can still see it even though this entrance has been closed off.

doing this film called *The Creeping Kid*, and you can be the lead part in that because you seem to be doing exactly that.'*

I wasn't actually creeping around, because creeping around the place would have made me appear to be obviously in the wrong place. So instead of creeping, I actually marched quite fast around Pinewood Studios. I marched at the speed of someone who was delivering something so that if anyone looked at me, they would think, *Ah, that fifteen-year-old is taking something somewhere.*

So there I was, marching around, scanning and looking but always moving because I couldn't ever stop, since that would be a dead giveaway that I didn't belong there, causing someone to surely and immediately approach me and ask, 'You're not supposed to be here, are you? Well, I'm sorry, but I'm afraid we're going to have to shoot you.' (Which is exactly what John Cleese said to Michael Palin in Monty Python's Cheese Shop sketch.)

I didn't know what the security system was, but I managed to wander around the whole of Pinewood Studios, even up to the famous Bond stage, where I stopped to listen at the door. I could hear people talking, which I thought meant there *were* people in there, which meant that if I opened the door they would ask me what I was doing there and then throw me out.

But if I didn't open the door, I wouldn't be able to interact with anyone and definitely wouldn't get into a film.

---

*We've all heard the stories of actors discovered in a line of extras (like David Niven) or at the soda fountain of Schwab's Pharmacy in Hollywood (like Lana Turner, even though it turns out she wasn't discovered there; she was actually discovered at the Top Hat Café, also on Sunset Boulevard).

In the end, I left without getting thrown out. Probably the best option.

I continued with the long shots to just try to get on to the first rung of the acting ladder.

I also tried at Elstree Studios, another British film and television studio, in Hertfordshire, but I couldn't find an easy way in, so in the end I went under the wire fence. Sadly, I was caught by a security guard almost immediately.

Later, in 1981, I saw *Chariots of Fire* and realized that David Puttnam existed as a producer. I was obsessed with trying to get to David Puttnam. I thought, if I could find out where he's filming, I could just turn up on the set.

Later still, in 1984, I joined the Association of Independent Producers when I'd finally come down to London with nothing – no projects and no money and no contacts. But I thought that if I was a member of a producing organization, then maybe that would help.

Again, I was just trying to get on the first rung of the ladder.*

This feeling has followed me throughout my career. I remember doing stand-up in Wellington, New Zealand, for the first time, in 2000, and hearing that they were filming *The Lord of the Rings*. Again, I remember thinking, *Oh, I'd like to be in that*, then realizing, *No, they're filming it now. They cast it ages ago, so it's just not possible.*

When I thought about it more, I couldn't see a role I'd be suited to play, not that the director, Peter Jackson, would have cast me anyway. At some later point, a fictitious story

---

*I have a few different ladders listed in my mind, but during my early years I couldn't get on the bottom rung of any bloody ladder anywhere.

got into Wikipedia that I had asked to be in *The Lord of the Rings* and was told no. But this isn't true. I just thought I would like to be in it, until I realized I couldn't be in it, because it was already cast and filming.

So that shows how serious I was about getting into the film industry from an early age.*

---

*I mentioned this story to the doctor on my 2016 Mandela marathons, Dr Gary, an old friend who I've known since I was thirteen, and he said to me, 'Yeah, I was there with you.' I seem to have left him out of my story. I apologize for this. However, Gary was in fact there, backing me up and giving me encouragement, and I would like to thank him for doing that and being a good friend. Therefore, when we walked past the drawbridge to get into Pinewood Studios, there were two of us, and we would have been talking to each other like Richard Burton and Clint Eastwood did in *Where Eagles Dare*, when they walked into the Schloss Adler in Austria dressed as German officers. Watch that film again and this will all make sense.

My Football Career

The last time I played team football (or soccer) was in the school's 1st XI, in December of 1974 at St Bede's School. I was twelve years old. That was it.

I absolutely loved playing football – the frenetic running about, the feel and sound of my foot connecting with the ball out on the playing field. So it's odd that the whole of my football career spanned only three to four years. The first year I wasn't really sure what I was doing. It wasn't until I got into the Under 11 team – The Colts – that I started having a sense for the first time of what I could do in football and of what football was doing for me.

To be one of the eleven best in your year in a school sport became very desirable to me. I couldn't do it in rugby, which was played in the Easter term, or in cricket, which was played in the summer term. I was good at running with the ball, as you do in rugby, but I was no good at the tackling. There is a certain skill to tackling someone in rugby, and a great exponent of this can pull down a huge rugby player, even if they are small in stature – using the proper techniques.

I never learned the proper techniques. I never asked anyone what the proper technique was. I just used to throw myself at people and get damaged. So that was rugby. A kid called Oliver Carter was brilliant at it at my next school. He was not tall but could take down the biggest player like a sack of potatoes.

For me, cricket was all about the bowler trying to 'throw' a very hard cricket ball at your head while you were standing there waiting to die. I was scared of the cricket ball.

And my eye never seemed to be good enough to see the ball coming toward me so I could hit it properly. I think I used to look away when the ball came near my body. And if you're not looking at the ball, there's no way you're going to hit it.

It'll probably hit you – and then you're obviously going to die.

So cricket never worked for me.

It was when playing football with the Colts that we played 'The Greatest Game Ever Played.' Normally, we played about ten other schools from surrounding towns in East Sussex. Sometimes we played at home, and sometimes we played away. One day, in 1972, we were playing a school from Seaford. I believe it was St Peter's School – a strong school for sports. That day the teams got mixed up and they sent their 2nd XI football team over to our school and we sent our 2nd XI football team over to their school. This meant that the wrong teams were in the wrong places, and our Colts team was lined up to play their 2nd XI team.

Now, me and the other kids on the Colts team were all about eleven years old. The kids in the 2nd XI team were a mixture of twelve-and thirteen-year-olds (as the 1st and 2nd XI's were made up of the best players in the top two years). If you think back, kids are really beginning to jump up in height at those ages, so if an eleven-year-old is coming into contact against a thirteen-year-old, there could be a massive height and physical difference in play.

At the other school, St Peter's, they decided that their Colts team would not play our 2nd XI team. Both teams just relaxed and had an afternoon off. At our school, though, something unusual happened. The teacher in charge of our team came and told us the situation. He said their 2nd XI team had been sent over and the only team available to play them was us. He pointed out that these boys were a year or two years older than us. And then he said:

'You don't have to play this game. It's up to you.'

We looked at one another. No one really discussed it, but then Mr Lord, our teacher, asked us 'Do you want to play them?' And we all said 'yes.'

For me, it was the greatest game ever played.

It was a blustery day, overcast, intermittently raining. These kids were big. And we weren't. Some of the kids on our team were bigger, but I definitely was not. That day we played our guts out. In the last fifteen minutes of the game, I do remember, our entire team was standing in and around our goal mouth, defending like lions from the onslaught that these frustrated older kids were unleashing. They were slamming the ball into us from all angles. Repeatedly. Endlessly. The rain was lashing down then. There were probably trumpets and violins playing as well (I may have added to this scene in my head). The final score was 0–0 and we knew when we walked off the pitch that we had broken the space-time continuum of football. It was such a beautiful day. It was such a hellish day. But what we did had been so beautiful. In my mind those older kids were two or three feet taller than us, but obviously they weren't quite that big. But there will never be a greater game in my mind.

Back to my football career. If you can really call it that.

As I said, I loved football. I was not brilliant at it, but I would run about a lot, do some pretty good passing and some really good assisting (passing the ball to someone else on my team who kicked it in the goal), and if I ever lost a ball, I'd go and win it back from the guy who'd beaten me in the tackle. I was tenacious at doing that. But I was no good attacking the goal – I was too keen to thump the ball in the back of the net, so I would take too big a kick and it would go all over the place but nowhere near the goal.

As I said before, in the preparatory schools (or prep schools, as they're called) of Great Britain, the pool of talent for the top two teams in each school (the 1st and 2nd XI's) would be taken from the top two years (twelve-and thirteen-year-olds). I don't know why this was done. Maybe the idea was that it gave kids who were a year younger the ability to interact with kids who were a year older, which doesn't normally happen in schools. So when I was eleven in the winter of 1973, I was playing football with kids who were twelve or who had maybe just turned thirteen.

I distinctly remember the last practice game before the first match of the season. Everyone who was good at football was trying to get into the 1st XI football team. The 1st XI had been essentially decided upon. The head teacher there (we called him 'Headmaster'), Peter Pyemont, was in charge, and all the best players were in the 1st XI and were wearing the green football shirt, the playing strip of our school. But at this final practice game before the first match, I was wearing a white football shirt and therefore I was going to be in the 2nd XI. Before we got down to the practice field, which was near the school, I decided to hold back while the other boys walked down so that I could call my father from the pay phone, an old British red phone box, just down from the school and slightly off the main road.

My dad picked up and I pushed in a twopence piece. Once the line opened up, I told him, 'It looks like I'm not going to be in the first team this year. I hoped I would be, but that's what it looks like.' I had thought, earlier in the week, that I would make the first team, but now I couldn't see how that would happen, as the team seemed to have already been chosen and time had run out.

After I made the call I joined the practice game. All the kids in the first team, in the green school colours, were obviously better and more confident. As they practised against all us kids – all wearing the plain white shirts – they knew that they were better than us and that they were already on the team.

At this point I noticed that Mr Pyemont, the team coach, was giving training instructions to some of the kids on the first team. I overheard that they were practising what is called 'the one-two' – a move where instead of trying to take the ball past the defender, you kick the ball to a fellow player off to the side, and as you run past the defender, this fellow player kicks the ball straight back to you.

Once I realized this, it seemed obvious to me that when

some attacking player from the first team came running up to me, he would always kick the ball to one side to this other player. All I would have to do was cut the ball out. I knew the kid wasn't going to try to take the ball straight past me, so I just had to work out which person he was going to kick the ball to, and then as soon as he kicked the ball, I would just put my foot out and the ball would be kicked straight to me.

So as the final practice game commenced, I started doing this.

Again and again and again, as the attackers came toward me, they would attempt to practise the one-two and I kept cutting it out. I must have done it three or four times in about twenty minutes of practice.

It was as if I'd gathered privileged information. In fact, it was like getting the cryptanalysis of the Enigma from Bletchley Park that Churchill had all the way through World War II. That's what I had. I had Bletchley Park working for myself. Really just me and my big listening intelligence-gathering ears.

After about the fourth time I did that, suddenly I heard the magic words from Mr Pyemont:

'Izzard, change your shirt!'

I can still remember that moment. I became right half (right midfield), and in my mind, being in the first team, I basically became godlike. Not big gods, not the gods in the sky, just on a school level. It was wonderful, and I played like crazy to keep that position on the team and to try to get better.

After practice, on the way back to school, I called my dad

again to tell him the good news. I was ecstatic, and while relating this story, I think I still am ecstatic. It's a bit bizarre, but I would really love to be back there right now, playing another game.

Now that I'd made the team, I had to be fast and I had to be agile. As I mentioned, if I ever lost the ball to someone, I would always tear after them to get it just before they kicked it into the goal. I'd usually get my foot to the ball in the nick of time and kick it away. I don't think they thought I was going to turn and chase after them that fast – but I was good at stealing back balls that I'd lost and heading balls off the goal line – which was another good place to be.

There were matches every Wednesday and Saturday. On Wednesdays, after lunch, there would be a school assembly, and in the afternoon there were no lessons, so we could all go and play our games. Mr Pyemont would read out the names of the kids who were playing on a team that day. He'd always start with the players in the 1st XI. If you were in that first team, it was such a wonderful feeling to have your name read out. You were on the list of the best. We had worked our backsides off to be on this team. He'd say, 'Okay, everyone on the first team, get your kit and your boots and meet up at such-and-such place to be ready for the match.'

Then the eleven kids, feeling somewhat godlike, who'd been appointed to this top team would stand up and walk out in front of the whole school. Nothing had ever felt as good as that. I don't know if anything that I have done since then has felt as good as that. That was a beautiful feeling. I can remember the taste of it now.

In the winter in 1973, I didn't win my first team 'colours' (a cloth badge with the school's crest on it that you would sew on to your football shirt – to show you were the best of the best). But I was in the first team and there was a photograph to prove it (it's all about photographs proving you were there). But it shows the amazing height differential: if you look at it you will see that I am quite a small kid and that I must have been going toe-to-toe with kids who were up to a foot taller than me.

In my final football year, the winter of 1974, I did get my school colours – in fact, the whole first team got their colours (which was very rare). Our team even got a blackboard with our match results written on it in white chalk. This was even more rare. Again, there is a picture, and I have shown it to everyone that I can, as if it is of a child of mine. But it was a beautiful time and I regret its passing. The day I was awarded my colours, I was sick for some reason – so when I was given my colours it was just in the school corridor by the head teacher as I was going into some lesson. Normally it was awarded out in front of the whole school at a school assembly. That would have been a fantastic thing. Not getting it presented in front of the whole school and just having it handed to me in a corridor on the way to some lesson was a massive disappointment. I have never got over that.

When I got awarded two Emmys for my show *Dress to Kill* in the year 2000, one for Best Writing and one for Best Performance, I was actually filming in the mountains of

Austria. They wouldn't let me leave the film set to go to LA to be part of the ceremony, so that also was a bit like getting my colours awarded in the corridor.

In the winter of 1974 I played my last season of football. We played fourteen games: won eleven, lost one, drew two. Those are good results. As I said, we got a blackboard in our photograph, and every single player on the team got their team colours, the eagle crest in red on a green patch that you sewed on to your shirt.

The enormous amount of joy and pride that playing football used to give me and to have lost that at the age of twelve was terrible, for me. I stopped playing football at twelve and didn't start again until I was at university. By then I was awful. And I found it so tragic to be so bad. I couldn't understand why I couldn't play well.

It was not until I developed the logic of analysis that I realized (though it should have been obvious) all the other university students I was playing against had had five years of extra training and matches and playing and confidence building. As they'd got better over the last five years, I had got worse – because I hadn't been playing any football at all.

So at university, I was too slow, I couldn't pass, I couldn't shoot, I couldn't do anything. It was humiliating. I don't suppose the other students playing noticed this – they probably just thought I was crap – but I knew I had once been good and I was now crap.

Much, much later, in 2008, I took up football again. I was performing at the Union Square Theater in New York City for a month and I asked my promoter, Arnold Engelman, to see if he could find anyone in New York who could teach me football. This is when I met up with Jennifer Meyerson. She was coaching a women's team at NYU, and instantly we got on very well together. I started training with her, and that's what I still do these days: I do training and practice sessions. If I ever try to play an actual game I tend to flash back to the twelve-year-old kid I used to be, and because I'm so competitive I tend to get injured. So that doesn't seem to work for me. But I have regained my love of kicking a football about.

In 2012, when I went to South Africa the first time to try to run twenty-seven marathons in twenty-seven days to honour Nelson Mandela, I brought some footballs over, and I gave them to kids at an orphanage. They started throwing them at each other, and I thought, *Okay, they don't want these.*

But then suddenly they went wild and they were playing football up and down, and I was playing with them.

I think football/soccer can help save the world.

The thing is, anyone can be good at it. You can be tall, you can be short, you can be wide, you can be thin – it doesn't matter. Even though America loves baseball, (American) football, and basketball, I feel it is the ultimate American game, really, because it's a pure meritocracy, and that is what America was designed as.

Scouts and Girls and Rock and Roll

My early teen years involved Scouts, girls, and sports. Let's start with scouts.

In my final year at St Bede's School, a new master turned up who was going to organize a Scout troop. His name was Mr Allen, and the word was that he had worked at the head office of the UK Scouts organization. He was the most hyperorganized person I'd ever met *and* he made things happen. I was in my last year and I liked the idea of joining the Scouts. To me it was a bit like joining the army or special forces, other things that I saw and thought, *I want to do that.* So I joined the Scouts.

We had two or three different patrol groups. I was head of one of them and we were going to 'do' some things. I didn't quite know what interesting things we were going to 'do' in the Scouts, but my mind was open. We must have done a lot, because by the end of my single year in the Scouts I'd achieved three full levels of scouting proficiency and had got so many merit badges that I had to take some off my shirt, as I couldn't fit the new ones on.

The levels I had achieved were: Scout Standard, Advanced Scout Standard, and then by the end of the 1975 summer term Ed Gearing and I had both become Chief Scouts. This was a difficult thing to do in one year, and when Mr Allen realized that two of us might be able to achieve this award, we were encouraged by him to go for it. And we were both up for it.

The scouting started with camping and lighting fires. This appealed to me – the ability to light a fire. This wasn't done by rubbing sticks or bashing flints together to get a fire going. These weren't prehistoric-survival-skills fires. These fires were just lit with a match, but still they were fires, and we learned how to build and light them.

But by the end of that year, we had canoed down the rapids of the River Wye, we had gone potholing (or spelunking) in underground caves, we had also done abseiling (rappelling), and rock climbing as well. And I had made a map of the village of Castleton in Derbyshire while camping near there, which is quite an intense thing to do.

Canoeing down the rapids was fun. Climbing up mountains was not fun. Going underground through dark caves starts off as a fun idea but then gets very cold and can get very wet, especially when you climb down a rope ladder underneath a waterfall – which is what we did. When a ton of water is crashing on your head and your headlight goes out (because we had naked flame lights attached to our helmets!), things get really miserable after that.

One kid in our group had a wetsuit on. I think it was Ed Gearing. The rest of us didn't. He was smart. Ed Gearing, in his wetsuit, seemed quite happy.

So this was the day I learned that swearing can keep you warm. We had got back to the top of the cave (having climbed down that rope ladder underneath the waterfall). I think we had to climb back up again (up the same bloody waterfall) and I remember we were waiting for the others to join us at the top, one by one. We were a total group of about twelve to fifteen kids, and all of us (except Ed Gearing) were freezing. So I decided to swear loudly to keep myself warm. This seemed to work – sort of. I would not advise it as a method for heating in the long winter months, but if you have nothing else, try swearing your head off. That's what I did. I did feel slightly warmer by saying swear words beginning with f, s, p, and l and z. Many times. Out loud. In reality, I probably swore for only five minutes, but at the time it seemed like a couple of hours.

Above all, this scouting year was a fantastic year. It was adventurous, it was sometimes scary, but I loved it. Unfortunately at the end of it, a bit like my football career, I never did it again.

The one part of scouting that I didn't like was rock climbing.

If I had gone into the real special forces, instead of teenage Scout forces, there would have been a number of things I would have found more difficult and scary to do. Rock climbing had fun involved in it: abseiling down a mountain is quite fun mainly because you're constantly attached to a bloody great rope. Climbing up a mountain is less fun. You have to drag yourself up. You can't see anything except a cliff face in front of you. Beginners are always attached by a rope from above, which is supposed to be safe, but you don't really want to test it. Hanging on by your fingertips to a vertical cliff face or letting go and trusting that someone's going to catch your weight on a rope – well, neither of those two options seemed much fun to me, even if we were only climbing really small cliffs: about thirty meters high (about ninety feet).

What I remember is that when I was halfway up, I used to think, *I shouldn't have started this. I don't know what I'm really getting out of this.* The other thing I remember thinking halfway up those cliff faces was: *Stuff this for a game of soldiers.* This is a brilliant British-English expression that I encourage people to use, though I have no idea where it comes from. Probably from soldiers who didn't want to do it anymore.

Rock climbing didn't make sense to me in the same way that football had. I loved playing football and I knew what I was getting out of it: I was getting fitness out of it, team spirit, the idea that we could win and then we would be sporting gods. Climbing was so solo, and tricky, and hard, that I didn't know what I was getting out of it. I think at the end of a good rock climb you get a good view, but that hardly seemed worth the fear of it – especially when you could just walk up the other side of the hill and get the good view anyway.

However, there *was* one rock-climbing adventure that was rather interesting for me. One day I was told that some Girl Guides were going to go rock climbing and that they needed some capable Boy Scouts to go with them. *Great.* Me and Ed Gearing were asked to go along.

I think someone thought it was a good idea to have two experienced Boy Scouts go with the girls, almost like a chaperone thing.

I probably tried not to look scared climbing the rock face. Probably I just stood at the bottom, shouting, 'Yes, that's right. Good idea. Look for the hand holes. Excellent.'

But because there were girls there, I think I rallied and

decided that I was going to be as heroic in my rock climbing as I possibly could.

It's what happened afterward that I find really interesting (in retrospect).

Of the Girl Guides, there was one who was very pretty, whose name was, I think, Caroline Lloyd. She was a year or two younger than me, which meant that we would never have normally interacted were we not on this rock-climbing adventure. Despite my being older, I didn't feel terribly confident, because I'd already begun to move into puberty and puberty is a major confidence killer. Climbing didn't offer much chance to chat or flirt, as you were halfway up a rock face, but at some point during or after the climbing, someone suggested we all go swimming in the outdoor swimming pool nearby, and that seemed like a great idea.

It all got off to a very nice start – a scene of playful girls and boys mucking about in the water. It was all very fun. What happened next was typical of my inability to be cool in these situations – situations of boy versus girl or girl versus boy.

As a straight transgender person (or a wannabe lesbian), all girl-boy interactions before I had come out were just like any other girl-boy interactions: full of normal insecurity and general ignorance and inexperience about how the love game was played. Basically I decided to try and flirt with Caroline Lloyd in a 'splashy-splashy, muck about in the water' type of way – all quite fun and easy if everyone's splashing water. But then I had the idea to try and get into a 'chase me, chase me' situation: that's when you splash a bit too much and they get mock angry and swim after you to try to catch you.

I don't know if I knew that this is what you should do, but this was the extent of my ability to chat to girls or chat up girls or try to get any sort of liaison going.

The few times I had done this before, mock chasing seemed to be a part of flirting.

I didn't really know what flirting was. I suppose I thought that everyone else knew about flirting, but probably lots of other people didn't know how it all worked, either.

So that day in the pool I decided to go for it and started playfully splashing water in her direction. Then, according to my vague plan, because I was 'splashing her too much,' she made like she was going to swim chase after me. So I turned to swim away and my 'let the chase begin' began.

But this is where I had no finesse. The speed of my swimming away was ridiculously fast. I swam as if a shark was after me. I just swam and swam and swam right to the other end of the pool, lengthwise. When I looked around, at the other end of the pool, she hadn't moved. She obviously thought I was a mad swimming idiot.

It might have worked, if only I'd been less of an idiot.

But that was it. That was the highlight of the afternoon. Nothing happened – maybe nothing was ever supposed to happen that day. Maybe she was just trying to splash water on my face because she was trying to drown me. Flirting was not a brilliantly confident area of mine.

I wonder what she is doing today. The editor of this book advised me that I should thank her for leaving me with a great comedy story, so I'm thanking her for this interesting story of unrequited love, and for some reason I do like this story because it's so pathetic. And I think she wouldn't even remember this.

I was a late starter in the girl-boy flirty-sex thing. Particularly the sex thing.

But I do remember, when I was seven or eight years old, the first time I overtly kissed a girl. I think her name was Jane Taylor, or it might have been her sister.*

Again, this involved girls and flirting and chasing. When you're a kid you get no instructions about how to flirt or make inroads with people you fancy. I did work out on a gut level (on an animal level?) that if you got into some sort of mock fight, that was kind of positive.

It wasn't actually a fight; it was more like you had to interact and, I suppose, tease in a flirty way, even though I didn't know what flirting was. So if a girl was pissed off with you, or mock pissed off with you, then that seemed to work – in a flirty way.

You could tell by a girl's reaction if they were smiley pissed off with you or frowny pissed off with you. Big difference. If they were frowny pissed off, then they were just pissed off and wanted to hit you (and quite often did). If they were smiley pissed off, then something good was happening.

On this occasion, Jane Taylor (or was it her sister)

---

* I'm not sure if I'll remember, or should remember, all the names of the people in stories about kissing – it's not as if I have a massive number of wild sexual stories to tell here, but I have noticed as one gets older that if one person has a memory of a situation, another person in that situation may have quite a different memory of it. This seems to happen again and again. So what I'm saying here is what I remember and how I remember it happening (not that these are great revelations).

appeared smiley pissed off, and a chase did happen. We ended up running around the back of a building where no one else was, and when she 'caught' me, I said:

'Kiss me. Kiss me on the lips.'

And she did kiss me.

And it was good (a biblical moment).

But then nothing much happened after that. Which was annoying.

It didn't develop into a girlfriend-boyfriend situation – even though I don't think I was looking for that. I don't think she was looking for that. We were seven or eight. She was a day girl and I was a boarder. It was one moment – just *boom* and that was it. It was a wham-bam-thank-you-miss with just one kiss but without any of the whatever-came-next. We were too young to do anything else. But it was a good experience.

For some people, usually the prettiest people, boyfriend-girlfriend and sex stuff becomes the big be-all and end-all. For me, it seemed a lot of fun, but it felt like playing with nitroglycerin and I was looking for the instructions.

Later on I decided the falling-in-love thing was horrible. Not actually horrible – the initial feeling is really great – but the out-of-control-ness of being 'in love' is horrible. You just don't seem to have any control of it. And so loving someone seems good, but I am very suspicious of *being* 'in love.' I believe a chemical gets released in the brain and once you've triggered it you can't get it back in the bottle. And it can screw you up. If two people are perfectly in love at the same time, syncing away, it's excellent. But how are you supposed to control that?

I do not know.

When I was about eleven or twelve, a game called 'kiss chase' started happening, which was a more organized version of the chasing and kissing I had done before and which had the whole flirting-for-beginners thing built into it, even in the name.

The idea was that every time somebody successfully tagged or touched you while the game was on – you owed that person a kiss. Obviously this had to happen between two people who wanted to kiss each other.

My partner in this game of kiss chase was a girl called Nicole Cunningham. She was slightly taller than me, or maybe somewhat taller than me, and very athletic. And as it is with all kids going through a number of years at school together, there just seemed to be a moment where we decided we fancied each other.* This, I believe, was that moment for us.

If you wanted to get kissed more in kiss chase, the trick was to get near the person you fancied so they could tag you while you looked like you were not wanting to get tagged, otherwise the game was not being played. I remember being in a classroom and queuing up next to the teacher's desk, which was near Nicole Cunningham's desk, which meant I kept getting tagged by her (even though I was seemingly trying *desperately* to avoid this), so it was all working for me and kiss chase was going very successfully. Which meant I owed her a whole bunch of kisses.

Kiss chase seemed a good and fun and – dare I say it –

---

* Maybe the actual Nicole Cunningham will remember this happening totally differently or happening with someone else – you'll have to ask her.

innocent but sexy game to play. But it was before puberty, which meant that it was the high point of my runabout, athletic, soccer-playing, confident-kid phase. After thirteen – after the end of my football 'career' (at only twelve), and after the end of my scouting year (the summer of 1975) – all that just disappeared (not that it was *that* wildly active beforehand). I was still a rather shy child – the idea of real sex hadn't yet got into my head. I don't think I had any clue what that was. Kiss chase was great to play, but I only remember playing it for a short, intense time.

Was it played for a day? Was it played for a week? Maybe it was played for a month. I can't believe we played for only one day and that was it, but that's pretty much how I remember it.

Nicole Cunningham – she was athletic and competitive. I was somewhat athletic and competitive, but I was not as good as her.

Now we come to the Under 11's athletics cup. Nicole should have won it, but I won it. I think Nicole Cunningham had won the Under 9's athletics cup. I think she had also won the Under 10's athletics cup. And she was definitely about to win the Under 11's athletics cup.

I was quite a small kid, but for some reason I was good at hurdles – that year. But Nicole had already done well in the other athletic events before that day, as she always had. There was the assault course and the long jump and the high jump and I think she had come first or second in all of those.

Coming into the final day of the competition, Nicole Cunningham had already stacked up a number of red ribbons,* so it seemed impossible that anyone other than Ms Cunningham could win the athletics cup. So on Sports Day, even if I could beat her in the hurdles, she would probably still get two first places in the only two running races, which meant she would win yet another athletics cup (which I think she didn't really need, since she'd won everything up to that point).

So that Saturday, the first race up was the hurdles.

I had no technique for this. Decades later, when I ran my forty-three marathons for the Sport Relief charity, I watched *Chariots of Fire* a lot of the evenings and days off, just to keep my head in the Endurian/Olympian mind space. And what I learned from watching it was that those runners had techniques: release and hold back, and turn it on, and then push to the last bit. All the technique-y stuff that experienced athletes have. But when I was eleven, I just had 'bang goes the gun and run like a rabbit.' And if it was hurdles, then 'run and jump like a rabbit.'

So that's what I did. The gun went off, I went for it as hard as I could, and I won the race (which surprised me). Ed Gearing came in second, and Nicole Cunningham was third. (There's a photograph of this – me punching the air with my hand in elation/surprise.)

But.

Nicole was feeling ill that day, and she was probably already ill in that race, so she was running that race not

---

* Red was for first place, green was second, blue for third. These would be handed out and you could win a whole bunch of ribbons. Well, let me rephrase that: *Nicole Cunningham could win a whole bunch of ribbons – usually red.* The rest of us just got other colours, coming in paltry seconds and thirds.

feeling well, which meant that she probably could have done better. After that race there were two other races to run, and I began to see that she wasn't feeling great and was not doing well.

Now, as a competitive little bastard, I really wanted to win these races and I really wanted to win the Under 11's athletics cup. I knew that if Nicole took part in the races and even just came in second or third she'd probably still win the whole thing. But I also knew that if she was ill and couldn't take part in the races at all, she wouldn't get any of those points.

So I decided it might help if I prayed to god for her to be ill.

I don't believe in a god now, but back then, well, I was told there was a god. Since then I've noticed that he or she never does anything, so I've decided to conclude that either they're not there or they don't care. But even with no moral reasoning behind it, I did decide to pray to god to make a bad thing happen.

Dear god, please let Nicole Cunningham continue to be unwell.

Now, this is a bad thing to do and I'm sorry I did it. But it didn't really do anything, since I'm quite sure he or she isn't there.

Whatever Nicole Cunningham had – a tummy bug, something she ate the day before, I don't know – she had to pull out of the last two races. In modern Olympics, the press would have gone wild: 'The athletics cup race is now WIDE OPEN.' I can't remember how the points broke down, but I won the last two races and so I won the Under 11's athletics cup. She would have won if she hadn't been ill, but she wouldn't have needed it, since she already had two cups. If there is a god, surely god would want the athletics cups to be shared out a bit. It's just boring if one person gets them all the time.

So I won the cup. I got a little silver cup, about the size of your hand. It was like winning a small silver eggcup. But it was really Nicole's.

I had prayed to god and god had answered my prayers, which I later felt guilty about. I feel I should say this. I do feel I am a determined little twit, so determined that I was willing to call a god. But I didn't spike her food or do anything truly terrible, so if there is a god hopefully I'll only get a suspended sentence.

The Scholarship Holidays

When I was about twelve, I realized that if you work hard, you get better results.

This might seem obvious to most people, but it was not apparent to me. Maybe it was because some kids seemed brighter academically or some worked harder than others and I never made that direct connection before, but when it came time to try out for the scholarship form* at St Bede's, I realized motivation was important and a key factor to success. Especially for someone like me, who I feel is a lazy but driven person. When motivated, I will move heaven and earth to get something done. When not motivated, I'll sit in bed and watch black-and-white movies and eat breakfast cereal.

To be in the top form, the scholarship form at St Bede's, you had to be smart or a hard worker, or both. At that point, I don't know if I had a view on whether I was smart or not, but I did feel that I was good at mathematics.

We all learned our multiplication table and I always got every multiplication problem correct. Every single one. From the age of six onward I never got any of them

---

*The scholarship form was a form for bright kids who were going to take a different exam to get to the next school (what is sometimes called 'Public School'). This exam was called the scholarship exam. It was harder than the 'Common Entrance' exam that most kids took to get into the next school. If you took the scholarship exam and did well, the school would offer you money (reduced fees) to come and learn at their school.

CLOCKWISE FROM TOP LEFT:
Dad and Mum in Beirut on their honeymoon in May 1959.

Mum, pregnant with me, in 'Adan (Aden) in 1961.

Me with my panda at the back door of 5 Ashford Drive, Bangor, N. Ireland.

Mark, Dad, and me (on the tricycle), in the garden in Bangor.

Playing in the back garden in 1963 or 1964 at 38 Windmill Drive, Bexhill.

Me with Mum and a 'kat' at Ashford Drive.

Mark, Mum and me in a car carousel in a Gothenburg park, summer 1965. Very happy times.

The whole family together in Gothenburg, summer 1965.
(We have very few photos like this – with all of us.)

Mark, Dad and me on a small boat ride, again on the Gothenburg holiday in 1965.

Mum was just well enough in December 1967 to make me this raven costume. My face doesn't seem to be overjoyed with the role.

In the small back garden at Grannie and Grandad's house. We would have baths, in front of the coal fire, in that tin tub. As did our dad and grandparents. This must be 1967 or 1968.

Playing on the breakwaters off the southeast coast of Ireland, on holiday after Mum had died.

Mark and me at St John's school in Porthcawl, Wales, summer 1968. The red rosettes meant we were both in 'Saxon' section.

Mark, Dad and me, in front of the Severn Bridge between England and Wales in 1968 or 1969, on a trip over to see Gran and Grandad.

Mark doesn't have the same sweet tooth as I do, so I probably
drank all the 'pop.' Outside the Beachy Head pub.

Me and Mark mucking about on a bench outside a pub in Crowhurst after
walking up the old railway line from West Bexhill station.

Playing in the fields of Skewen in 1968, with a cheap helicopter thingy. I always loved the gadgets.

Mark and me in our St John's uniforms – off to a wedding (note the white flower) in '68 or '69.

Mark, Gran and me – photo taken in Skewen. Gran with her Gran hairdo.

Mark and me on the South Downs which I love so much, in front of the Seven Sisters Cliffs near Beachy Head, early '70s.

Great photo of Mark and me, packing Dad's VW, outside the Atherton family house in Bishop's Stortford, where we had a wonderful time. It was there we all watched Neil Armstrong set foot on the moon in July 1969.

Winning the Under 11's hurdles race in summer 1973, against Ed Gearing and Nicole Cunningham (she would have won but she was ill).

The whole 1st XI got our colours (and a blackboard with our results) in the winter of 1974. This was very rare, but I would never play competitive football again.

I really wanted to play the drums, and so I did. Here probably in 1976 or 1977.

Me with Ian Rowland – our first Edinburgh Fringe, summer 1981. Taken on 'Fringe Sunday,' where everyone performed on the High Street and I discovered street performing.

In 1982, in Bexhill wearing a suit. The watch and chain belonged to my great grandfather.

wrong. I knew the whole times table when I was six. From two times two to twelve times twelve. They even came up with a new times table for me to learn: one times one is one, two twos are four, three threes are nine, four fours are sixteen, etc.

I was dyslexic with letters, but I liked numbers. As there were a lot of different subjects, I was better at some than others: namely, mathematics and languages.[*]

It started with the game of I Spy and spelling tests. I remember Mum working with me back in Bangor when I had just started going to Ballyholme Primary School. Spelling seemed weird to me. It just didn't make any sense.

The word itself – *dyslexia* – is ironically very hard for dyslexic people to spell correctly.

I didn't even know what dyslexia was until I was doing stand-up comedy in my thirties. Someone at the end of a show came up to me and said, 'I think you're dyslexic; you talk about things in a dyslexic way.' I'd heard of the word, but I had no idea what the traits or symptoms were. 'Well, your writing would be all over the place.' Which it is: I have bad handwriting – the size of the letters are always different – and there are a number of key things that dyslexic people do that I seem to do, too. So I started feeling I was dyslexic just because of what this person had told me after a gig.

There came a point when someone wanted to give me an award for being dyslexic, but I felt slightly fraudulent

---

[*] I remember reading about Churchill being a bad student and then teaching himself what interested him. I totally understand that and think there must be quite a few kids at school who are bright enough but who can't find the motivation to endlessly work at learning things. If there is no application for the things you are learning, it can seem pointless. And kids get bored.

because I thought, *Well, I* think *I am dyslexic, but I don't really know. Can somebody test me?*

When I was finally tested, I was told afterward that I was *severely atypically dyslexic.* It seems that I have a big mental memory map but I'm rather bad at other things. They still gave me the award, which was very nice of them, but since half of the world of dyslexia didn't seem to trouble me and half of it did in a big way, I still feel slightly fraudulent. I have since been retested for dyslexia and, basically, I'm still dyslexic.

I can sight-read fairly well (these days), so it's not as bad as it could be. I was a very slow reader when I was younger, and I am a faster reader now. I can sight-read, not brilliantly well, but quite well. Well, enough to appear like I don't have dyslexia. If there are large words, unusual words, or words with *f*s and *th*s and *ph*s, I have to slowly go through the words to work them out and then I have to repeat them again and again. Out loud. Which is one of the traits of dyslexia: vocalizing as you read.

I know people who can read a novel in a night, but for me, it's tricky. Reading scripts is tricky: I just take longer than anyone else. With film scripts, it is better for me to read them out loud.

I do think that a lot of creative people are dyslexic. Maybe if you're dyslexic, you think sideways rather than forwards. I'm sure there are other aspects involved, but I've always felt like I've looked at things and done things slightly differently from other people. If you're a logical thinker, A to B to C to D: that's how you move through tasks or how you move through the steps of your career. Dyslexic people like me are more: *A* is an upside-down *V* with a handle on it; *B* is two *D*s stuck on top of each other; the letter *O* is a number; the letter *E* is the same as the letter *B*, but the front bit's been cut off. Things like that.

Anyway, my brother got into the scholarship form at St Bede's and what I remember most about that was that they went on holiday during term time! When I found this out, I thought that this was un-fucking-believable.

How could this be? How could you go on holiday when everyone else had to do lessons? Is this not joy beyond all joys?

Because the holiday thing just blew my mind, I was determined to get in, too. If other kids had been doing lessons and exams and I had been in a class that just sat around drawing pictures and relaxing, that would also have been fine, but the idea of some kids doing lessons and exams and the rest of us going for a holiday in France was just too much.

So at the end of the summer of 1973, I found that I'd got into the scholarship form. I was very happy now that I knew I'd be getting a holiday in term time. Especially while the other kids were working.

At the end of the first term in the scholarship form, approaching winter, my report cards were bad. At the end of the Easter term of 1974, my report cards were equally bad. I was at the bottom of the heap of the six people in my year in the scholarship form.

That year, my dad had been asked to go out to work in Abu Dhabi, in the UAE, so during the Easter holidays my brother and I went to stay with him there for four weeks. Which was great. We flew from London by Gulf Air, a long,

long flight with one extra stop for refueling. We also had to be chaperoned on the airplane because we were traveling without an adult, since Dad was already out in Abu Dhabi.

This was scary but exciting. We were taken to what is now the Holiday Inn right next to Heathrow Airport. We stayed in a twin room for one night and it had a minibar. We were told we could help ourselves to anything from the minibar or from room service. This was the first time I ever had a free minibar and expenses in a hotel room and it blew my mind. I must have drunk one, if not two, Coca-Colas. I didn't care. It was so rock-and-roll. And then I went downstairs and Auntie Trudy (a good family friend who had known my mum when they were both nurses) came to see us and we had a meal, which we extravagantly charged to our room. I had sausage, egg, and chips! Well – when in Rome . . . I just went completely wild. I must have run up a bill of almost five pounds, which seemed like a king's ransom to me. The next morning we flew to Abu Dhabi, and while flying was always a nightmare to me – I'd normally throw up on every plane – on this, one of the maiden voyages of Gulf Air, I didn't throw up!

About a week after we arrived I got shingles. It was a sort of scratchy disease – your nerve endings get all flared up. I was sprayed with plastic skin and told I couldn't go in the water, which is the main thing you want to do when in Abu Dhabi because the seas are blue, crystal clear, and it is very hot. Shingles is normally very painful, but for me, it was just annoying and scratchy.

We stayed in what was probably called the European or

American section of Abu Dhabi* at that time, in a very nice house that belonged to a family who was away on leave. The kids had left a lot of American comic magazines – *Batman*, *Superman*, *Spiderman*, *The Green Lantern*, and I remember finding those fascinating and exciting. Americana! This crystalized my fascination with America. They had the records of the first-ever *Batman* episode and the first-ever *Green Lantern* episode in their house – which we recorded on my brother's state-of-the-art Sharpe cassette-tape recorder.

Whilst on this holiday, the school report cards came out. Mine said that I was a bad student not doing well and that if things didn't change that summer term, I was going to get moved down into the common entrance form instead of the scholarship form.

This would mean I would not get the term time holiday in France. So I decided, *Hell, 'not working' is not working. I better try working.*

That next term I paid clear and distinct attention to everything. I remember it was a little tricky, because after two terms I now had to play catch-up. But at the end of that summer term, the school reports came in and I ended up coming first or second in my year in most subjects. Once I started working again it was much easier: I was paying attention, so I stayed in the scholarship form long enough to get two holidays in France: one in the summer of '74 and one in the summer of '75. But I must say, once they allowed me to stay, I stopped working again.

---

* Otherwise known as the Place Where You Don't See Any Local People. You had to go to the markets and bazaars to see real local people.

In the summer of '74 we went on holiday to a place called Camping Indigo Paris. It's where I almost set fire to myself in my dad's single-person canvas tent using an international camping gas lamp with the wrong gas cylinder: what was supposed to be gas-powered turned into a kind of flamethrower when I put the wrong gas into it. I managed to get it back under control after twenty or thirty seconds, but it was touch and go.

I went back there recently, to see the camp site again, while I was performing my show *Force Majeure* in Paris, nearby, all in French! The camp site is right by the Bois de Boulogne (the Woods of Boulogne), which is famous for being an area where prostitutes, who just happen to be transgender, hang out at night. It was weird for me to be there, since I feel I'm at the more action and executive end of transgender, but I decided that I should do a symbolic walk, in heels, from my old camping site to the place where I was now performing comedy in nearby Boulogne-Billancourt. I walked this journey in heels, in what I call 'girl mode,' just to prove that not all transgender people in heels in the Bois de Boulogne are working in another particular industry.

It was quite a long walk. I walked for an hour, but it was a meaningful walk, as it drew a clear line from where I had once been (a kid in a camping site) to where I am now (an openly trans person doing stand-up in French). There are very few times in life you get to see the progress you've made as clearly as that.

The Magic Ian's Nephew

(PROBABLY WRITTEN IN 1970 – WITH THANKS TO C. S. LEWIS)

Edward I.

Our Story ① 31th Ianary

One day a girl named polly was outside in the garden, and a boy looket over the wall the boys name Digory he had a dirty face, the boy and the girl sone made friends. One day Digory said letts explore your hous so polly and Digory went up into a place wen there was a hole and you can carol threw into a long passage at the end of the passage there was a empty house polly said letts go to the empty house but how dow we no that we are in the rite house said Digory polly said we will measure how long it is, so polly and Digory measure after that thay went and got lotts of wood and steks and put tham across the hole, and so wen thay had a long hole with wood and steks, so thay went along the passage till thay came to a door so thay opend it and

②

thay came into a rome with furniture
and a fire and a tray with green
and yellow rings but Polly did not
touch the rings but the chair was
mooving and a man came up and
than Digory said that is
Uncle Andrew, his face looket
cruel, Polly said I have to go
to dinner Uncle Andrew said
wate a minite let me give you
a little present first, i wil
give you a yellow ring.
Polly said can i have a
green ring no you can't
have a green said uncle
Andrew with a smile
only the yellow rings
polly was just going to
touch it and Digory
said dont touch the ring

③

dont be a fool, but it was
to late polly had disappeared
Digory said wie did you do
that, Uncle Andrew said I wanted
to see wote was in a nuther
wold, wie dident you go to
the other wold said Digory,
because I mite be kild, than
your a kowerd if you
want polly yode beter go
and get her but how
do I get there, you
put a yellow ring on
and put two green rings
in your rite pocit than Digory
put on a yellow-ring
and Digory disappeared
Digory found him self in a
dark place a bit like a
passage and he thort he

128

④ PLEASE tune to the next page

was in a pole of water
and he found himself geling
out of the water and
than he saw a girl, Digory thort
that he had sean that girl bofor
and the girl thort that she had
sean the boy bofor and than
thay remembered you are Polly sa
Digory, and you are Digory
said polly than Digory said
there is a ginepig with a Yellow
ring Polly said lets go home
Digory howe do we get
there I have two green
rings the green rings take
you back the the other Wold,
so thay put on the green
ring and said one two three and
jumet and than polly said
caje rings Digory wantid to

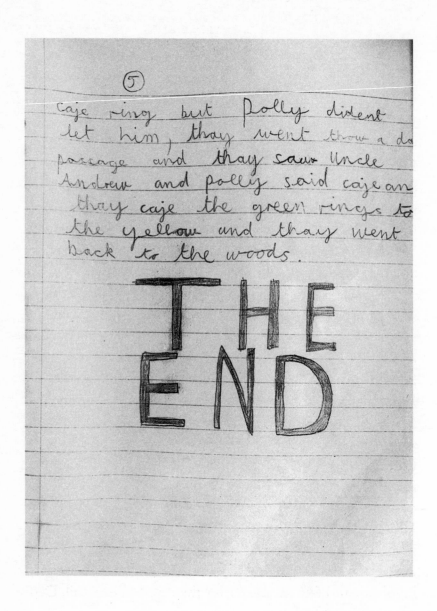

⑤

caje ring but polly dident
let him, thay went throw a do
passage and thay saw Uncle
Andrew and polly said caje an
thay caje the green rings to
the yellow and thay went
back to the woods.

THE
END

Three Each

In 1975, when I was thirteen, Kate Tomasetti became my stepmother. She and my father met in a rather odd way: Dad was volunteering on the Samaritans phone line, which people phone when they are depressed and need to talk to someone. Dad had been rather isolated since Mum had died but had decided by that point to stop looking for a partner. Instead, he decided to try to help people who were having an emotionally tough time.

In January of '75, midway through a call with a woman who was separated from her husband, he realized from the smattering of details she'd revealed that he knew her: Her name was Kate, and her first marriage, years before, had been to his cousin. They had even holidayed together in East Anglia in 1957 when she and his cousin and he and his first wife, Joy, had all still been married. He said nothing about this during the call, but the next day, unable to stop thinking about her, Dad contacted Kate, even though he knew it was against the Samaritans' rules to make personal contact with clients. He revealed that he was 'Harold of Hastings' – his identity from the call line – and when she invited him over to her house for a visit, they realized they lived quite close to each other. Soon after that they became involved, and two months after their first phone call, Dad proposed and they became engaged.

They got married in September, on the first Saturday of my first term at my brand-new school. I was now at East-bourne College, a boarding school for thirteen-year-olds to eighteen-year-olds, and after just four days of being there, I had to disappear for a day – on Saturday – to go to my dad's marriage.

At this boarding school, we did school lessons every Saturday morning, which meant that I had to miss the first French lesson that Saturday. The next week, when I went to the next French lesson on my schedule, I managed to say a funny line:

'I'm sorry I wasn't here on Saturday, sir – my parents got married.'

I do remember thinking of it as a funny line. Which is interesting, since my whole time line as to when I thought I was funny or when I started cracking jokes is hazy to me. And I never actually cracked jokes. I never did a 'two men walked into a pub' kind of thing. I couldn't tell jokes. I could only make quips, like the one about my parents getting married. They appealed to me.*

So my dad had finally remarried, something I know he had wanted to do, and later I came to understand that Kate, too, was happy to be married again. I don't remember much about the wedding itself, but I do remember that something very unexpected happened at the reception. At some point Kate said, 'Well, that's three times for both of us.' Meaning

---

* I liked comedy, but I didn't think I could perform it. Until I was sixteen or seventeen, people said that I wasn't funny at school. I know I became consciously funnier in chemistry lessons when I was seventeen or eighteen. But at this stage, when I was thirteen, I was just lucky to get off the occasional quip.

that both she and my father had each been married three times. Then I chipped in and said, 'Actually, it's only two times for Dad.' But Dad confirmed it:

'No, it's actually three times.'

This totally blew me away. Because I had never known that my dad had been married before Mum.

The news of this earlier marriage had a huge effect on me, as if everything I'd known about the world and my place in it had shifted. Which it sort of had. I had to sit down in a corner of the reception room to try to process it, which didn't really work because I simply couldn't understand why I hadn't heard of this other woman until now – at Dad's third wedding.

In actual fact, I later realized, it was none of my business, but as someone's child, I suppose, you feel you should be allowed to know everything. Dad was not happy about his first marriage, so he'd written it off, as if it hadn't counted, and his marriage to Mum became the only marriage he ever mentioned.

Years later, when my career had taken off, I was playing the Congress Theatre in Eastbourne.* I played it for two nights, and on one of the nights, Dad's first wife, Joy, the one I'd never known about until I was thirteen, turned up at the gig. I remember she was there with her two children, whom she'd had after she and Dad split up. By that point I'd learned that Joy hadn't been completely faithful to my father during their brief marriage and that they'd got divorced because Dad had eventually found out, so I can't

---

* The Congress Theatre is the biggest theatre in Eastbourne, where I'd watched *The Sound of Music*, years before. When I got to play it and fill it, it was a dream come true.

say that I was wildly happy to see her. Dad, who was there, too, and Joy seemed to be getting on very well, which confused me. To make matters even more confusing, one of Joy's children had told me that their father had been a big fan of mine. Assuming this is true and I didn't just dream it all up, I was terribly thrown by that. And I was about to go onstage but feeling rather pissed off by Joy because of what she'd apparently done to my father.

But afterward, I realized that if Joy hadn't caused their marriage to end, my mother, who turned up in 'Adan in 1958, probably would have met someone else on the refinery base and married him instead of my dad, and therefore – I wouldn't exist. So I really had no reason to be pissed off.

I feel Kate had had a tough upbringing. She'd grown up in North Shields in the northeast of England, near the city of Newcastle, and she later told me that she'd suffered sexual abuse as a child, which is a very rough way to start out in life. She was quite ordered and capable and intelligent, and I heard that when she took the exam for the UK Foreign Office of the civil service she came in fifth in the country. Quite a feat. But for all her abilities (she worked in the SAS doing Morse code in '44 and '45, and later even went on to visit Russia during perestroika before it was completely open), she seemed to fear being given too much responsibility, refusing promotions in the Bexhill tax office where she worked for many years before she met Dad. I really don't know why, but for reasons I never quite understood, she had a great deal of potential she didn't use.

Kate seemed to have an unusual combination of attributes:

tremendous ability and a fear of ambition. I was quite the opposite: I had tremendous ambition but with questionable ability. We both looked at the world in opposite ways.

Becoming the stepmother to Mark and me couldn't have been easy for Kate, either. Being a stepparent must be one of the hardest gigs in the world. When she arrived we'd lived seven years without a mother. And we'd been seven years without a father for two-thirds of each year because we were at boarding school. So her presence suddenly made a massive difference.

In their new home in Bexhill-on-Sea, which Dad and Kate would share for almost forty years, always with two black poodles (which were Kate's passion), she was very particular about certain things. For instance, she had a rule that we weren't allowed to drink milk in the house or have it as a drink (I still don't quite understand why – something to do with it being 'foodstuff'). She also insisted that we say, 'I have had sufficient,' instead of 'I'm full up' when we'd eaten enough. This may be better English but I didn't see what was the problem.

Initially, having a new stepmother who wanted things done her way was horrible and I did a lot of disagreeing. As a teenager, it certainly was not easy to follow new sets of rules, especially during holidays when my brother and I came home from school for our breaks. Dad would be at work and we would be at home, all trying to get along.

During my brother's eighteenth birthday, Kate said roughly this to us: 'You've got to understand that you are a cog in the machine. As soon as you understand that, you can fit in and get on with life.'

Now, that is an opinion, but there is no way that I agree with it. You could argue that some people in life end up being cogs in the machine, but I would wish them not to feel like that and not to have to live thinking that way. Lots of people work for companies, and I suppose if you are in a company, you are part of a machine. Maybe that's what she was talking about. But I was of the opinion that you should never feel like just a cog in a machine, you should always go for your dreams.

I would have said that even if I were a cog in the machine, I would not like to see myself as a cog in the machine. I would like to see myself as a cog who is shooting for the stars and could go into any machine I want to and become a bigger cog or a cog shaped like a different cog. I would redefine the whole cog argument, that's what I'd do. But her view was a hundred and eighty degrees different to what I believed. Kate was very easy to get along with, as long as you agreed with her. And I didn't most of the time. This would cause friction, so I did my best to just shut up and not say anything for the five years of teenagehood I had left before I went away to university. I had a lot of energy and Kate had a lot of energy but we thought in completely opposite ways. With hindsight I could probably see her point on a number of disagreements we had, except for the fact that she gave away all our childhood toys, including teddy bears.* That's just not right.

---

*Not too long ago, my brother, Mark, said, 'You know, she gave away our toys?' I mean, you are getting older, the toys and teddy bears have been put to one side, but still, you should be the one to decide when you lose your own teddy bears. I did meet someone at her funeral who received them. He said, 'I got all your toys.'

I'm sure our arguing was hard on my father. I'd had quite a lot of training for arguments in boarding school, where argumentative kids of the same age were constantly debating everything.* I'd had seven years of this, so when Kate said something I didn't agree with, I wouldn't lie down. And if I did disagree, after a while, there would be tears (not mine). And once there were tears, there was no more arguing. The discussion was over.

Therefore, at a certain point, we never discussed anything.

Not about the makeup I'd been caught shoplifting.

Not about my denials that I'd been trying on her clothes.

Not even when she asked me the same question for years and years, after I'd left university and come to London to become a professional performer – which was, 'When are you going to get a proper job?'

Dad was much more easy going with me. He would just say, 'As long as you're happy.' That's really what he's most cared about for us. Only once, about four years after I'd dropped out of university, do I remember him saying, 'Are you not a little bit disappointed? You could have had a well-paid job with a company car by now.' I said no. Dad knew that I wanted to earn decent money, but he could see that my mission had changed. He could see that I was going for my dreams, and while he felt he could never advise me – my dreams were far out of his comfort zone – he was never anything but supportive of me.

---

* Especially when someone said that you were an idiot and then you said that he was an idiot, and then you had to explain to him why he was an idiot, and then you'd explain why you weren't an idiot, and it would go on and on and on.

Kate, however, wanted me to be an accountant. When I dropped out of university, she felt I should repay my father the money he'd spent on my education. You can see the logic behind this: so many parents tell their children, 'Get a proper job, have a backup career, become an accountant, do something professional. It's too difficult being an actor, or a performer, or a musician.' But as I hadn't asked to go to a boarding school in the first place, I felt different.

But my key career idea was not only not to have a normal career backup plan but to actually have an active no-backing-out backup plan. I thought that was very important. My motto was: Don't burn your bridges – flame-throw your bridges. Absolutely completely destroy them. Because then the only way forwards is to go for your dreams. It suddenly hit me that, for me, this meant not getting an accounting degree. That's how I made sure there was no way back. Eventually, when I was working in a restaurant, first as a barman and then as a waiter, I told someone that I wanted to be an actor, that my dream was to perform. 'Yeah, yeah,' this guy said. 'That never happens.' And I thought, *I can't be here. These people don't believe that you can do what you want to do, so I cannot hang out with non–dream believers. I quit within a week.*

When my career began to pick up, Kate started to get a bit of recognition (as her last name was Izzard) and occasionally receive odd things like free sandwiches in a pub, or something. It is a weird thing, celebrity, having people point at you and say, 'Oh, is that that bloke?' I think suddenly she rather liked the fact that people knew who I was and, by default, knew who she was – as my stepmother. Kate did once ask me in to her hairdresser's to meet the people who did her hair, which I was happy to do but I found rather strange because she'd been so dead against my career at the beginning. Once my career took off, she was into it. I kept expecting her to say, 'Well, you've still got to stop this!' But she never did. Kate told me that, at one point, she was turning up to my early gigs without my knowing it and apparently once signed an autograph as my stepmother when asked if she would do so by someone she was chatting with.

When I told my father in 1991 that I was transvestite (now we define it transgender or trans), he and Kate were in the midst of an eight-year rocky patch in their relationship. They eventually repaired things, but at the time of my coming out to Dad, she and I were not really in touch. She had wanted my brother and me to side with her over this rocky patch, but Mark and I refused to take sides, especially against Dad, which didn't sit well with her. She decided not to communicate with us for a period of time, which meant that I didn't talk to Kate about being TV (transvestite/transgender) until years after that, when it was already out in the press. By then I was wearing makeup and whatever clothes I wanted to, so I never got a direct, upfront reaction from her as to how she felt about it. I'm sure she probably would have frowned upon it, disliked it, maybe even hated it. She was from a working-class background and she liked Mrs Thatcher and nearly always voted Tory, which was absolutely not my politics or my father's politics. Plus, she had been dead set against me performing – doing comedy and acting – so I was pretty sure she wasn't going to like my being transgender as well.

By the time communications started up again between us, the truth about my sexual identity was already a done deal. I was who I was and that was it.

One time later she said to me, 'Well, you just like dressing up, don't you?' The implication being that my identity was all about the clothes, which it wasn't and isn't. Clothing and makeup are part of the way I wish to express myself (as they are for everyone), but I feel I express myself in response to my built-in boy/girl genetics. The idea that we would get into a big confrontation over this was not somewhere I was going to go. I was at home for the weekend and I knew that the topics of sex and sexuality were not things she wanted to consider or discuss in a deeper way – in a way where we could talk about LGBT+ people and their rights in modern civilization. That just wasn't going to happen. Which was odd, since one of her really good friends – a man she'd met in San Francisco when she was on holiday there with my father – was gay and he and his partner lived there together. I think she definitely must have known that they were gay, but somehow it didn't bother her.

I think lots of people in the world behave similarly: they can like individuals for who they are, despite the fact that they don't necessarily agree with or approve of the bigger issues and ideas related to their sexual or gender identities. It's a strange disconnect to me – not wanting to let facts affect your opinions – but it seems to work that way. I've been on the receiving end of this kind of thinking. I may seem more acceptable as a transgender person to some people, and they may be more accepting of me because of my charitable marathon running and perhaps being on the telly, but they won't necessarily change their mind-set about LGBT+ people in general.

The younger generation is much cooler with this – acceptance has been somewhat built into their zeitgeist – though it wasn't always that way. About twenty years ago, in the early 1990s, I remember having a huge row in a passageway (Goodwin's Court) off St Martin's Lane in the centre of London, with a young woman who had said to me, as I walked past, 'You're sick!' because I was wearing makeup, heels, and a dress. Her reaction didn't make sense to me, because she happened to be a young black woman and she was with her boyfriend who was white, and I thought that, seeing as how she was to have her relationship, she might be cool about me existing. It was clear that her reaction to me was coming from her gut, and I wanted to try to understand why she was so opposed to me. As the argument continued, I shifted the conversation around and said, 'Well, what about gay people?' To which she replied, 'Oh, no, gay people are fine. I've got gay friends.' So while she was 'okay with' gay people, she was not okay with transgender people.* When I tried to explain the connection between how she was harassing me and how she herself must have been harassed throughout her life as a young black woman, it seemed as if she started to see my point.

I soon realized, though, that she didn't have the gears to back down without losing face, that she could not apologize

---

* I thought this was a quite positive situation, because at least gay and lesbian people were accepted in her worldview, even though we transgender people were still poor relations and hadn't quite made it yet. Maybe now, twenty years later, she's cooler about us. I hope so.

even though she had come round to seeing that she'd probably been wrong. By discussing it with her, she had seen that I was a human being, so she didn't have as much of a problem with me anymore. It's the humanity that gets lost in these issues. In the end, I decided to apologize to her – 'I apologize for this situation that has just happened' – even though she was the one who had insulted me. And then she apologized back.

It was an interesting human interaction on the streets of London, not seen by anyone in that quiet little passageway. One that has stayed with me all these years. Something important had happened there: I learned that some people can't apologize first, if at all, even if they know they're in the wrong, because they can't allow themselves to feel or look weak, and I think maybe she learned that day that no matter how you self-identify or what clothes you're wearing, you're still a human being.

Another time, something even worse happened:

I was in a small town in the UK, and at the entrance to a restaurant someone stopped in front of me and looked at me and said, 'What the fuck is *that*?'

I've never had anything said to me in public that was worse than that. I didn't have anything pithy to say to him at the time, but hopefully he has had a rotten life since that day.

So if people wonder how I can do things – how I have the grit and perseverance to run marathons, to perform on the streets of London, to play the Hollywood Bowl, and just to keep going, no matter what, it's because of this:

If you are an LGBT+ person and you come out, you

have to go through your knight's quest to create ground for yourself, to create a space for yourself, to stand there and say, 'I exist. I have no reason to feel guilt or shame. I am proud to exist, and while I'm not perfect, I deserve to exist in society just like anyone else.'

That became my first big fight.

While I consider myself to be fantastically boring, I realized that if I took on my own sexuality and came out and just told people about it and tried to have a chat with them, tried to be offhand and casual about it, and tried to build our place in society and humanity, then that would be a good mission. This is where I exist in society. I am just this guy. I am transgender, and I exist. But that is just my sexuality. More important than that is that I perform comedy, I perform drama, I run marathons, and I'm an activist in politics. These are the things I do. How you self-identify with your sexuality matters not one wit. What you do in life – what you do to add to the human existence – that is what matters. That is the beautiful thing.*

In the end, my stepmother got cancer and she had a tough fight with it, but I did respect her fight against the dying of the light.

She fought very hard. In May of 2011 she was diagnosed with ovarian cancer that had spread to one of her lungs. She was given six months, but she carved herself out three more years.

One of the things she loved most was playing and

---

*I'm quoting myself here from a video I made during my marathons in South Africa. Just Google it: *Eddie Izzard Marathon Man-Nails.* ·

listening to the violin. Serious classical music. She would follow her favourite violinists, especially Joshua Bell, and go to many concerts on her own, even though she was ill. After she got cancer, I decided to turn up at some of the concerts she went to without telling her, as hopefully a pleasant surprise. I'd use all my connections to get a seat in the row behind her, and right before the concert started I'd just tap her on the shoulder and surprise her, which I think made Kate happy. I think we ended up in a fairly decent place.

A Life in Retail

I've always had an instinctive feel for retail. That sounds like a weird thing to say. But not if you're in retail, I suppose. Though I didn't articulate it in this way when I was younger, I realize now that I've always felt I had a head for business.

I started in sales.

I remember selling crayons to a kid called Kevin at St Bede's School when I was about ten or eleven. I said something like, 'Kevin, you need crayons. Everyone needs crayons. There might be a nuclear war. How are you going to write "help" without crayons?'

Kevin bought the crayons and I was seventy pence richer.[*]

One time we were told there was going to be a charity festival day at St Bede's. Everyone was asked to think of ideas for stalls that they could be in charge of, and I very quickly said:

'I would like to run a stall with lots of small round goldfish bowls.' The very small kind that holds only one fish and are now understandably deemed bad for fish.

'And I also need a whole bunch of goldfish and some Ping-Pong balls.'

---

[*] And I bought a tiny house with it.

I'd seen this before: people would pay money to throw a Ping-Pong ball and try to get it into the little opening of a round goldfish bowl, and if they got the ball in, they would win a goldfish.

My stall was a big hit from the moment the day started – it was crowded with people playing and watching all day. I was taking a lot of cash and people were occasionally winning goldfish. Everything worked out perfectly: money was made for charity and, except for the fact that the goldfish didn't do too well in this, everyone was happy, especially me, as I was running my first shop.

I also got a post office book, which is a savings account with the UK post office, when I was about ten. I used to nip down to the post office in Meads Village, about ten minutes' walk from school, and I would take out a small amount of money – maybe three pounds. I'd then go and buy something in another shop for, say, seventy-five pence, but then I'd go back to the post office and put two pounds twenty-five pence back into my account. All this would happen within an hour. I really liked the idea of trading and commerce even though this wasn't actually trading or commerce. This was some kind of weird speed-shopping thing. I think I got the idea of 'money goes out and money comes in' very early on – I just wasn't making anything to sell at this point. But I did know that I understood it on a gut level.

The mathematics of money has always intrigued me, too. I was fascinated with what happened when the UK changed to the decimal system. This will not make much sense to people who have grown up with a decimal financial system, which just means a financial system where you have a hundred units to the main currency unit, be it dollar, euro, yen (most currencies of the world have this hundred-unit system now) – but until about February 15, 1972, we didn't in Britain. We had a 240-unit system!

We had pounds, shillings, and pence. I was good at the mathematics of pounds, shillings, and pence. I could work that stuff out.

The pound symbol is the same as the weight symbol, and from my knowledge a pound meant a pound of silver in the old days. A pound of silver was broken up into twenty shillings and then each shilling was broken up into twelve pence. So the mathematics could be rather complicated, which I was okay with because I understood it.

When we changed to the decimal system, we had to take that system – the pounds, shillings, and pence system – keep the pounds as they were but change the shillings and the pence into a system of a hundred units. If you're good at mathematics (or even if you're bad at mathematics) you'll see that this isn't an easy fit.

But back to my love of commerce.

In my early teenage years I had a paper round, which I liked, but because I was in a boarding school, I only did it on holidays, mainly the summer ones. I would go down to the post office in Collington, Bexhill, which, like most post offices in the UK, sold stamps and did registered post and delivery, but also sold sweets, magazines, and drinks, among other things. My bicycle would get loaded up with the newspapers all in order and I would deliver them.

This is not a terribly exciting story,* but I liked having a paper round. Mainly because I liked having extra pocket money.

When I was sixteen, in 1978, I had been working for the last few summers at the De La Warr Pavilion for around thirty-eight pounds a week. The De La Warr Pavilion is a fantastic-looking building that was built in 1935 as an arts centre and performance space for shows and dances, and it also had a café and a restaurant. By the late '70s, when I worked there during school holidays, it was a rather tired old building.†

I went to work in the self-service cafeteria of the old pavilion. It was on the ground floor, right next to the main restaurant. Both establishments had seen better days, but I liked working there and I earned a bit of money and it was my first real job.

The clientele were mainly retired and older people. In the summer months many of them would take their teas and coffees outside to sit in the open air. And as people will do, they all added a lot of sugar to their drinks. This meant that when they left to go home, the residue of a lot of very sugary drinks was left in the teacups on the tables.

---

*I would need to have been attacked by a gorilla to make this paper-delivering story more interesting. But there were very few gorillas in Bexhill-on-Sea. I did one day go to deliver my newspapers and dropped all the newspapers in the street, so they all went out of order and I just had to go back to the post office and the lady in the post office had to put them back into the correct order. But still I'd have to have been attacked by gorillas for that to have been more interesting.

†A lot of amateur productions happened in the big theatre, but back in the 1970s none of the big shows came to Bexhill-on-Sea. Now it has changed. Since the mid-2000s, the De La Warr Pavilion has been rebooted and is now a powerhouse in the area of arts and performance.

Wasps really liked this.[*]

At the end of each day, someone would be sent to clear away all those cups with the sugary residue inside and the plates with bits of leftover food. We called it 'the wasp run' because you had to very slowly pack up all the crockery and trays and bring them back inside to get washed up without doing anything too dramatic – otherwise, the wasps would turn on you and kill you.

We felt this. We weren't sure of this. But we just sensed that if you moved slowly enough the wasps would go, 'Oh, he's okay. I don't know what he's doing here, but let's not sting him to death. Let's just fly around and be annoying.'

Wasps are actually like The Borg from *Star Trek*.

After a while, I got sent over to Egerton Park, which was also owned by Rother District Council.[†] The man in charge of the self-service café at the De La Warr Pavilion said to me, 'It's a sunny day, so there's going to be people in the park. I want you to open the café.' This was the first thing in the real world that I'd been in charge of (after the Ping-Pong goldfish). It was like a promotion.

I was going to be in charge of the café. I was the only one *at* the place. It was all down to me. I found this very exciting. It was retail heaven.

When I got there I opened up the café. I switched things

---

[*] As I've said in my stand-up before, wasps are the SS of the flying-stinging brigade. Bees make honey and wasps make nothing – just attack small children. I don't know what wasps do. If there is a god, why would he create wasps? Apparently they do something to flies, but they're not doing it very well.

[†] The council owned the De La Warr Pavilion and Egerton Park. Being council-run enterprises, they were not really run in a dynamic way at all.

on – I didn't really know everything that I was supposed to do, as I hadn't worked there before. But I guessed I had to switch everything on, and I knew how to sell things for money – I could do that, I could work the till, I could give change – but I hadn't run a whole café before.

This became a problem when my first customer arrived. A man came in and asked for a cup of tea. I'd never made tea before. This is because I hated tea.* I don't know what I did – I must have boiled the water, put too few tea leaves into the pot, poured the liquid out, put some milk in, and given it to him, like it was an actual cup of tea which clearly it wasn't. It was probably just milky water with a hint of tea.

He sat down, took a sip, and brought it right back. 'This is no good,' he said. 'It's awful. I want my money back.'

That was my first sale and return. I got the hang of it after a while, but, in court, my excuse was I had never made a cup of tea. It never actually went to court except in my mind.

I ran the café in Bexhill's Egerton Park only once or twice, but I was asked to sell ice cream for many weeks at an ice cream kiosk at the foot of Galley Hill.

Galley Hill is at the far end of the promenade at Bexhill-on-Sea. Like many seaside towns in the UK, Bexhill had a

---

*There's this American belief that goes, 'Hey, you British, you love tea!' But no: some of us do, some of us don't. Now I quite like tea. I'm okay with tea. But back then it tasted awful. It tasted all tea. And real tea shouldn't have milk in it. At St John's School that was all they drank. You had to have tea. And I thought this was disgusting. I was six and I didn't want to drink tea. I just wanted to drink sugar. Anything with sugar in it. You could add sugar to your tea, which sort of made it more bearable, but I didn't like tea. The more I drank of it the more it became okay, so from the summer term of 1968 until the end of the summer term of 1969, I drank tea. After that I didn't drink tea until I was about forty. (There you go. 'My History with Tea.')

long promenade (which is the French word for 'walk'; *promenade* just sounds better). The interesting thing about this kiosk was its proximity to Galley Hill. At the top of Galley Hill in 1940, the one and only Spike Milligan* was stationed as part of a group in charge of a gun that was going to stop Hitler when he invaded.

I was stationed at the bottom of Galley Hill, in that kiosk selling ice cream in the late 70s. The ice cream kiosk is not there anymore because they never sold many ice creams. Sometimes I would have only one window open of my two-window kiosk, because very few of the senior population of Bexhill-on-Sea could make it all the way down to the end of the promenade.

So the kiosk was positioned in just a position that no one would come. The three rules of retail are: location, location, location. They got all three rules wrong.

With so many ice creams and sugary drinks and chocolate bars for sale, this was a booster pack for my sugar addiction. Let's just say that not all of those chocolate bars made it out the window.

It was like being addicted to crack and working in a crack-cocaine kiosk. It was never going to end well.

---

*If you don't know Spike Milligan, I consider him the godfather of alternative comedy. He did most of the writing for a radio show called *The Goon Show*, which ran on BBC radio back in the 1950s. He and Peter Sellers and Harry Secombe were the stars of this radio show and it was very surreal. It hugely influenced the Monty Python team, and I think they did televisually what *The Goon Show* had done on radio. *The Goon Show* happened in the 1950s and Monty Python happened in the early 1970s. When I started watching and listening to Monty Python in the '70s, my dad also started playing me audiotapes of *The Goon Show*. So I got a double injection of surrealism into my comedic sensibility. I think this is unusual and somewhat fascinating. (Listen to the audiobook *Adolf Hitler: My Part in His Downfall*, written and read by Spike Milligan. Bexhill and Galley Hill feature in it.)

Creative Beginnings

My brother, Mark, and I arrived at St Bede's School in September of 1969.

In January of 1970, headmaster Peter Pyemont directed a play called *The Boy with a Cart*, by Christopher Fry. There were about ten characters in this play and one of them, the mother, was played by a boy called Peter Champion (what an amazing name), who was about two years older than me. I haven't seen that play since that day, but I still remember that his performance really made me decide to be an actor.[*]

The character of the mother was not the lead role, but this kid got a great reaction from the audience. I recall, though I may have made this up, that he was causing the audience to howl with laughter as well as occasionally emotionally stopping them in their tracks. When I saw the play, in what was then the gym/theatre/hall underneath the school chapel (yeah, we had a chapel!), I decided there and then that acting was what I would do in life.[†]

It was not as clear to me then, the articulation of that feeling, but I do know that it all stems from that moment. I would guess it became clear gradually so that now when

---

[*] Boys were playing the male and female roles in the production, but this story has nothing to do with my being transgender. It's just about the effect his performance in the play had on me.
[†] This hall has since been separated into different rooms, one of which is a dance/movement studio at Bede's School. I would like to do a show in that room, to bring things full circle.

I look back at it I think, *Yes, that's it. That's where my whole crazy performing life started.*

From that point onward I tried everything I could to get into shows.

I was brilliantly unsuccessful at this.

When I was probably eight or nine, kids at school were offered the chance to learn to play a musical instrument and, if we wanted, to choose *which* musical instrument we would like to play. My brother, Mark, chose the flute, which I thought was very tricky, and I was persuaded to play the clarinet.

I say 'persuaded' because I'd wanted to play the piano because my mum had played the piano.* Mum, though, had never taught me how to play the piano. I wish she had, but maybe I was too young to start playing an instrument before she died. I suppose if you're a musical family you might start your kids early, but that didn't happen with us. Dad didn't play an instrument, but as I said Mum played a bit of piano, which was actually a little Hammond organ, the kind with legs that screwed into the bottom and that had maybe three or four octaves. When you switched it on, it made a noise like a cat being inflated (a happy cat, not an unhappy cat).

Mum would play songs from sheet music. I'm pretty sure she wasn't playing chords, improvising, feeling her way

---

* She had played the organ, but to me it was the same thing. (And it really is the same thing, because it's got black and white keys and letters for notes, unless you're Italian and then they have *Do Re Mi Fa So La Ti Do*. Which I only discovered three years ago. I knew the *Do Re Mi Fa So La Ti Do* existed, but I didn't know that's what they called the actual notes. I just thought it was a song from *The Sound of Music*.

through her music, like I ended up doing. I think she occasionally played some set pieces, and that's really it. Music wasn't a massive thing in our house. We didn't have sing-song sing-alongs. Most of the time the little organ would just sit there, with the legs screwed on, and occasionally Mum would play it, and sometimes my brother and I would muck about and press the keys and play it, too, if you call making discordant noise on a little portable organ 'playing' the organ.

So when it came time to choose an instrument at school, Mr Pyemont said to me: 'Hey, what about the clarinet?'

I agreed, even though previously I'd never heard of the clarinet.

The story of why I swapped my choice of instrument is a bit weird, but the way I remember it is something like this:

The school had three clarinets (just lying around?), so Mr Pyemont wondered (understandably) if someone would play them. Now, why he had three clarinets is a mystery. It felt to me like someone – a pushy drug (and clarinet) dealer – had said to him, 'Hey, mate! I've got three clarinets. You want three clarinets? I'll give you a good price on three clarinets.' And Mr Pyemont obviously said, 'Well, I suppose so. If I have to. Do I have to?' To which the clarinet drug dealer replied, 'Yes.'

This would explain why I, another older kid, and also Mr Pyemont himself got roped into playing the clarinet. What's more, I remember having early lessons with the older kid and the headmaster in the same room with me and the clarinet teacher. This is just an odd way to start to learn an instrument, don't you think? Why were we all learning the clarinet? It just doesn't quite make sense. This may just be my memory going bonkers, but I don't think so. I think this actually happened.

Anyway.

That's how I got stuck with the bloody clarinet, which prevented me from ever being in a school musical. Let me explain that.

The clarinet I learned on was a cheap, not terribly good one. I went on and on and on, taking lessons on it and making a very bad noise.* When I was thirteen, I felt obliged to continue learning how to play the thing because by that time I had taken grade five theory, which was necessary in order to go on to grade six in any instrument. I quite liked musical theory. I was even able to write basic three-part harmony.

I passed grades six and seven on the clarinet, and ended up achieving grade eight, with merit. You could get a pass or a merit or a distinction, but I never got a distinction because my sight-reading was so crap.† I hammered my way up these endless grades playing music that really didn't interest me at any time, though the occasional Mozart clarinet concerto was quite beautiful and created a wonderful sound even if I was making it. If you watch *Out of Africa* you can hear Mozart's Clarinet Concerto in A Major,

---

* Later on, I did try a very expensive clarinet and I made a better noise. A bad workman blames his tools, but apparently not with the clarinet.

† Sight-reading is an amazing thing, and if you're going to be in an orchestra, I think you need it. If you're going to be a creative musician, make your own stuff up, it's not so needed. In fact, it's not needed at all. Maybe it's actually detrimental to know how to read music (because you may end up playing other people's music most of your life – and that will not help you to make your own music).

which is beautiful. Even the animals think so. I think I could play that now and achieve a more beautiful sound, because you have to put emotion into it, and I feel that I can now play with emotion. I even listened to a recording of Mozart's Clarinet Concerto in A Major in the mornings in Africa when I was there running my marathons in 2016.

There was one big musical a year, I remember. Performances were always in the spring term, and the first one the school did when I was there during the Easter term of 1971 was Gilbert and Sullivan's *The Mikado*. I was not allowed to act in this production, as I was learning the clarinet and it was compulsory for all instrument players to play in the school band (orchestra?) accompanying the musical. The rule was that if you played an instrument, you couldn't have an acting role instead.

The next year, in 1972, we did another Gilbert and Sullivan musical, *H.M.S. Pinafore*.

In this production I again played the clarinet.

In the Easter term of 1973, we did our first musical in a new gym/theatre that had been added on to the school. Yet another Gilbert and Sullivan musical, *The Pirates of Penzance*. This is a wonderful musical for kids to perform, as most of them can play pirates. In this production again I played the bloody clarinet, even though I went to the headmaster's office and pleaded with Mr Pyemont, who was directing the musical, to let me act in it. He told me no, you have to play the bloody clarinet.

The next year, in 1974, we performed *Oliver!* the musical. One of the kids who went to the school had a dad who was a semi-professional actor. He sometimes performed in real professional plays, but since that was something he only did part-time, he was able to play the lead role of Fagin in our production using his own makeup and props. *Oliver!* is such a great musical, with such good and catchy songs, and it was a wonderful thing to be involved in, even though I was still playing the bloody clarinet.

In *Oliver!* the place where the band/orchestra sat was on the same level as the audience – the stage being above us and behind us. I was at the front playing 1st clarinet by this time (the 1st's were the best players), and given my proximity to the stage, it was my job to hand props to Fagin during the show.

During this period of not getting any decent roles in any productions, handing two or three props to Fagin in *Oliver!* was as close as I got to performing and to being onstage. Fagin would just put out his hand for the props, and when I handed them to him, it felt like I almost entered the musical.

The thrill of proximity aside, handing props to a parent-actor was such a long, long, long way away from even a small speaking role, and I was incredibly frustrated that, after deciding years before, when I was seven, I was going to act or perform, I was now twelve and this was as far as I had got. It was just not going right.*

There was a point when the school choir performed *Joseph and the Amazing Technicolor Dreamcoat*. I was now fairly senior in that school, but I still didn't want to be in the school choir because that was too 'girly,' too not-football-

---

* Patience has never been one of my virtues. I'm obviously not a saint.

playing-rough-and-tumble-boy-stuff (I am an action transvestite, if you'll recall). But *Joseph and the Amazing Technicolor
Dreamcoat* was different. I must have heard them playing the
catchy songs, and I decided I had to be in that.

So I just kept turning up and standing there when they
were getting things ready: if something needed to be
moved, built, or constructed, I would move it, build it, or
construct it. I made myself 'necessary' and would be there
and available until eventually I wheedled my way into the
show. I even got one solo line – a spoken line, not a sung
line – to the charismatic teacher Sam Gray,* who was playing the Pharaoh/Elvis role. It was just one line, but I'd got
into the show.

Despite that small bit of progress of getting one spoken
line in *Joseph and the Amazing Technicolor Dreamcoat*, my successful run didn't last long. In the Easter term of 1975 – my
last year at St Bede's School – my final musical was *Stalky
& Co.*, which was based on a Rudyard Kipling story and
adapted by two schoolteachers.

Of course, I played the bloody clarinet.

There is a repeating motif in my life of trying to do something and being told no.

No no no no no no no no no no no no no.

Just endless amounts of *no*.

I don't know whether other determined people all came
through a Big Wall of No to get to the Land of Yes. I do

---

* Apparently when Sam Gray got married, he'd already decided to do a motorcycle holiday of
South America. So he went and did that before he did his honeymoon. That's kind of interesting.
And he was also in charge of the scholarship form.

know that sometime after having to endlessly play the clarinet instead of acting in school productions, I began to realize that a professional creative life would require endless stamina (which I had already learned).

And I wonder how good I would be now as an actor (as opposed to a comedian) if I'd got parts in all five of those musicals.

I suppose the clarinet was part of my life, but I ended up getting to do dramatic acting after all, and now I feel I'm doing decent work in acting and comedy, even if my early work (in both areas) was not good.

Playing the clarinet taught me how I could be forced to do something and still be able to circumnavigate it eventually. It does seem in my life that a number of my plans took about twenty or thirty years to work. Maybe that actually *was* the best training. I'd accidentally learned stamina, and with that, staying power, which is how, in the end, you get a plan to work.

Interestingly, as I mentioned with Peter Champion, we had some boys playing girls' roles in plays and musicals at St Bede's. This happened even though we had girls at the school. I think there just weren't enough girls to go round, especially in big musicals where there would often be a whole chorus of girls that needed to be cast.

With me, knowing that I was transgender at that point (even though I didn't call it that then – I didn't call it anything), I would have been very happy to play a female role. Or a male role. Or the role of a gorilla. *Anything* in this production or any bloody production.

But it was not to be.

A few years later, though, when I was sixteen and at Eastbourne College, I was cast in the Pennell House[*] Christmas play.

I was cast in a girl's role.

It was a comedy sketch play that had been written by Tim McHenry, who is a friend I've kept in touch with since that time.[†] Having been cast in the girl's role, I thought, *My god, I am now sixteen and I've been hoping this would happen since I was four.* I couldn't have cast myself in this role because I would've had to admit I was transvestite or transgender. But when someone just said, 'Hey, this is your role,' it seemed to be the perfect cover: acting.

What happened next was very interesting.

I got ill.

I got absolutely one hundred per cent psychosomatically ill.

My brain was overloaded because it was 'taboo,' 'wrong,' 'not what you're supposed to do.' And suddenly, despite having the perfect cover to do what I'd always wanted to do – wear a dress, put on makeup, heels, whatever – I was sick as a sick dog.

My body and brain could not deal with it. There had been no slow buildup to it.

---

[*] Pennell House was one of several 'houses' at Eastbourne College. A 'house' was an actual house which people were assigned to: If they were boarding houses the boys (or girls) would sleep there as well as work there. If they were day houses, students would just work there and go home at night to their parents' actual house somewhere in the Eastbourne area. There were five boarding houses, two day houses, and one girls' boarding house (the girls were all seventeen and eighteen) at Eastbourne College.

[†] He is, at the time of this writing, the director of programs and engagement at the Rubin Museum of Art in New York City.

Just one day prior I wasn't 'allowed' to wear a dress, and now for several nights during rehearsals and performances, I was going to *have* to wear a dress.

So my brain made an executive decision. I got ill. So ill that I couldn't perform in the show.

I wasn't scared of doing it. I wanted to do it. I wanted to play this role.[*]

My mind was simply too blown away to do it. So my mind and body shut down. *Nope*, they said. *This isn't going to happen.*

Some other kid was given the part at the last minute, and while I didn't actually see the show because, as I might have mentioned, I was ill, I remember hearing bits of it from upstairs. But I do know that I got well again that night! Maybe even by the time the show was finished.[†]

I've just been reading this bit back through and I realized this sounds rather fantastical. Could you really get ill just for the time of the play and then get better again? I'm checking back through my memory and it really was that stark. Even if I had played the role, it wouldn't have helped me get closer to 'coming out.' I don't actually know what I would have done. It was an opportunity I clearly wasn't ready for, so my brain took over to protect me.

Now let me tell you about my learning to play the piano, the instrument I love. It happened like this:

After three years of clarinet, playing songs like 'Snug as

---

[*] Male or female, it was a role, and I was still trying to get as many of them under my belt as possible.
[†] That seems a bit too quick, but definitely by the next morning I was fine.

a Bug in a Rug,' I thought, *Why don't I take lessons for piano?* I liked the piano then and I still play it – I will jump on any piano and just start banging away (even one rather old one at Osborne House on the Isle of Wight while filming *Victoria and Abdul,* which will be about to come out when this book is published). I call it 'banging away' because I like the idea of being able to impose yourself on a piano. I like the idea of playing a piano with gusto, rather than picking out notes while looking at sheet music so that you get no sense of the flow of the music (because I can't read music). I want the music to jump out of the instrument. And it's quite an instrument. A grand piano is quite a thing.

So I took some lessons. About a year of lessons. The teachers wanted to teach me 'Snug as a Bug in a Rug' – the piano version. This was not good. It felt like déjà vu. But I think I passed grade two piano.

Then I decided to stop taking lessons. I decided to just teach myself. I don't think I actually had that concrete thought. How do you teach yourself an instrument? When I was a kid, I didn't think that was not possible. But on the piano, I was going in a direction I didn't want to go in – the Snug as a Bug direction. It wasn't fun, and I knew somehow that I'd have to go about learning this instrument in a different way.

The thing about learning an instrument is you always have to go away and practise. That is the key thing. And if you don't like what you're practising, how the hell are you going to want to go away and practise it? What is the motivation to learn some music that bores the crap out of you?

Kids learn rock-and-roll music because they want to hear

it back. They want to play the music that they want to hear. They first start by learning the songs of bands they like – music they want to hear – and then they start making their own stuff up. And they're highly motivated because they like the sound of it. You can't be creative making music you don't want to hear. That's obvious. You have to create what you want to create – in any artistic arena.

I remember the feeling at the end of each clarinet lesson where they'd say, 'That's it for the day,' and I'd think, *Phew.* And then the music teacher would say, 'Practise this piece and that piece for next time,' and I'd say, 'Yes, Mrs Badcrumble.'* Then by the next week I either come back with no practice done or maybe some furious practice done just half an hour before.

When I got to Eastbourne College in 1975, there was an upright piano in the recreation room of Pennell House. One day, when I was about fourteen, after I had been there a year, I decided I wanted to play a bit of piano. Maybe I had mucked about on the piano a little bit, because I could play some basic songs, and I know that I then went to a music shop in Eastbourne and bought a couple of pieces of sheet music: the *Pink Panther* theme song, 'Bridge Over Troubled Water,' and Scott Joplin's 'The Entertainer.' I learned 'Bridge Over Troubled Water,' and I learned the *Pink Panther* theme song, but I don't think I ever quite mastered the left hand of 'The Entertainer.'

So I just sat at that piano in the rec room, stared up at the sheet music, and picked away at one note after another –

---

* In the back of my mind I'm thinking, *You'll be lucky.*

slowly putting it together. I was motivated to practise these songs because I liked the sound that was coming from the instrument. This seemed so obvious to me.*

As I got these tunes into a decent state of playing, I became a bit bored with the slow pace of the learning process, but I got more confident with the piano. I started to just play around with chords and, without really planning to, began teaching myself how to improvise. And at this point, I realized what I was doing and I encouraged myself to keep doing it because it took all the work out of it – all the arduous learn-this-by-rote stuff.

It seems I've applied this approach to stand-up comedy, and to performing in different languages. Stand-up comedy can only be learned by doing stand-up comedy, so while writing stand-up comedy can be arduous, at least you're writing jokes you want to hear. Then you get onstage and workshop ideas around until they're in good form. Which is what I was doing with the music back then. I would play around with chords until I thought I had a shape to a piece.

The piano in the recreation room didn't have a great sound, but I did find a fantastic old grand piano in the big hall of Eastbourne College. The big hall was called – Big School. What a terrible name for a hall. I mean, call it Big Hall, or Great Hall, or Eastbourne College Hall. But 'Big School'? That just sounds weird. Its terrible name notwithstanding, it was a hall in which exams were taken,

---

*Why doesn't all music get taught like this? Before you even persuade kids to learn an instrument, find out what kind of music they like. Maybe kids don't know what music they like until their teenage years, but that's the way to do it. So many kids are practising music they don't want to hear and that doesn't work. They should learn music they want to practise. It's so bloody obvious that I don't know why it's not shouted out from the tops of tall buildings.

assemblies took place, and plays were performed.* But during most hours of most days, its door was open and it was empty and unused. A grand piano stood in one corner, and the lid of this piano was not locked.† This big old warhorse of a piano was unlocked. And rather unloved. I don't think anyone ever played it much.

But I did. I'd go in there often and hammer away on the keys, making a fairly decent sound. I was a sucker for playing major chords rather than minor chords. My style of playing was somewhat Elton John influenced, like I was doing a simple version of his style of playing.‡

I also started teaching myself music by listening to tracks. Bob Geldof's band, the Boomtown Rats, had a big hit with the song 'I Don't Like Mondays.' I taught myself how to play that on piano by picking out the chords, the notes, and working out where they should be on the piano. Quite often I would end up with an approximation of the song, but it was still very good training.

---

* It also had the entire Bayeux Tapestry painted on wood all around the hall just below the balcony.

† There was another grand piano in the music center – this school had quite a few facilities – but that was a very new grand piano and was permanently locked shut. Even if some musical piano-learning kid was wanting to play the piano, that piano was still locked. Every time I tried the lid of it (because you could get into that room from time to time), it was locked. I didn't quite understand why you locked a piano. No one wants to steal the piano keys. They just want to play the piano. It's locking creativity away from people who might create it. It's a real non-creative thing to do, to put a lock on a piano. In train stations around Europe they now have pianos sitting there and people can just come and play them. That's what I feel should have been happening in my school. But instead, a piano was just locked up.

‡ Basically my left hand played octaves and my right hand mucked around playing different chords. I never pushed to learn really intricate left-hand stuff. Instead, if you just thumped around with octaves, it gave a real weight to the sound, and then you could just stare at your right hand and play around trying to get interesting chords and individual notes. That's how I developed my confidence to play the piano.

By age sixteen, I thought I'd like to get an electric key-board. That way, I could play anytime without making a lot of noise (because you can adjust the volume). I'd seen one in the window of Birds' Music Centre on Sackville Road, Bexhill (the shop is still there) when I was working that summer of 1978 at the De La Warr Pavilion's self-service café. This electric keyboard I think cost about one hundred and twenty pounds, and as I mentioned, after three years my wages were around thirty-eight pounds a week. Now that I had something to save for, I knew I would save the money.

So I remember my dad came home from work in London one day – and when he did, I asked him if he knew of any music stores in London, near where he worked.

'I want to buy an electric piano,' I announced.

Kate immediately said, 'Why do you want to get that? You'll just get it and use it for a bit and drop it.'

Now, if you'd looked at my track record, that could well have been true. I, and many other teenagers, did get into things and then get bored with those things. But she was so sure of this and she put it to me so strongly that I found it hysterically funny and I couldn't really say anything back to her. As I said, my stepmother and I quite often thought in opposite directions.

Refusing to give up, I thought, *Okay, well, I won't go to London and get an electric piano: I'll find another shop around the Bexhill area.* That's when I remembered the electric keyboard in the window of Birds' Music. I put down a deposit to hold it and I thought, *I've got to get this keyboard back to school where I can have it without my stepmother knowing that I've bought it.*

According to my dad, it was from this point on that I just started doing what I wanted to do rather than doing what adults told or advised me to do.*

Whilst working in my summer job, I'd met a teenage girl about my age working in the ice cream kiosk up by Galley Hill. I found out that her mum liked to go shopping in Eastbourne.† So I asked if her mum would mind taking me and my electric piano over to school the next time she went shopping there. The young girl said she thought her mum would be cool with it, and she was, so I managed to get transportation for the electric piano back to school without my stepmother knowing.

This was a perfect plan. It all worked very smoothly. I'd earned the money, put the deposit down, bought the electric piano, taken it back to Eastbourne, and got it into my room at school. All was good. Until:

One day, about three months later, my dad and stepmother turned up unannounced at Pennell House – a surprise visit. They were ushered into my room, where my stepmother suddenly discovered I had bought an electric piano. So she was pissed off and she steamed a bit about this, but it was a fait accompli, as the French say.

I never really liked the sound that came out of that electric keyboard as much as I liked the sound that came out of the grand piano in the Big School. But I did play that electric keyboard in a band at Eastbourne College – we

---

* I do actually listen to advice, but sometimes I will go against it if I feel I just have to try something I feel strongly about.
† My school was in Eastbourne, twenty kilometers away (about twelve miles) from Bexhill, where the family home was.

played various songs from the Commodores (not really my taste in music) to Elvis Costello (much more my taste in music). I particularly liked Elvis Costello's song 'Oliver's Army,' which I played live with that band.

Later in life, I met Elvis Costello. He's a really decent human being. He even came to a gig of mine, which was a great feeling: to have played 'Oliver's Army' on the piano as a kid and then to meet the guy who wrote it. We both actually played in Milwaukee, Wisconsin, on our separate tours on the same day in 2014, and we talked to each other on the phone even though we couldn't meet up. I then phoned him when he played the De La Warr Pavilion in Bexhill, the place where I had worked through the summers in the late 70s to earn the money to buy the piano to play his song 'Oliver's Army.'

I've come to the conclusion that if you can find the centre of your creativity, you can use it to create almost anything. At school I was probably more creative with my piano playing than with my performing. Since school, I have been more creative with my performing than with my piano playing, as I haven't been playing in a band. The stories I have just told show that I was relentlessly trying to get acting roles but not succeeding terribly well.

Meanwhile, I was allowed to play as much piano as I wanted to, and therefore I came up with some interesting creative techniques that I have since applied to my performing career. I remember once hearing that paper clips were given to kindergarten kids, who were then asked, 'What can you do with these?' The kids came up with so many different inventive ways of using the paper clips that their actions were recorded at a genius level. Kids who are older become less inventive with the paper clip. It could be that we're all very creative when we're young but that we're just encouraged to push creativity out of our lives as we get older.

Lord Nuffield's Syllabus

One holiday, when I was about sixteen, I was at home watching television and a revue show came on. A number of comedy performers were doing sketches. I didn't know who these people were at that time, but the style seemed very much like Monty Python. I watched it all the way through and thought:

Who are these guys and how did they get on television?

They were part of the Cambridge Footlights Revue at Cambridge University. Now, half of Monty Python had come from the Cambridge Footlights, so I thought:

That's what I've got to do. I've got to go to Cambridge University.

I was very logical about this.

Just at the point when I realized that I needed to work very hard to get into Cambridge University, so that I could join the Cambridge Footlights and have a future in comedy, I also suddenly decided to *stop* working very hard. Which was not very smart or useful.

I decided to stop working because I had passed twelve O-level exams. O levels are the 'ordinary' level exams that we took in the UK in the 1970s when we were sixteen. Normally one takes eight or nine O levels. I decided to keep adding extra O levels so that I could seem really clever. My brother had taken eleven O levels and my dad had given him an umbrella. I wanted Dad to give me an umbrella, too.

Maybe a bigger umbrella. An umbrella that was a one-O-level-more umbrella.

So I took all these O levels and I got seven As, four Bs, and a C.

And that was fine – pretty good. My dad said he was *surprised.* This wasn't quite the reaction I was looking for. I then asked if I could get an umbrella. I think he then bought me a hat. I can't actually remember. I do love my dad, but he felt Mark was cleverer than me. This is because my brother, Mark, *is* academically cleverer than me. I'm just somewhat relentless. That's the thing I have.

The next two years, one moves on to the A-level exam – the 'advanced' level – which means more studying and more work. This made me think: *Why am I doing this? What's going on here? This is not terribly interesting! It's just a lot of effort.* I could do the work, but I was losing motivation.

Why was this? Well, there had been no girls of our age (thirteen to sixteen) at Eastbourne College from 1975 through 1978. Then, when we were seventeen and eighteen, girls appeared at the school. So about thirty girls came in to a year of about ninety boys. Not good numbers for the boys (very good numbers for the girls). So if you were good-looking or good at sports, girls paid attention; if not – forget it.

Girls weren't terribly interested in what I was offering.* I was just some nerd at school who was pretty good at math, physics, and chemistry. I was no good at sports because my school didn't play football. Boarding schools in the UK in

---

* I should mention at this point that I'm a male lesbian. I've always fancied girls and not boys. I don't know why this is. If you have a problem with this, please complain to the United Nations.

the late '70s didn't play football as a major sport. Hopefully they now do, and if they don't they should change that immediately.

So to make myself appear more interesting, I decided to try to become a rebel – surely that would work with the girls.

I couldn't become a punk – but I could at least just stop working. This was my interesting radical idea: I'd stop working and then I'd become a rebel and then girls would find that interesting. A non-sporty, non-punk-music-listening, not-doing-any-work type of rebel.

This idea did not work.

I was just a nerd who wasn't working. And that package was not terribly appealing to anyone. Including me.

I did find some social acceptance in, of all places, chemistry lessons with the chemistry teacher, Dr Edmondson. He talked in a very slow and measured way as he wrote on the blackboard. He would leave gaps . . . between what he was saying . . . in order . . . to write more clearly . . . on the board. In his wonderful gaps, I would throw in silly words that would fit quite well and that would make the class laugh. He was a perfect straight man for me, an unwitting improvising partner, and I quite consciously used these lessons to practise my comedy. I have never met him since I stopped studying chemistry in 1980, but he really did help get my funny-line hit rate up to a very high level.

By the summer term of 1979 (during the third term of A-level chemistry lessons) my funny lines were getting so good that one girl did turn to me and say, 'I didn't know you existed until this term.' These days I am still good at dropping funny lines into conversations. I don't often get the chance to do this, but I am very good at it because of Dr Edmondson's chemistry class.[*]

My dad very much wanted my brother and me to go to university. He had never been to university, so that was an important condition of our upbringing. As exams got closer I realized two things: my 'rebellious' attitude was not working with girls and that, also, I had better start working again otherwise I wouldn't pass any exams. Once I decided to start working again, I managed to get back up to speed to eventually achieve an A grade in mathematics A level! This was with the help of Nick Pendry, our teacher who gave us such really great notes. I also got a B grade in chemistry and a D grade in physics.

I blame my physics grade partly on the fact that Eastbourne College had decided to adopt a new system of learning (maybe just for physics A level) called the Nuffield syllabus. I think now that it was quite a brilliant system. It asked the pupils: *What kind of experiments would you like to do in physics? What problems would you like to solve?* It made the students think for themselves. But at that stage of my life I was used to learning things by rote and regurgitating everything I had learned on to an exam paper. The idea of

---

[*] I am reviewing what I have written before we publish this book, and at the moment, in November 2016, I'm now performing in Barcelona. In talking to my brother, Mark, I've just found out that he did the very same thing with Dr Edmondson. Maybe not as intensively as I did it but in exactly the same way. Apparently Dr Edmondson, who was a rather heavy man, had been trying to teach my brother's class what rust was – Fe_2O_3 (iron oxide). Doc Ed, as we called him, said to my brother's class:

'So I'm riding along on a bicycle and my bicycle falls apart. Why is this?'

And my brother called out, 'Because you're a bit too heavy, sir?'

'No, Izzard,' he said. 'It's because of Fe_2O_3.'

Now I know that Dr Edmondson was a gift to all comedic minds, if only kids knew it.

seeking out problems and then trying to solve them – by experimentation – was just not part of my brain psyche.

I now think that the Nuffield method is wonderful. It's what I do in life all the time: I decide what direction I'd like to head in and then I experiment to figure out how to get there.[*]

Which is to say that I now seem to live by the Nuffield syllabus.

But when I was seventeen and eighteen it was a completely alien concept and I hated it.

So I passed my A levels with an A, a B, and a D.

Not bad. Not great. But, in the end, my grades wouldn't really matter: I was already planning for my next step and figuring out how to get there.

On the fast track to nowhere

Early on, I hoped that I would be a performer (actor or performer – I merge these together). There was no way I was going to be a chemist, or a physicist, or a civil engineer, or an accountant.

There was a book that existed that listed all the courses at all the universities in the UK. It was called the UCCA book (Universities Central Council on Admissions). In it, I found a course called Accounting and Financial Management with Mathematics. It was a dual degree. I didn't know what a dual degree was, but it seemed more impressive than a single degree. I'm pretty sure it was the longest degree title in the book, though I didn't choose it exactly for that reason. I thought: *My dad's an accountant, and I like finance, and*

---

[*] The French word for 'experiment' and the French word for 'experience' is the same word – which is quite beautiful and a little confusing – *une expérience*.

174

those two subjects, along with mathematics, are surely within my skill set. It shouldn't be too hard. And then I can get to Sheffield University, do comedy shows, and then take the comedy shows up to the Edinburgh Festival.

Luckily for me, I didn't have to worry too much about my father having a problem with me pursuing a career in performing instead of accounting. While his *job* may have been traditional, he always had a great philosophy: *As long as you're happy in life.* That was what I remember him telling us. And so I pursued a career that made me happy in life.

Somehow I had this all worked out already: that going to the Edinburgh Festival was the key piece to the puzzle of my future.

Going to Cambridge University and being in the Cambridge Footlights (like half of Monty Python) would have been good, but it clearly wasn't going to happen for me. So getting to the Edinburgh Festival was now the most important part of that plan. It seemed that's where you could become a big star. When I say the 'Edinburgh Festival,' I really mean the Edinburgh Festival Fringe, which was and is a massive fringe festival, and anyone is allowed to go and perform there. In fact, there are multiple festivals that happen at the same time as the Edinburgh International Festival. There is the Edinburgh Festival Fringe, the Edinburgh Jazz Festival, the Edinburgh Book Festival, the Edinburgh Poetry Festival, and others. I believe it is one of the largest, if not the largest, collection of international arts festivals in the world. If you chose to, you could just go to the Edinburgh Festival Fringe and take a show to perform there. It was the Nuffield syllabus of comedy and theatre production. And

I strongly encourage all world stand-up comedians performing in English to play the Edinburgh Fringe.

After my exams, I was accepted by Sheffield University. I
wanted to go to a university in the north of the UK because
I felt that if I had grown up in the south of the UK, I should
at least go to a university in the north of the UK and get to
know the people there. I didn't find my first year at Sheffield
easy. Like at most colleges and universities, students lived in
halls of residence during their first year, with communal
dining halls. I lived in the annex of Sorby Hall, the annex
being an extra building attached to the main Sorby Hall. I
found most of the students staying in the halls of residences
rather juvenile, to be honest. I think it was the first time most
of them had been away from home and their parents. They
ran about and had high jinks and behaved, I suppose, like
normal university students. I had been at boarding school
since the age of six, so I'd already had twelve years of this
kind of existence. I didn't talk to almost anyone in my hall
of residence. So they all thought I was weird, which I didn't
really mind because I thought they were weird.

My main focus was taking a show to the Edinburgh
Festival.

During my second term, in the spring of 1981, I auditioned for a Howard Brenton play. Brenton is a serious
playwright, and *Weapons of Happiness* is a serious play. It was
described as one of his more comedic works, but it was
really a drama with comedic elements in it, as opposed to
a comedy with some drama in it, so I was probably in the
wrong play.

Sheffield University had a society run by the students

called the Theatre Group. Not a very imaginative name, but that's what it was called. Theatre Group was the big thing if you wanted to do theatre at Sheffield. They had the resources to provide you with a decent production for a show if they chose by democratic vote for your show to be produced. But it was essentially theatre, as opposed to comedy. I didn't really want to do theatre or drama at this point. I just wanted to go to the Edinburgh Fringe and do comedy. So I went to their office/room in the students' union – some people would always be hanging out there – and popped my head in. After talking to someone for a few minutes, I said, 'When you go to the Edinburgh Fringe next summer, can I come with you and help?'

There was no question in my head as to whether they were going to the Edinburgh Fringe, because in my head every university took shows there. But one guy said something totally unexpected:

'No one goes to the Edinburgh Fringe from Sheffield University.'

'What do you mean, no one goes?' I said. 'Surely somebody goes? Surely some group takes a show up?' But apparently not.

'No, a few years ago we took a show up and they lost a lot of money, so no one goes now,' he said.

Oh.

This was a baseball bat to the head of my plans.* My whole career strategy was to go to the Edinburgh Fringe. What the hell am I going to do now that nobody goes

---

* As someone who is English, I should probably say 'cricket bat,' but I'm afraid I just prefer baseball to cricket. Sorry, cricket.

there? I'm at Sheffield University, I'm doing Accounting and Financial Management with Mathematics, and I can't get my actual career started – because nobody goes to the Edinburgh Fringe.

No one is going.

I have to go.

Therefore, I will go.

How many shows had I produced before this?

None.[*]

I like planning. I had wanted to be in the military.[†] At that time, I still sort of wanted to be in the military, and the

---

[*] Except for the teddy bear show I'd staged on my dormitory bed when I was ten. Getting all the teddies to do an improvised story that the headmaster found entertaining was obviously an auspicious beginning, but I hadn't put on a show by myself since then.

[†] Since I was very young I had considered being in the military. Probably in the army, but then I discovered the paratroopers, so I thought that would be great to be accepted for, and then I discovered the commandos in WWII and I thought I would have been very happy to be a marine. At Eastbourne College they had a Combined Cadet Force (army/navy/air force cadets). When I was sixteen I had done a special extra course, with other cadets from around the country, to practise and do training for kids who were really considering being in the armed forces for a career. That's how serious I was about getting into the forces. I then learned you could do an officer cadetship at university. You could get paid at the rate of a second lieutenant for three years, and then you had to do three years in the forces as a payback. I had already got the forms to do this and was seriously considering it. In the end, I decided to back away from joining the armed forces because I didn't know which war I would be sent off to fight. WWII was very clear to me. The evil of the Nazis had to be stopped, and so I would have absolutely volunteered to fight in that war. But since then and before then, wars have been much less clear-cut. I also knew I wanted to perform, I knew I was transgender (but I didn't have a name for it then), so in the end it seemed more logical just to leave the idea of being in the military behind and forage on with my creative career. But I do tend to run my career on military lines. I have said in public that I did want to be in special forces. I'm sure some people think this is an odd thing to say. But now, having come out as transgender thirty-two years ago (in 1985), having run over seventy marathons for charity, and having performed stand-up comedy in four languages in forty-three countries (by the time this is published), I feel that this is me doing Special Forces: Civilian Division. And I am nothing special to be able to do this. All I prove is that we can all do more than we think we can do.

military needs plans. So this was my radical plan.

I sat on my bed in Sorby Hall annex and in my head I talked myself through the logic of it all. This was a real 'cards on the table' moment. This means for me you just lay all your plans (cards) out there, and as long as you've made the decision that you're going to do something, all you have to do is play out your hand and try and win with the cards that you're holding. That's a much easier thing to do than trying to decide what it is you want to do in the first place.

I had the luxury of knowing what I wanted to do. So I just sat on the bed and I came up with a plan for myself:

'I have to go to the Edinburgh Fringe. But I don't have the confidence to do a production there because I've never gone before, and I don't even know how to get there or what to do once I get there. So I will just act as if I do have the confidence to go to the Edinburgh Fringe. I'll just borrow confidence from a future version of myself. Once I've been to the Edinburgh Fringe and performed a show there, then I *will* have the confidence to go to the Edinburgh Fringe. I will go to the bank manager of confidence (in some part of my brain) and I will borrow that confidence from the future, and then I can wear it like a cloak, and I will talk to everyone with this confidence.'

It was out there as a concept, but it worked.

The first thing I had to do was get to Edinburgh. So I called the Festival Fringe office and got information about their opening hours and location. I thought, *I have to go and sit in that office and beg them to advise me what to do*. I knew this bit couldn't be done on the phone. In the early eighties, calling long distance, city to city, you would be pushing ten-pence pieces into the phone box and every ten to fifteen seconds the ten pence would run out and the phone would go *beep beep beep beep* – to tell you to put another ten-pence piece in. There is no way you could have had a decent conversation with anyone with that system.

But I also needed them to get to know me. And me them. I had no money to travel to Edinburgh.* So I got a bus to the Tinsley Viaduct, which was a motorway junction where the M1 motorway met the M18 motorway. There, I just put out my thumb and started hitching my way up to Edinburgh. It took me a whole day, but I finally got there at about ten p.m. There was a guy named Jimmy Ogglesby who I had known at Eastbourne College and was now studying at Edinburgh University. My idea was to find his hall of residence, try to find him, and then ask him if I could sleep on his floor. I took a train for the last part of the journey to Edinburgh's Waverley Station, then I walked up the Royal Mile (the High Street) to the castle near where his hall of residence was. It was a beautiful but cold February evening and all of Edinburgh was lit up with street lamps. When I got to his hall of residence, I asked if anyone knew where Jimmy Ogglesby was.

'Yes, he's in that room, watching television.'

Jimmy just happened to be in the hall common room watching *Fawlty Towers*. The room was packed and everyone was laughing. It was comedy, it was John Cleese, ex-Python, doing his sitcom. I said to Jimmy, 'Can I stay on your floor?'

---

* I also had no money to put on a show in Edinburgh in the summer of 1981, but that is for later.

And he said, 'Yeah, okay.' It was a great break for me, and I'd like to thank him again for his hospitality.

So I slept on his floor, and the next morning I presented myself at the Edinburgh Festival Fringe office, where I think they thought I was bonkers, and I said, 'I want to do the Fringe. How do I do it?' They were very helpful and they gave me forms, they gave me a brochure, they gave me an old Fringe programme, and they told me essentially what to do, which was that I'd have to do it all myself. So I just sat on the floor for the rest of the day and read all the forms and the brochure and asked them a whole bunch of questions.

There were people who ran the Fringe venues, but if you wanted to get a slot at a venue, you had to bring your own lights (or pay to use their lights), you had to get your own tickets printed, and you had to find your own place to stay. It was a lot of production. Even thinking about it now, it was a lot to do and organize, and I'm a little surprised that I was so certain that I was going to make it happen. With that visit to Edinburgh – turning up at the Festival Fringe office, endlessly asking questions in their office* about what it was that I should do – I somehow managed to turn all my determination into an actual show.

The only fly in the ointment of this entire story is that the show was crap. (It had moments of good stuff, but generally we weren't brilliant.)

I remember meeting the man who ran our Edinburgh 1981 venue, which was in Brodie's Close, an alleyway

---

* Alistair Moffat was the head of the Festival Fringe at that time, and Jenny Brown was his deputy, and they were both very helpful to me – as were their staff.

opposite Brodie's Tavern, a very famous tavern at the top of the Royal Mile. And when I met him again, in 1983 or 1984, and he said to me, 'Yes, I remember you, your show was crap.' He actually said that. And he just said it because it was true. And I thought, *Well, it wasn't that bad!* But he seemed quite certain it was crap, and that was the only review we got.

My first Edinburgh Festival Fringe show took place in the summer of 1981 in a twelve noon to one p.m. slot, which is a terrible slot for comedy. I had called it 'Fringe Flung Lunch.' I had to come up with a title for the show that would stand out, and I had to come up with a title before we had even written a word of the show. This is the way it worked out with every comedy sketch show I did. After that February morning in Edinburgh, I went back to Sheffield Uni armed with leaflets and an old copy of the programme and got started. I talked to everyone I could and I said, 'I'm taking a show to the Edinburgh Fringe. Do you want to come?' In my mind I was definitely going, and it was definitely happening – I just wasn't sure who would want to come or what show we were going to do.

As I'm thinking about this now, it does seem quite fantastic that it actually happened. Was it desperation, or passion, that turned this dream into a reality? I like to think I was passionate with just a hint of desperation, like one of those ice creams with a hint of desperate pistachio in it.

I had sorted a venue in Edinburgh with, unfortunately, a terrible time slot. I had an entry in the Fringe programme and I even managed to get a loan out of the students' union by impressing them with a passionate and eloquent speech

(I hid the desperation). I was quite impressed by the speech myself, which went something like: 'Lend me four hundred quid, will you? It will be good for Sheffield University! One day the story might even end up in an autobiography!' There was a woman in Sheffield, Jo, doing English and Drama, who I'd heard was interested in going to Edinburgh. So we arranged to meet and she seemed happy to join me and Ian Rowland, the one other writer and actor I'd already got on board. As soon as I met her, as well as really needing her energy and skills for the Edinburgh show, I also found her very attractive. So it was great when she agreed to come and work on the show and also that meant we would be working together – which I was very happy about.

I needed about six people to be in this show and to help with the technical aspects of it, and by this point I had maybe three. As I said, I was writing the show with Ian Rowland, whom I had met from putting a notice up on a board in the English literature department asking if anyone would like to write comedy. Ian got in contact, said he was up for it, and even though I don't think he had ever done this before, his ability to perform and write funny stuff was amazing. I think I was a bit unnerved by his confidence. He just walked in ready-made.

I did one show at Sheffield in the term before the Edinburgh Fringe of 1981. It was called 'The Gazebo.' I did it in Lecture Theatre 4, in the Sheffield Uni Arts Tower, which is a very weird place to do a show. The only way to control the lights was with a single switch in a soundproof booth at the back of the hall, and if you flicked the switch one way, all the lights went off, and if you flicked it the other way, they all came back on again. That's not what theatre lights are supposed to do. That's some lights in a room. The guy in the soundproof booth couldn't hear what was happening unless we taped a microphone to the stage wall so he could hear through a speaker in the booth. Then he would know when to turn the lights on and off. That's how weird that was. One guy played a dead body. He was a friend of ours called Ozza O'Toole. I think his character died about five minutes into the play and Ozza had to lie there for the remaining forty-five minutes. At one point I had to pick him up, which was almost impossible, since he was over six feet tall, so it was kind of hysterical.

Tickets for the show were thirty pence. It was also not a good show. (If the guy from Edinburgh Fringe had known me earlier and had been there at the venue he would have said, 'This first show is crap, and I think your next show will be crap, too.' But I knew this one was crap. It was an existing play and I had rewritten it a bit, but I think I just made it worse.

It was on the heels of this 'great success' that I left Sheffield for Edinburgh. I went up there in July, five weeks before the festival started in August. I worked as a waiter in a café to make some extra money, at Crawford's Bakery on the Royal Mile, and I ended up blowing what little I earned on phoning old friends around the UK and encouraging them to come to Edinburgh to be in the show. I phoned everyone I had ever heard of (it felt like that). I spent about a hundred pounds on phone calls in what must have been just four weeks (a lot of money in those days).

In the end, I persuaded my brother, Mark, and two school friends – Gary (who is Dr Gary from my Mandela marathons) and Chris Bucknell from Eastbourne College. Also, along with Jo and Ian Rowland, Steve Goodman from Sheffield University, and maybe some other people, but apologies if any names have escaped me. Another school friend, John Ryley (now head of Sky News in the UK), also came up for a few days as well.

A small team, but we were up for it.

Ours was a sketch show, a not-terribly-good sketch show (apparently we were crap, which I have already mentioned). We had one funny sketch written by Ian that was a parody of Jacques Cousteau and his boat, *Calypso*. I put on flippers, and a snorkel, and shorts, and that sketch got a good reaction. It was recorded for BBC Radio's 1981 'Aspects of the Fringe' show and then dumped from the final broadcast. That was a huge disappointment.

The other sketches were not so good. There was one I quite liked that never took off – a mash-up of Chaucer's *Canterbury Tales* and the Nativity story. It had the Wife of Bath and the Knight and all the characters on Chaucer's pilgrimage trying to find somewhere to sleep in a town on the way to Canterbury. But the guy behind the desk says, 'I'm sorry, there's no room at the inn, but you can stay in the barn. I'm afraid Herod has called a census, and so there's a lot of people staying in the town at the moment.' I thought it was interesting, to mix the Christian Nativity story and Chaucer's *Canterbury Tales* together, but maybe it was just one big joke and the sketch never really took off.

Ian was playing the innkeeper, and Steve Goodman, who

was one of the pilgrims along with the rest of us, suddenly said he had an idea for how to make the sketch work better: 'Why don't I do my Jimmy Cagney impersonation?' And I said, 'What?' He said, 'When I get there and there's no room in the inn and Ian says we can use the barn, I'll do my Jimmy Cagney impersonation. "You dirty rat, you dirty rat!"' I said, 'Steve, you're not doing Jimmy Cagney. There's no comedic reason for Jimmy Cagney to be in this scene. That's just mad.'* He insisted, but I said, 'No, you're not doing a Jimmy Cagney impression in *The Canterbury Tales*.'

Then we got onstage, the scene started, and someone said, 'We would like to stay for the night. We are tired and we have been on this road a long time. Is there room to stay at the inn?' Ian, the innkeeper, said, 'No, there's no room, mate, but you can stay in the barn.' And then Steve actually started his Jimmy Cagney impersonation. It actually sounds quite funny to me now, but at the time, the audience of four or maybe seven people at twelve noon on a Tuesday was deathly silent.

Basically, all we heard, during most of our shows that summer, was silence. Then more silence. Mainly just different versions of silence.

Another sketch we did involved acrobats. Normally, of course, in real acrobatics, two people doing amazing feats of strength onstage would produce great rounds of applause. But Chris Bucknell and I would run around and do three or four different attempted athletic stunts that were just pathetic – just very silly non-athletic poses. One day, during the second week of the show, Chris and I, because of the total

---

* Reading this now, I think it's quite an interesting idea. But back then it just seemed unhinged.

lack of reaction, became totally hysterical and just could not stop laughing. Normally our lame athletic poses would get a small amount of laughter, but on that day it got just total silence for about five minutes and we couldn't deal with it. We just laughed and laughed and then had to run offstage.

So that was Fringe Flung Lunch. One good sketch and a sea of troubles. We had quite a nice place to stay, but the landlord, Mr Bungara, kept calling me David. That should not really be a bad thing, but it just didn't make any sense. I kept saying, 'It's Eddie.' 'Of course, of course. Now just sign this, David.' In the end, I just agreed to be David. Sometimes you just have to. He made me sign a legal document so he could get a lot of money out of us. Our crap show actually broke even, but we ended up losing money because of Mr Bungara's steep accommodation costs.

The achievement of putting on that first show was rewarded the following year by members of the Theatre Group back at Sheffield Uni coming to me and saying, 'How on earth did you put on a show at the Edinburgh Fringe?' So I sat them down in a pub and I told them what I had done, and then they went and did it. It was no big deal – as soon as someone had done it, anyone could do it.

The next year I went again to the Edinburgh Fringe, but now, as I hoped, I had the confidence that it could be done, so it wasn't that hard to do. We got a bigger venue but further from the centre. We also got a better time slot – in the evening – but still our show did not take off. I remember stamping around backstage before every show, going, 'Why is no one buying tickets? What have we got to do to get people to come?' We just couldn't get many people to come to our show. During the day, we were all out in the centre of Edinburgh, performing sketches and jumping about, handing out leaflets, and putting up posters. But still, we couldn't get many people to come. Not the first year, not the second year, not the third year. It went on and on. The shows got slightly better and slightly more people did come, but none of those first three shows ever really took off.

But there's one positive thing that I have taken with me from this whole kit and caboodle, which is that if I had worked harder academically and got into Cambridge University and their Cambridge Footlights, I would never have learned how to build a show out of thin air.

The confidence I'd borrowed I could now legitimately have for myself. The technique of pushing myself to do things I'd never done before was actually working, however slowly, and it is that which would help me to eventually start doing street performing, then start doing stand-up comedy, and then twelve years later have the confidence to bring my comedy to the West End of London.

Instead of embarking on a military career, at some point I began trying to run my comedy career on military lines (or at least using analysis). I'd set my sights on an end goal, and try like crazy to get there.

At first, all I thought I had to do was get to the Edinburgh Fringe, do a comedy show, and someone would say, 'Hey, you! Come be on this national television show!'

That didn't happen the first year. Or the second year. Or the third year.

Then I got quite confused. Because that's as far as my forward thinking had gone, and I hadn't worked out that I had to have backup strategies – on what to do next, after your first attempt doesn't work. So, rather despondent, I took a year off and didn't go to the Edinburgh Fringe in August 1984.

Instead, at the end of that year – I came out.

PART TWO
The Wilderness Years

Invited to the Party

Some people are really good at dating and relationships. They are probably lucky enough to have aesthetically good-looking genetics.

They are born 'Invited to the party.'

They grow up invited to the party.

They go through school as people invited to the party.

And then, when they're old enough to go to real parties, they are of course invited to the party.

These people are maybe 5 per cent of the world. Maybe less. The rest of us would just like to be invited to the party. We just want to be part of the fun things. The rest of us have to develop our personalities and our looks and our attitudes and our abilities in order to get invited to the party.

The 'pretty' people don't.

As the 'pretty' people get older, their looks start to fade and then some of them end up in the boot of a car.

Not necessarily dead, just sitting in the boot of a car (or the trunk of a car), shouting at people and saying, 'Where is the front of the car?' Because they haven't developed the ability to work out which end of the car to get into.

At school, I think we all want to be the person who is invited to the party but we can't just press a button and make ourselves wildly attractive or popular.

America had a war of independence (I just noticed that

as I was passing a history book), and in that war of independence, Americans said no to royalty. No to monarchy.

No, no, no. 'Hereditary power and privilege is a bad thing.' And I agree with that. America had a war about it and that was that.

Since then, Americans have never been into monarchs – that is, unless they're 'pretty.' 'Pretty' monarchs? America loves them to death.

'Oh, you're 'pretty' and you're a monarch? Then come here, and we'll go down on bended knee and we'll invite you to all the parties.'

I have been in America when this happened, and America went absolutely batshit crazy. When Princess Diana turned up, it was 'Come and stamp on my tongue, why don't you?' It was just off the hook.

Cleopatra got a lot of press. She really did. She was cute and got off with Julius Caesar and Mark Antony, and I think she shot her brother, who was ruling before her, with a Luger pistol. (I think she probably used whatever the Egyptian weapon equivalent was back in her times.)

Anyway, about my relationships.

I was fascinated by girls from a very young age, starting in primary school. Not that there was much interaction at that stage, because there comes an age for a boy when you're not allowed to hang out with girls, but when you do you have to pretend not to like them:

'Girls? Ugh.'

You actually had to say that. You had to go, 'Girls? Ugh.' Not because you felt 'ugh' but because some other older boy had said 'ugh' and you fell in line. 'Yes, "ugh." What he said. My speechwriter has written the word *ugh* down for me.'

My first kiss, as I have already mentioned elsewhere in this book, was a decent first kiss, I suppose, as first kisses go, or seem to go in films, except it was between seven-or eight-year-old kids. There was no follow-up. No relationship, no wine, and no flowers.

What is it, by the way, with flowers?

Because I am transgender, people buy me flowers, and when they do I say to them, 'I don't know what to do with flowers.' I say, 'Thank you for the flowers, but do you want to keep them? Or do you want them back? Because you can have them back, if you want.'

I can do flowers if someone puts them in a vase. Flowers are great in a vase; they do look bright and colourful – which means I can appreciate them. But when people send flowers or give me flowers, loose flowers, flowers in a bunch, that are now in my hand, I just go, 'I don't know what to do with this.'*

Judi Dench (Dame Judi) sends me a banana whenever I do a show. I think she was going to send me a bunch of bananas, but then she ate some of them and decided to send me just one banana with *Good Luck* written on it. She's

---

*Sometimes I say, 'If people feel they have to give me something (which I'm not advising), then get something like one of those windup things with teeth that bites its way across the table. I like gadgets. I just can't do flowers.'

Now, flowers have their place. Bees speak very highly of them. When I look at flowers in the garden I like them; I'm okay with them in the house in a vase, but they don't blow me away. I don't have the flower-appreciation gene. Some people do. They are predisposed to like flowers. If flowers are in the garden, sitting there growing, I like that. I think I could grow flowers. I think I could do plant husbandry. I could make those plants do okay. I should do that at some point – take up gardening. But first I've got to get a garden.

got a wonderful sense of humour and she likes my comedy, which is totally bonkers and a great honour for me.*

Flowers, and Judi Dench's banana gifts, of course, have nothing to do with my thoughts about dating and relationships. As usual, I'm just stalling and digressing because I'm not that comfortable talking about dating and relationships.

Is anyone who isn't good at dating and relationships comfortable talking about them? I don't think so. I think the only people who like talking about dating and relationships are the people who are good at them. The rest of humanity has to spend the rest of their lives figuring that stuff out and overcoming shyness.

I believe shyness has a lot to do with flirting and dating and relationships, too.

I think I was shy. It would have been nice not to have been shy.

And I am still shy.

There are some people who are not shy, who have confidence when it comes to relationships, even when there seems to be no reason why they should be confident. Some people have great physical genetics and therefore are very confident at saying, 'Hey, should we just go and have sex now?' (Obviously, this is something you say when you are older rather than when you're seven.) But you can under-

---

* I just finished filming *Victoria and Abdul* with Judi. She was playing Queen Victoria and I was playing her son, Bertie (later, Edward VII). Judi had already come to opening nights of my comedy shows – *Stripped* and *Force Majeure* – which blew me away, but now I was acting with her in a dramatic film directed by Stephen Frears. The whole experience was wonderful for me. As a kid of seven who wanted to act, and seeing *The Boy with a Cart* in 1970, it is wonderful to have acted face-to-face with her and such a great cast and crew on a film like *Victoria and Abdul*. I enjoyed every minute of it.

stand that, because they have a certain look and it's all terribly easy. No work, then. No struggle.

But sometimes struggle is good. This is something I tell myself. I will say, 'This is good training. I will spin this scary thing around and decide that if I can learn to do this thing that is terrifying, then I will get to a place where it no longer terrifies me.' Then the scary thing becomes a new extra thing that I have the ability to do.

If you have flirted in a pathetic way or failed in your flirtations, it's quite good to talk about them because then you can conquer them. You stick a wooden stake through the heart of your failures and they become successes. And while I slowly got better at my boy-girl chitchat, and while there are certain things I've got pretty good at in life, being good at relationships is still not one of them.

The beginning of puberty and the arrival of Captain Acne during my adolescence didn't help with my confidence and flirting. I believe Captain Acne came to stay (on my face) due to my enormous sugar intake. Now, a lot of the people who didn't get acne were the attractive kids. (I remember one good-looking guy in my house had one acne spot *once*.)

Nobody tells you that Captain Acne is coming. Nobody says, 'Now that you are thirteen, your sugar intake and hormonal imbalance will cause acne to appear.'

Nobody tells you that you will develop lanky, greasy hair, and that you will have to start washing it rather relentlessly, and bathing, and washing your clothes relentlessly if you want to get anywhere with dating and relationships.

If you don't have the confidence to walk out the door

and say, 'Hey, who wants to have a relationship with me? I'm a teenage guy with no real experience or confidence! But it's going to be fun,' then it's just not going to happen. If you don't think there's a chance of something happening, then you don't bother with attempting to make it happen. Instead you get on with the rest of school life.

And what was school life?

I hadn't been allowed to play football, which meant I had no confidence in my sporting ability. I was at a school that didn't admit girls for three years, which meant I couldn't develop confidence in my flirting ability. And I had puberty activating and acne coming and going.

Mysterious and fascinating, I was not.

I tried to get into school plays, but that was sporadic. There was no kiss chase anymore, so there seemed to be no way in to having sex with any girl, even though that phase of things (the sexual phase) was getting more and more real.

'Hey, at some point, you have to have sex.'

'Really? How does that work?'

'I don't know. Get a book out of the library.'

Yes. All that information to learn and the stranger- than-usual sex chat with your father in the car. That all happened, but still, I wasn't getting to a place where I was saying, 'Yes, I will be going out to have sex tonight with Shirley.' Or anyone. It just wasn't happening.

After three years of going to Eastbourne College with no girls in our year, the school now changed (for the seventeen-and eighteen-year-olds) and had a few girls. If you were a sporting hero, then fine. If you had a certain look, fine. If not, well, your chances were limited.

I decided I wouldn't even get involved in the sexual chase/game. Now, if I performed in a play where there were girls involved, I realized that would be much better. Like when I acted in *Cabaret* (the musical) at seventeen, which was great fun and probably the biggest boost to my confidence since playing football when I was twelve. But despite the acting and despite making girls laugh in advanced chemistry lessons, I wasn't really getting anywhere with them.

The pressure was building. I knew I had to lose my virginity, but it wasn't happening.

In the end, I lost my virginity at twenty-one, which is late. And you should never mention such a late loss of virginity to anyone, because it's embarrassing. And you shouldn't write it in your autobiography, either.*

I would have liked for this milestone (millstone?) to have happened earlier. If you're a boy, you want to say, 'Yes, I lost my virginity at fourteen.' I think David Niven lost his virginity at fourteen with a prostitute, and I think most boys would like to be able to say that, to get it done and say, 'Well, that's when I lost my virginity,' even if they didn't have sex again for another five years. Seventeen is a good age. Sixteen, seventeen. Eighteen. All better than twenty-one.

For me, things were very complicated, gender-wise. I had decided that I shouldn't say anything about my alternative sexuality (being transgender). I wasn't dealing with it at that time. I was essentially straight – I fancied girls or women – which seemed fine, so I decided not to talk about or think

---

* Oh crap. I just did that.

about the rest of it. I suppose I thought I was just going to lie about it for the rest of my life.

My relationship with Jo was a bit fragmented. Jo was never that certain that she wanted to have a relationship with me to begin with, while I was certain that I wanted to have a relationship with her. I was very attracted to her and I thought, *Maybe this relationship will work.* It turned out I was too clingy. Or too effusive. Or too obsessive. I wasn't brilliantly experienced at relationships, and I didn't know how to control my emotions at that point – not that one wants to necessarily control one's emotions, but I needed a certain amount of control over what the hell I was feeling, otherwise I became too emotionally attached to people in a way that they felt was too needy. And needy is not very sexy or rock-and-roll. Needy is not very punk. I am not so needy now, but I was rather damaged back then. Just damaged from the trauma of Mum dying when I was very young. And the trauma of not seeing my dad for two-thirds of every school year after that.

At some point, Jo said something important to me that has stayed with me. She said that when I was producing and performing a show was when I was most interesting. I felt that this meant I was sexually – or relationshippy – interesting.

Therefore, I realized, when I was not producing and performing a show, I was not those things.

At the time, I felt very pissed off about that. I thought, *Oh god, that's awful. That means I will have to be doing a thing to be considered an interesting and attractive person and when I'm not doing a thing, I won't be considered an interesting and attractive person at all.* That didn't quite make sense to me. I thought that meant that the only time I was attractive was because of an action, because *I* – just standing there – wasn't terribly interesting. I had to be doing something.

It threw me, but later on I changed my opinion and saw that it was an accurate observation: it meant that when I was doing things, I had to use any charisma or any commanding ability I had, and that I had to be driven and confident. And 'driven' and 'confident' certainly do sound like more attractive behaviors than 'clingy' and 'obsessive.'

Attractiveness is part of the dating and relationship equation. What is it about people that one finds attractive? At school, when you're young, it's all about looks. It's 99 per cent about looks. Athletic ability also seems to figure in, also if you have that 'bad boy' thing (I don't think 'bad girl' works so well).

Later on in life, it becomes more about personality. But they don't teach you anything about how to have a personality or how to improve your personality in school.

I think they should teach you that. I'd say it's one of the most important things you can learn. Why not spend a little less time on geography and a little more time on developing a confident personality?

It'd be interesting for someone to do an examination of all the 'lookers' from school and what they ended up doing in life and all the average people from school and what they do in life.

To do great things in life, I believe you have to be an average person at school. The curse of the 'lookers' from school is that they don't have any incentive to develop any other abilities. This is not a perfect science, but I think it is true. Once I realized that it was good for me to be doing things and making things happen, because doing this made one more dynamic and attractive, I think I tried to make things happen as much as possible. I can't say it's made me any better at dating or relationships, but making things happen is still better than just letting life flow by, so that's what I choose to do.

It does get better, kids. But until it gets better, it's hard not to look at the tiny, instantly socially successful subgroup of 'pretty' humanity and wonder if they're always going to have it so easy.

Now, having style and a look can definitely help with dating.

I, unfortunately, was sartorially challenged.

When I was at Sheffield University I bought a 'good' overcoat. It was a fawn-coloured camel-hair cashmere coat that looked quite business-y and you're-doing-all-right-y. The kind of coat that says you've got it all figured out and that you're making it happen. Whatever 'it' is.

I was never that good at figuring out what to wear, and I was even worse at things like laundry or cleaning my room. While I was still at Sheffield Uni, there were huge washing machines in the students' union that were very cheap to use. People would come down to the union by bus from their halls of residence with huge bags of washing, and I did as well. One time, I did my washing only when I got to the point where everything I owned needed to be washed: everything except this fawn-coloured cashmere coat and my Wellington boots. I just threw everything into one massive washing machine and sat there reading a book in my overcoat, underpants, and Wellington boots.

For years I just didn't see the point in spending time and money on clothes. I had no idea about clothes and how they worked. I had no idea what to wear. I had no idea what style was or how colours worked, and I knew nothing about tailoring. Tailoring is something you learn about later in life, if you're lucky. It's an amazing thing to see what expert tailoring – the precision of it, the craft of it – can do, how it can transform something that looks good but doesn't quite work on you into something that does work on you.

As I got a bit heavier in my twenties and thirties, I used to think, *Well, this doesn't fit, but there's nothing I can do. Some people look good in clothes, other people don't, so I won't worry about it.*

And that was my attitude. What you really want and need in life is a guide or mentor, someone constantly helping you out, saying, 'Don't wear this with that.' I think maybe your parents are supposed to do that, but given how my life had been going, my dad could hardly have advised me on these things. And I wouldn't have asked.

Some people get mentors as they grow up, but I don't think I've had one in my entire life.

Of the 'moves' I've made, many were made using the Nuffield syllabus method of thinking shit up and trying to work out the strategy for the next step in my life. While I haven't always known exactly what to do next, I've always felt that it would be better for me not to take the easy route. The path of most resistance – not least resistance – has always been the way I've ended up getting from one point in my life to the next. Plotting out the next destination has always been my strategy, even when I didn't have a fully formed plan of how to get there. It's made my career incredibly interesting but unfortunately rather slow to show results.

For example, when I started doing stand-up comedy, at a certain point I decided not to do television. Doing television would have been an easier way forward, but I decided to block that route and just progress using word of mouth as the main engine. Then, I refined this and decided that I would use television to do TV chat shows and to show recordings of my stand-up but that I just wouldn't use television to be in a comedy sketch show or a comedy sit-com, which I had for ten years been ardently trying to get into – especially a comedy sketch show. There were three reasons for this: The first reason is that if you feel you have the 'it' thing, that you're doing something that people really want to see, and you build your profile up by just touring and doing videos/DVDs, your career is much more in your control. The second reason is that if you are not in a comedy sketch show or sitcom, you can never have that show cancelled. Therefore, though it's harder to progress, in the long run your foundations are on firmer ground.

But the third reason was the most important. If you become 'Mr Comedy' on TV, it's very difficult to be accepted by audiences in dramatic roles. And once I finally felt my stand-up taking off, I wanted to go for dramatic roles as well. I sometimes wonder why I seem to set the bar higher the minute it's in reach. It seems I'm never content with what I have. In my early career, as soon as I became a decent street performer, I wanted to become a stand-up; as soon as I became a good stand-up, I wanted to play theatres all around the UK. As soon as I played theatres all around the UK, I wanted to play London's West End. Then I wanted to do gigs in New York. And then tour America. And then tour the world. It seems I keep moving the bar higher. To be honest, I feel quite content most of the time, but if I wish to do something, I am quite happy to go back again and again and attack the brick wall of 'no' and find a way to push through to the other side.

I'm sure one could look at my career and say, 'Ah, it was luck.'

And there has been some luck along the way. But not a truckload of it. Maybe a small car boot of it. I've just been able to work out where it was best to be positioned and then wait for some luck to turn up. It's always good to be well positioned.

But I can't say I've ever been lucky when it comes to relationships.

I think I was in love back then, with Jo. When we stopped doing shows together, we sort of split up and I got terribly distraught about it. Immediately I wanted the relationship to start again. I'm not sure what would have happened if it had. It was a bit like I had some sort of terrible 'grass is always greener' thing.

I'm sure lots of people examine relationships much more assiduously than I am doing here. But I believe this is a human pattern: wanting what you don't have, not wanting what you do have.

After Jo, I had a relationship with Kaite O'Reilly. She also studied English literature and drama at Sheffield, got a first-class degree, and has since become an acclaimed author and playwright.* She was very open-minded and positive, and I tried not to be too clingy. I think she probably started the relationship, since I was never direct and on the front foot about that kind of thing – I was always slightly on the back foot when it came to starting relationships.

Once I left Sheffield University for London in 1983, I stopped trying to have relationships. In early 1985, I had dropped out of my degree course four years before, I had given up on the Edinburgh Fringe, I didn't feel great about myself, and I couldn't get a performing career going. So after six months of doing nothing, I did one positive thing: I decided to come out as being transgender. But after expressing this for a number of months, I then went back into boy mode and went into street performing in about July of 1985. I hadn't stopped being transgender, but I just didn't feel that my performing was about my sexuality.

When I started street performing, I temporarily put my sexuality back in the closet. I thought, *I'm not going to perform on the streets of Covent Garden wearing a dress. Because they are going to say I'm a drag performer, and this isn't drag. This is my sexuality. This is a different thing.*

I feel the word *drag* means something more like 'costume,' and drag is expressed by gay men who wear clothing expressing a heightened and glamorous female look. I feel

---

* I cast her as Fräulein Kost, the prostitute character in *Cabaret*, at Sheffield Uni, and while comedy wasn't her natural thing, she did it really well.

this is different from how I as a transgender/transvestite person express myself.

I feel drag is a more theatrical experience, while being transgender is about expressing yourself day to day, showing how you self-identify. It's more about your identity than a theatrical sensibility.

I knew I did not want to perform in that way (what I call 'girl mode') on the streets of London, not just because I was afraid I'd get my head kicked in but because I would have been misunderstood.

I also knew I was transgender (even though back then I was calling myself 'TV' (short for *transvestite*), so I thought, *Well, I won't do relationships, because they would be too confusing.* For me and for them.

And that has always been a tricky thing, the 'gift' of my sexuality. It is tricky and it is difficult.

I've talked to women who have said, 'Yeah, that's just not my cup of tea, and therefore, end of story.' They might find me attractive in boy mode, but when girl mode becomes part of the package, they feel 'That's not for me.'

And that is quite understandable.

Crying

Starting to cry, falling in love, and feeling sick in cars are three things that, once you start doing, can't be switched off. If there were a god he'd surely give us controls for all of them.

As I mentioned earlier, from ages eleven to nineteen I didn't cry. Just paint all those years in using a non-crying paintbrush. I would get pissed off, I would get angry, but I would not allow myself to cry.

Interestingly, I don't think I allowed myself to be home-sick after that point, either. In the early years of my life, in boarding school, I used to cry on the first day back. I always felt very sad. It reminded me of my mum being dead, not being able to see my father for weeks – and so I was sad – and so I cried. I know after the age of eleven I didn't cry, so not crying was a safer way to exist in the 'jungle' of boarding school.*

It is easier to survive in a tough emotional situation with no emotions. I worry that most kids who go to boarding school, like I did, have to switch off their emotions and

---

* Again, if you cry you can't control it. Once you start, you tend to cry more after you've begun. The brain cannot work out how to rewire itself back to the non-crying place you were before, and your eyes 'bleed' water. Falling in love and feeling sick in cars seem to work in the same way. I'll leave it to some expert to do a study on this.

become emotionally dead people as adults.*

I started to cry again when I was nineteen, at Sheffield University. One day I saw a cat trying to cross the road rather too slowly for the cars that were bearing down on it. I made a noise to try to scare the cat out of the road and get it to safety. But I quickly realized it wasn't going to get out of the way fast enough from the cars that were traveling very fast and it was run over.

The cat dragged itself off the road and through the little gate of a walkway leading up to somebody's house.

It lay there, dying.

I remember I tried to comfort it. But I don't know if he ever had a chance.

The cat died and I picked it up but I felt absolutely nothing. And I realized then that I was emotionally dead. Maybe I had blocked all the connections to feeling anything. It was a safety mechanism and it had served me quite well. It's what happens in extreme circumstances like accidents, but in that moment I thought, *This is wrong. I need to be able to feel things. I need to be able to empathize again.* So I forced myself to cry. Not in a fake way of crying as if I didn't care for the cat but because I did like animals and I wanted to cry and I'd just forgotten how. So I took the cat back to my room in the Sorby annex and called a vet.

'I don't know what to do,' I said. 'I have a cat who has died.'

They told me to bring the cat down to them and they would take care of him, which, in part of my mind, I hoped

_____

*Seven per cent of kids in the UK go to boarding schools/private schools/independent schools, and many of them may have probably lost the ability to feel emotion.

meant they would save it, even though I really knew they couldn't, because the cat was already dead.

Since then, I feel my emotions have reacted more like a real human being's.

It is sad that it took a cat's death to get through to me.

I'm Going to Tell Everyone

I was twenty-one when I first told someone how I felt about my sexuality.

The person I told was Kaite O'Reilly. By the time I told her, we were separated, but we still got on well. She was, and is, a very open-minded woman. She had a brother, Jim O'Reilly, who was openly gay and who was also a talent manager in London. These were amazing things to me: It was the first time I knew someone who had a family member who was openly LGBT+.* And someone with a proximity to the entertainment business.

I can't exactly remember what pushed me over the line to tell Kaite that that was how I felt about myself. I remember the room we were in, which was in her flat on Crookesmoor Road in Sheffield, and I do remember that she was positive about it.

Kaite was very relaxed and calm about everything I told her, and it was pretty amazing to be accepted like that (for the first time).

I don't think I ever thanked her quite enough for being that way.

So I would just like to say: Thank you, Kaite O'Reilly.

---

*I should mention that the term *LGBT+* didn't exist back in those days in 1983. I think *L* and *G* existed, *B* was questionable, *T* had not yet turned up and the *+* was the rest of the alphabet just waiting to come and join.

I told her about every experience and feeling I'd ever had about being transgender.

I told her how the first time I wished to wear a dress was when I was four or five, living in Northern Ireland, when a new family had moved into the neighborhood. There were a number of girls and a boy in this family, and for some reason (probably because they were new to the area and not for any religious reasons – at five, what the hell is religion?) we wouldn't let any of them in our gang.

The kids in our gang had heard (but did not see) that these sisters had encouraged their younger brother to wear a dress. There was a lot of laughing and talk, like, 'Oh, what an idiot, he's wearing a dress. This kid is obviously a loser.'

But I remember thinking right at that particular moment, *This kid seems to be winning to me.* Because a dress felt like something I would have liked to wear.

I knew something was different right then.

I think most LGBT+ people know early. My dad said that around the same time I used to adjust the garter straps on the stockings attached to my mother's girdle. I didn't even know what a girdle was, but I remember being fascinated by the garter straps and adjusting them; though, like most memories, it's a very hazy one. Years later, in the *Believe* documentary, my dad would say that my mother, Dorothy, had told him about this. But he never told me that he knew. The first time I heard it was in the documentary. Which was quite strange. And all he said was that my mother had found me in the bathroom wearing her clothes. He didn't say what her reaction to that was, but in the documentary he told me that he 'wasn't best pleased.' It proves that I had these feelings before she died, and that the feelings were not brought on because she died when I was six, as some people like to speculate as being the 'cause' of my *alternative sexuality*.

I talked to Kaite about visiting my mum's good friend, Trudy, who we called Auntie Trudy,* and how Trudy's daughter Sally had a wig on a wig stand in her room. The wig stand was a Styrofoam shape of a woman's head, and the long-haired wig sat on top of that. I remember going into Sally's room and being fascinated by the wig, which I really wanted to try on. She realized that I was wanting to try it on (I don't think I overtly came out and asked her), but when I did try it on, of course it didn't fit (I was only about seven).

I also told her how, when I was a prefect at St Bede's, I found costumes being stored in a big box in a classroom that wasn't being used. No one was supposed to be in that room, but I was deputy head of school at that point,† so I was allowed in any room. Having discovered that box of costumes, I decided to go back down to that room after everyone was in bed because there was a dress I'd found there that I thought might fit me. That was quite something, to have a dress to try on, because I didn't have access to many (or any) dresses back in those days after my mum died. There was no mirror in that room; it wasn't a dressing room or a room designed for trying things on – it was just a classroom that had a big box of costumes in it temporarily.

---

* She and Mum had been to nursing college together.
† In British boarding schools (in my day, and maybe still today) all prefects and heads of school were appointed by the head teacher (headmaster). I was deputy head of school (assistant head of school), much like a class vice president in an American public school.

I told Kaite the story about how, when I was thirteen, my father got remarried and my stepmother arrived, which gave me access (but not permission) to her dresses and heels and makeup when I was home visiting. When I was fifteen, I started trying on some of her clothes when she went out, which I had to do while constantly checking to make sure she wasn't driving back up the street to come home. I don't remember quite how I thought I'd get everything put away in time if I'd seen her coming – how I'd get my makeup off in the few minutes it would take her to park the car and come in – but I had some sort of plan worked out. (She'd probably have said something like, 'I'm driving over to Eastbourne now to do some shopping,' so I'd think she'd be away for at least half an hour.)

One time she did turn to me and say, 'Have you been adjusting the straps on my bra?'

And I said, 'No!!!' with as many exclamation points as I could get into it.*

Which, of course, was not true. I had been adjusting the straps on her bra. I had just forgotten to readjust them when I put her bra back in the drawer.

Another story was that when I was fifteen I would steal makeup from Boots the Chemists. I came up with a technique where I would go in with a loaf of bread, hide some

---

* I felt that being accused of trying on women's clothes was the worst thing that could be asked of you. One of the medical students living at 37 Calabria Road, where I was living when I finally came out, had at one point, just in passing, asked me, 'Have you ever worn women's clothes?' And I tried to get as much tone into the response as possible, and said, 'Nooo!' You're trying to say no in a strong way, but it's got to be casual as well. If you protest too much, then they think, *Oh, you have worn a dress.*

makeup under the loaf of bread, and then walk out. It's a bit of a weird technique, because you have to go in with a loaf of bread and then leave with just the same loaf of bread. I think sometimes I might have bought something else, but you didn't really want to go near the cash till when you were stealing a lipstick. I had a bit of pocket money, but I couldn't buy the makeup because that would risk the cashier looking at me and saying, 'Why are you, a boy, buying makeup? Are you a transvestite?' I couldn't face that, so I just thought stealing it would be easier.

And it was. Until the store detective gets you and hands you over to the police.

Before then, I'd been stealing makeup, bringing it home, and putting it into a shoe box – with a false bottom! I thought my stepmother might decide to take a look inside the shoe box. In the end, when the store detective caught me stealing makeup, it was probably the third time I had stolen. He handed me over to the police.

They said, 'Have you done this before?'

And I said, 'Yes, there's more, it's at home; it's in a shoe box with a false bottom.'

My stepmother was there when the policeman brought me home. I handed over what I had taken and he walked off with all the makeup.

What happened afterward with my stepmother later became part of a stand-up routine. After the policeman left the house, she said, 'Has this got something to do with your obsession with the SAS?'

I should add that my stepmother had been a Morse code operator for the SAS (Special Air Service) Brigade, special forces in 1944–45 (something that blew me away when she told me). I was really interested in the special forces, and I had a serious plan to try to join the marines or the para-troops, and then do 'selection' to try and get into the SAS. I'd even bought a blue SAS belt that had their dagger em-blem and motto on the buckle – *Who Dares, Wins* – and I knew quite a lot about the history of the SAS. So I was into football and was in the Army Cadet Force – I had even done a special course where I had to go on maneuvers in my army uniform – but now, here I was, stealing makeup. I didn't know how to explain this, so when my stepmother said, 'Has this got something to do with you and the SAS?' I thought this was a lucky diversion and immediately blurted out, 'Yes. Absolutely.' I stole the makeup as part of an improvised, covert operation (this I should have said but didn't).

Then she asked, 'But why do you always steal makeup every time?'

Oh crap! What kind of secret operation would require lipstick?

But then I suddenly remembered there was this very cute girl I'd met in France when I'd gone there for two weeks to learn French and had stayed with a local family, and she was in some of the group photos I'd taken. So quickly I said, 'Actually, I stole the makeup for this girl.'

It wasn't true, but I didn't know how else to explain or admit that I was a transvestite or transgender – I didn't know how to articulate it in a positive way or even spell the words!

At that point my stepmother got bored with it and said, 'Oh, just use your pocket money and buy her a scarf.'

So I did, and I sent it to her in France in Châlons-en-Champagne. She would have been surprised.

And finally I told Kaite how at university I'd worn a long, blue dress during the 'Pyjama Jump,' a cross-dressing evening of partying for all the students, which was part of Rag Week (an annual week where students organize stunts and fund-raising events for charity). Why it's called Rag Week I do not know, but the Pyjama Jump was a huge party where everyone came wearing pyjamas.

The women usually came wearing men's pyjama tops with stockings and heels – and the men came wearing women's clothes, but in a garish, deliberately nonfeminine, clumpy, Cinderella's-ugly-sisters-type way, allowing them to keep their male sexuality intact and not have it questioned.

I realized that only on this one night could I throw on a dress without having to answer questions. I had been in Sheffield for over a year and was already doing shows, so I knew there was a costume wardrobe in the English literature department, which did a lot of productions. There was this blue dress that seemed to be suitable and that seemed to fit, so I borrowed it for the Pyjama Jump.

That night when I met up with everyone else who was going, I arrived with my makeup already done and with my heels already on, but no one was asking questions. I just looked slightly more put together than the other guys. It happened to be the time of the New Romanticism pop movement in Britain, and people probably thought, *Oh, he must be part of that.*

But I wasn't part of that.

Whenever there was a movement where guys were wearing makeup in rock-and-roll and pop music, I was not part of it. For me, they always felt like a fashion thing, which was not the same as really expressing sexuality. So I was never part of those movements. But my first Pyjama Jump was a fun night. You could walk around town in a long dress and no one questioned you because everyone was doing it.

I do remember I was so empowered by this situation that, after unburdening different thoughts, feelings, and experiences to Kaite O'Reilly over a period of half an hour (or maybe four hours), I went to the window of her flat and, looking out over the whole of Sheffield, where she was a student and where I had been a student, I said, half to myself and half to the world outside the window:

'I'm going to tell the whole world about this!'

When I said this, I was quite sure I was not going to tell the whole world. But I just blurted it out.

And having said it, the moment passed. I left her flat, life went on, and time passed.

But that line stayed in my head.

The Art of Self-Analysis

Coming out didn't happen overnight. It was a process.

I have found this a few times in life: Someone says a thing to you that is pertinent and you absolutely resist it in that moment. Then later you decide that that was absolutely right.

After thinking for some time about the unthinkable idea of telling everyone about my sexuality, I decided I had to act on it. I was living at 37 Calabria Road in Islington, London, just by Highbury Corner. I was living with a bunch of medical students, one of whom was Gary, who became Dr Gary, my doctor friend who came with me to South Africa in March 2016 to help me with my twenty-seven marathons in twenty-seven days.

I was living on the top floor of the house, and my room was shared with a big water tank. Half the room was a water tank, and the other half was me.

It was 1984 and I was trying to get my career going, but nothing was happening. I had no work, no prospect of work, and no job. I'd dropped out of university three years earlier, I'd done a number of projects and shows at Sheffield University* and at the Edinburgh Fringe, but now I

---

*Even though I'd left Uni without finishing, I'd sort of hung around, done projects, and made up my own course at Sheffield. My time at Sheffield was tough, but everything changed for me when I was there. Sheffield is a city I am very fond of.

was in London. It had to work in London. But I had no clue of where to begin.

When I looked at my calendar then, it was so empty that all I was doing was breathing – compared with when I look at my calendar now and it is so busy that I can hardly breathe.

A distinct part of starting out as a freelancer, or doing any kind of job or thing you set up on your own, is listing work, or for us 'gigs,' in diaries.* And also saying to bookers that your diary is really full but you could squeeze them in. A lot of my early days of gigs involved me staring at completely blank pages and saying to bookers, 'I don't know. This Tuesday? Yeah, okay, I'll move things around and let's do Tuesday.'

Empty, empty – months of emptiness. Just empty, blank pages of no work at all.

Much later, I managed to do my first tour when I found that my diary was quite full with individual gigs that I had got in different ways. So I realized that if I wrote all those gigs out on a poster – that would be a tour. And then people would say, 'Wow, he's doing a tour,' and then I *would* be doing a tour. It was the active use of confidence. It was the first time since Edinburgh Fringe of 1981 that I had used this logic.

My first tour in the early '90s was called 'The Loose Connection of Dates Tour.' But in '84, going into '85, I don't think I even had a diary.

*

---

* Sometime in the '60s, rock-and-roll people started calling live concerts 'gigs' in Britain and America. I don't know who started it, but when we in the UK started alternative comedy in 1979, everyone decided we would be doing 'gigs' and not 'concerts' or 'shows.' The word *gigs* just sounds cooler, and I'm very happy to use that word. It really just means 'shows.'

But back to coming out.

The process started with self-analysis. Which meant lying on my bed to see if I could work out why I felt different: why I felt like I had boy genetics and girl genetics instead of just boy genetics.*

Why self-analysis instead of traditional professional psychiatric analysis?

Well, because my attempts at actual analysis – with an actual psychiatrist – didn't ever work out.

Before I came out to Kaite O'Reilly, I had tried to seek 'professional help' while I was still at Sheffield Uni. I'd got an appointment with a doctor, a GP at the University medical centre, and went in and sat in front of him. Then, in a way that I found easier than I'd thought it would be, I'd said:

'I am a transvestite, I need to talk to someone about that.'

The GP said, 'Okay, I'll get you an appointment with the psychiatrist.'

It was so easy that I left the medical practice very happy, within about five minutes. But I waited and waited and waited, and no appointment was ever sent through.

So I went back to the medical centre thinking, *God, I've got to do this whole thing again.* Luckily I ran into the same GP I had seen before, coming out of the centre just as I was going in.

'Do you remember me?' I said. 'I came in here and said that thing about being a . . .' I wasn't going to say the word

---

*In those days I didn't think of being transvestite/transgender as a matter of genetics. I hadn't yet come to that conclusion. This hasn't been absolutely proven, but it's the only thing that makes logical sense to me.

outside of his office. 'But the appointment never came through.'

Again he sounded helpful and said, 'Oh, I'll get right on it.'

But that was the last I heard of that appointment (I do feel that GP should have followed up on me).

When nothing happened the second time, I decided not to go back again. A few years later, down in London, I decided to try to analyze myself.

Analyzing myself was a very interesting experiment. It was, again, the Nuffield syllabus: figuring out what I needed to understand and how I was going to find it out. Can you do an experiment where you lie on your bed and analyze your brain? Well, I tried.

The great thing about this experiment was that I didn't have to publish any results. I just had to report back to my own conscious brain later about what I found out.

That's my kind of experiment.

Actually, I could have done it with a stopwatch and actual figures, but the things I discovered about myself were a bit intangible.

Here's one thing I found out:

If you have been told your entire life that you have a sexuality that is 'not correct,' you quite logically build up a negative attitude toward those feelings. You think you are doing something wrong because society is saying that you are doing or feeling something wrong.

When I tried to examine those feelings – *Why do I feel like this? Why do I want to do this? Why do I want to wear makeup or wear a skirt?* – my brain wouldn't actually let me concentrate on them. I couldn't hold the ideas and the thoughts in my head. I found it was really difficult to break down that wall to find the answer.

What would happen was that I would think about it for a while but then I'd start thinking of something else. The brain has powerful defense mechanisms that can push big questions like that away. I tried it many times, lying on the bed with the curtains drawn: no other interference, nothing else going on, door closed. Just me and the water tank. But again, my brain couldn't focus and I couldn't get anywhere with my thoughts and with the big question: Why? Why is this feeling happening?

The why was elusive. The why is still elusive. Why do I want to self-identify as both 'boy' and 'girl'? I still haven't figured it all out.

Who is supposed to wear heels? Are women supposed to wear high heels? If you think about it, you could go to seven billion people in the world and say, 'Who is supposed to wear high heels? Men or women?' And probably seven billion – probably all of them (except for three of them) or some ridiculously high number – would say, 'Yeah, women are supposed to wear high heels.' Then if you say, 'Well, why are women allowed to wear high heels and men not?' then probably they would say something as innocuous as 'Because that's what women do.'

If you get down to it, there is no overt reason.

Native tribes of men and women do not wear high heels; there are no high heels out there. I believe that high-heeled shoes, in fact, originated historically with men (at least in Britain) around the time of the prince regent who became

George IV of England, but there is no essential logic for women wearing high heels. If you analyze clothing, skirts were worn by the Greeks and Romans at war and (arguably) by the Scots at war, even though they called them kilts. In different societies we create our own rules about clothing and makeup and ornamentation. I've just come to the conclusion that all women should wear whatever they want to wear and that all men should wear whatever they want to wear. If they have a problem with that, they should take it up with the United Nations.

As for heels, I happen to think they're fun and sexy. And I happen to feel that wearing high heels allows me to express a more feminine side of myself.

That wish to express my feminine side has been in me since I was four. And if any woman or teenage girl has ever thought, *I want to wear high heels*, that is the exact feeling that I have. There is no difference in the feelings.

When women started putting on trousers, or 'pants' as one says in America, back in the '30s and '40s, people said to Marlene Dietrich and Katharine Hepburn, 'You women are dressing as men.' They and other women disagreed with that and said, 'No, we're not. We're just wearing pants [or trousers].' And now women have that right to wear whatever they want to wear whenever they want to wear it.

Therefore, I claim the same rights. To wear whatever I want to wear, too.

So I don't say, 'I'm dressing as a woman.' I say, 'I'm wearing a dress, I'm wearing a skirt, I'm wearing some heels.' As we don't say (anymore) that women are 'dressing like a man' when they wear trousers.

High heels are deemed sexy, but is there more to it than that? It gets to the real fundamentals of the problem of trying to define gender. I tried myself to define what *feminine* and *masculine* are, but when you get into that, you can get really stuck.

You can say, '*Masculine* is strong and determined and brave and physically tough.' But then, many women are also strong and determined and brave and physically tough. If you say, 'Men have bigger muscles,' is that it? That's the whole bloody thing? That is masculinity? Just bigger muscles in your arms, your legs?

When you try to break down femininity and masculinity into little definition boxes, it's tricky as all hell. I didn't get anywhere with that. If you try distilling the idea of femininity and masculinity, I don't think you'll get to any clear conclusions, either. But meanwhile, I was still trying to lie on the bed and work out why I felt I was transgender, and the conclusion I finally came to was that while I may never understand the why of it or be able to live neatly within either a feminine box or a masculine box – but not both, the way many people do – guilt and shame were two feelings that I felt I should let go of.

If you have an 'alternative sexuality,' which is my way of saying 'LGBT+,' you should not feel guilty about it or ashamed about it, because you did not choose it.

I say that. I claim that. I believe that. Because I believe it is about genetics and the genetic codes we are given.

Obviously I'm not a scientist, or a geneticist, or a psychiatrist, but through the reading I've done and my own self-analysis, I've come to understand it this way. Which is why I feel that women who like to throw on a pair of heels, a skirt, and makeup have, in some of their genetics, the same genetic coding that I have. Exactly the same. We know that the human genome is massive, and whatever that bit is – that bit that encourages us to wish to express ourselves in heels and skirts and makeup – I have that bit. I feel it's exactly the same for me as it is for those who also have that same genetic code.

We need to become more open-minded to the idea that many of us exist on a spectrum – a continuum – of gender. That for some of us the choice isn't just one or the other – completely male or completely female – but often a combination of both.

In fact, it seems there are three different lines on the sexuality spectrum: how you self-identify, who you're attracted to, and what you look like. And it seems the dial can be at any place on any of those three lines. That seems to be how humanity is made up.

I have talked to a number of LGBT+ people, and the vast majority of them say that they knew they were of alternative sexuality from when they were very young. I, myself, knew when I was four or five. To me, it now seems that it was built in. Nature rather than nurture. One should not feel guilty or ashamed about it. It's just how it is.

We all get dealt our genetic cards when we are born. In life, we have to play them as well as we can. Sometimes I think I had a lucky escape by not going to the psychiatrist. I found that all the thinking on being transgender was very much based on psychiatrists talking to people who were having a very bad time dealing with their sexuality. Everyone talked about gender dysphoria (gender 'confusion'). I remember talking to one psychiatrist who said, 'Oh, I'll look up *transgender* in a book and see what information I get.'

Well, I certainly didn't need to talk to a person who was going to look up my 'condition' in a book. And I didn't feel that my gender was 'confused.'

That's why I don't like the word *dysphoria*. I refuse to be confused about this. It's confusing, but I am trying to be not confused. Which is why I made up my own terminology – being in 'girl mode' or 'boy mode' – it's how I describe where I am on any given day on that nonbinary continuum of gender identity, a concept that psychiatrists and sociologists and politicians and religious types don't seem able to explain with any degree of medical or biological certainty why I wish to wear skirts and heels on certain days and trousers on others. I don't know why, and neither do they. And I suppose, in the end, the why of it really doesn't matter. It's just who I am and the way I was born. That's who a lot of us are and the way a lot of us were born.

The self-acceptance I gained from that time of self-analysis gradually started to take root in me. Once I decided to not feel guilt and shame about who I was, I felt less conflicted about my identity and more committed to my mission of being wholly myself, whomever that self was and whatever that self looked like. When I finally came out in early '85, I came up with a plan to wear a dress and heels and makeup and go around expressing myself that way every day for six months. Not something most twenty-three-year-olds would decide to undertake (back then).

At the time I came to this decision I didn't have a job. I suppose that helped.

Not having a job during that period was also why I watched a lot of television. Australian soap operas, mostly: *Sons and Daughters*, *A Country Practice*, and *The Young Doctors*. When I didn't have enough money, I would take a bit of butter or margarine, some sugar and egg, some flour, and make a whole bowl of cake mix. And then I'd eat the whole bowl of cake mix without baking it.

Now, this is a very piggy thing to do, and obviously very reprehensible, and I could go to cake prison for having done it, because as far as I know there is no statute of limitations on cake crimes.

But again, applying the Nuffield syllabus to experimenting with cake, I found that if you make cake mix, and you put the cake mix into the oven, and the oven makes the cake mix rise and expand due to the heat and other scientific things, that cake comes out tasting *less good* than when it went in. The spoon and all the turny bits of the electric whisk, covered with the last vestiges of cake mix on them before the main cake mix went into the oven, tasted fantastic. This pure-cake-mix taste was unbelievable heaven. But I always thought that when the cake came out and you tried a bit of it, it was fine but nowhere as good as before it was baked. Which is why you have to put some cream and icing onto the cake to try to make it taste as good as the cake mix did before it went in the oven.

So yes, I did eat the cake mix, sometimes entire bowls of cake mix, because you could make as much as you wanted to (and I didn't know how much you were supposed to make): I just added the ingredients, mixed it with a spoon, and off I went. It did taste fantastic.

But it had what Madame Curie would call a radioactive half-life. Well, not really a radioactive half-life – it's more like you lit a fuse. I'd eat the cake mix and then I'd think it would 'cook' in your stomach. I know there are chemicals in your stomach that break things down. I think if you eat the cake mix too quickly, it will process in your stomach until your body informs you that you have, in fact, eaten a massive rock that's just going to sit in your stomach, so now you can't walk. So it's not a good idea to eat (too much) uncooked cake mix. But it's the kind of thing that, once you've done it, you think, *Oh, I will never do that again.* And then you go and do it again a week later. Anyway, I don't do cake mix anymore. So that's all gone. No more cake mix.

The next step after self-analysis and cake mix was finding a help group.

I somehow knew that there were other people who realized they were TV and TS (again, the terms for transvestite and transsexual in the 1980s) and that maybe there were support groups to help them.

I say 'somehow' because I am trying to imagine, back before the Internet, how one learned about anything. How I had learned this, I don't know. I must have read it somewhere.

When we want to learn something now, we just go to the Internet and type in: *I want to learn about soup in Afghanistan.* And it gives you all the soup variations in Afghanistan. If you remember the early search engines, like, say, Alta Vista, then you know that when you'd type something in like *Soup in Afghanistan*, it would show you *porn, porn, porn*, etc. And you'd go, 'No, I was after soup in Afghanistan.' *Porn. Naked men, women, porn nakedness?* 'Nope, just soup, mainly in Afghanistan.' You couldn't use words; you just had to say, *Soup. Afghanistan. Not porn.* As soon as you said 'not porn' it would say: *Ah, you meant porn, Afghanistan porn. Soup porn.* They must have just put the entire dictionary into their search request. Anyone who wanted to look for *trousers* – porn. *Go to the moon* – porn. These porn people will attach the word *porn* to anything to make money.

Actually, mentioning the word *porn* here is interesting, because in the old days, whenever you said you were transgender, other people felt you were essentially saying you were pornographic. Perversion was implied and assumed – and that's what I, and everyone else who has come out with any kind of alternative sexuality, have had to deal with. We've all had to fight these negative words and say, 'No, actually – member of society.'

It was initially just a mission for myself, I suppose. Because I didn't feel I was on a mission to become an activist for all transgender people. I didn't know how to do that. I didn't think I *could* actually do that. I just thought:

I'll try to create some space for myself where I can exist.

I thought then, if anyone could make use of the space I'd made, that would be great.

I had heard that there were essentially two support groups in the UK for people who were coming out as TV or TS back in 1985.

One was the Beaumont Society, which appeared mostly

to help older men – male-to-female transgender people and their wives who often came along to meetings – express themselves. It sounded like something positive for them, but it didn't sound like it was for me.

The other group, the TV/TS Help Group, seemed more focused on younger people like me. I think I got the number for the TV/TS Help Group from the Yellow Pages and then went to one of the old British red phone boxes and called them up. That's what we did in those pre-Internet days. Looked things up in the Yellow Pages and then made calls from phone boxes. I called from an old red phone box because the phone boxes were great for having private, tricky conversations.

Remarkably, the TV/TS group met on Upper Street, Islington, in London (bizarrely, right next to a police station), only a half mile from where I was living.

The first thing I remember thinking when I found out where they were located was: *Right next to a police station? Are we still considered illegal? Can we be carted off to prison, like Quentin Crisp, back in the day?*

No, my sexuality wasn't actually illegal at that point (1985), but you just weren't really sure what the rules were then.

The second thing I remember thinking when I found out that they were just down the road was: *This is fate. This is fate telling me to go. The only help group in the UK that I feel might be right for me is just down the road from where I'm living? I have to go!*

So I went.

Now, that was before I was really at ease throwing on the dress, the makeup, and the heels because, fashion-wise, I was a mess at that point. Which is evidenced by the fact that the first time I went to the TV/TS Help Group, I turned up in green military trousers, Jesus sandals, and maybe a corduroy jacket. Back then, I just put on whatever clothes were lying around.

If you are on the cutting edge of style, you can look really way out there, off the map. Some people might say you look like a dickhead. One of my stand-up pieces is about fashion being circular: It goes from people actually looking like a dickhead; to people looking okay; to looking trendy; to looking cool; to looking cool, hip, and groovy; then back to looking like a dickhead. It goes full circle. Very advanced fashion almost joins up with having no fashion sense at all.

So back then, I turned up in combat trousers and Jesus sandals and a corduroy jacket. It was not a good mix.

The group was run by a transgendered woman named Yvonne Sinclair, who was very helpful to me and to everyone there. I remember there were husbands with their wives being supportive. I remember there was one wife there whose name was Helen. We got on very well. I regret that I've not met her again since those days, because we had some good chats, and I hope she's doing okay.

There was also one young lesbian woman there, just hanging out, I presumed, again being supportive or maybe just curious. I found her very interesting, and I thought, *I would like to get to know her better*, but I didn't know how to start that up.

One guy I met there said he was going to be a lawyer but that he couldn't wear a dress while doing his job – being a transgender guy in a conservative law firm just wasn't going to work for him. But then he said something amazing. He said:

'It's a gift. This is a gift.'

And I said, 'Being TV is a gift? I don't think I would use that word, *gift*.'

'No, you have to look at it as a gift.'

That stayed with me, and though it took me a few years I eventually realized that he was right. Being trans – LGBT+, whatever you want to call your alternative sexuality – *is* a gift.

It's just a really tricky gift, one that's quite difficult to handle, but, as I've said, we're all given these genetic cards and we have to play them as well as we can. It was a most unusual gift to me, since I don't look terribly girly. Which should mean that hopefully most people know when I walk down the street in girl mode that it's not been an easy journey. I did not just casually jump to my decision to come out and I always have to be ready to deal with the possible negative reaction of others.

But it has made me stronger. It has made me know what it means to stand up and try and speak openly about sexuality and life. I wear my gift now as battle armor. I came out thirty-two years ago, which means I've fought my way through for a bloody long time. I didn't get helicoptered into this place where I am now. I had to fight my way through. And at times it's been a bloody hard fight. And so I just keep going, trying to find a space for myself, and for anyone else, who is on the same path.

I went to the TV/TS Help Group regularly for a number of weeks, maybe even a number of months. Eventually I was working on the phone help line, encouraging people who called to come down and visit the group.

The first time I went, I just hung out. The second time I went I brought a dress, heels, and makeup for me to wear. Back then, I bought my first dress from a catalogue, not from a shop, because you have to have a lot of guts to go into a regular shop and say, 'I will try this dress on in this changing room now.' And most trans people won't have that kind of confidence at the beginning. In fact, we are, understandably, at the bottom of the confidence mountain. To come out takes a lot of guts and determination, but at the beginning it's very difficult to have confidence.

Because the fear of coming out and getting negative reactions in the streets is so unbelievably high.

Which is why I say the defining moment of my life was walking out the door in a dress and heels from 37 Calabria Road, Islington, in 1985.

It took me twenty-three years to develop the guts to do that. Anyone who's ever done it knows that it is just so fucking hard that anything else you do after that seems almost easy.

You think, *If I can do something that hard, but positive – maybe I can do anything.*

And maybe you can.

My First Day Out

I'd been going to the TV/TS Help Group for about two months before I actually left my flat wearing makeup and a dress. At the help group I had been talking to a young lesbian woman I liked and I had thought, *Hey, can I have a relationship with a lesbian woman? Does that work?*

But at that point of my sexuality-and-confidence-advancement mission, I wasn't quite up for pursuing a relationship. So instead I just asked her, 'Will you come with me and just accompany me the first time I go out wearing makeup and a dress?'

Luckily she said yes, so we agreed to meet somewhere in town for tea or coffee and have a day in the centre of London.

I knew I could get out of the house in a dress because I was living with five medical students and I was familiar enough with their schedules to know when they wouldn't be home. Getting ready and leaving when no one was there didn't seem too difficult.

Getting back in the house without being noticed would be the challenge.

So I made a plan to go to the ladies' loos on Highbury Fields to change my clothes before returning home.

Most of what I remember about my first day walking around outside in makeup and a dress was fear. The fear of being stared at, which I knew I would be. This was partly because I wasn't that good at applying makeup. I'd bought a book about how to do it and then tried to teach myself, but I didn't have older sisters to practise with, or on.

So I went out and hung out with my friend from the help group, and I made it through. Until it was time to go back home.

I had a little bag I'd brought with me with my other clothing to change back into. So at the end of the afternoon, I came back on the Underground to Highbury Corner in Islington and went to the ladies' loos as planned. I'd expected to go in, quickly change my clothes, wipe off my makeup, then slip back out in boy mode so I could go home with no one the wiser.

What I wasn't expecting in the ladies' loos at about three o'clock in the afternoon were three teenage girls smoking cigarettes. They were probably just skipping school. So there they were, smoking cigarettes, while I was just trying to find a stall, change clothes, and get out of there.

But the first cubicle I went into didn't have a lock.

Actually, it's the kind of public loo where it's surprising that they've even got doors. And I'm sure the men's loos were even worse than the women's.

I thought, *Oh shit, I cannot change in this loo and be constantly trying to hold my hand against the door.*

So I decided to find another stall.

I opened the door of the stall I was in and zipped across the middle passageway to the stall opposite.

I closed that door. It didn't have a lock, either.

I thought, *Oh crap. I've got to try for another one now.*

So I went across a third time, and by that time these girls were quite obviously whispering about me: 'Who is that? What are they doing? Is that a he or a she?'

I could hear the whispering going on. In the third cubicle there was a lock. So I locked the door and quickly managed to change my clothes and wipe the makeup off my face, not using the handy makeup wipes that you can buy today, but probably with liquid makeup remover or something else incredibly inconvenient.

Finally, the dress was off, the heels were off, the makeup was off, and jeans and flat shoes were back on. Now I had to make it out quickly before the girls could react.

But that was impossible.

The girls were ready to act. They were just waiting for me. And when I finally came out of the cubicle, they shouted, 'Hey, mate! Hey, mister! Why are you wearing makeup? Why are you dressed as a woman?'

I was out the door, heading back toward home, but they were following me. 'Hey, why are you dressed as a woman?' They were still following me across Highbury Fields, which was when I thought, *Don't go home, they'll know where you live, you'll never hear the end of it.*

So I was heading *away* from home, walking and walking and walking, around Highbury Corner, down Canonbury Road, while they continued to shout at me. Finally, I thought: *Screw this. They're just going to shout at me forever. Let's confront this.* So I stopped and I turned around to face my teenage inquisitors.

I shouted back, 'You want to know why I'm wearing a dress? I'll tell you why.'

But before I could say anything else, the girls just screamed and ran off in the other direction. I was stunned. *Wow. That wasn't as hard as I thought.*

I think that was the first time I was overtly intimidated because of my sexuality.

You assume older people intimidate younger people, but those three thirteen-year-old girls had power over a twenty-three-year-old man.

Maybe they turned out to be wonderful human beings. Or maybe they all now live in a tree. Whatever.

I learned something that day when those girls ran off: If you confront aggression – sometimes just standing your ground or even with cheeriness and politeness – sometimes you can shut it down. It's not a perfect science, but it feels better than being scared. I also learned that you could feel empowered by facing people down. They were only thirteen or fourteen, but the turning around and saying, 'All right, I'll tell you,' felt almost like a second coming out because I had to say, 'Okay, you want to put me in a corner? I'll face this down as opposed to screaming and running.' Which I always thought I might do. But I didn't scream and run – in the end, they did.

I went home and didn't tell any of my housemates for another few months. When I did tell them, brilliantly, they were all very cool about it.

I remember filming *All the Queen's Men* in Hungary in late 2000, on an old Soviet airfield near Lake Balaton. Hungarian extras were there dressed as German soldiers, waiting for their next call to do more filming, and they were sitting on a part of the runway where planes used to taxi along.

I was actually playing a transgender character, so I was wearing a black dress, heels, and a turban!

During shooting I had learned a few words of Hungarian, and as I walked past the thirty or forty Hungarian extras that day, I could see that they were all nudging each other and talking about me in what was obviously a negative way, or at least a non-positive way. I'd learned how to say 'good afternoon' in Hungarian, so as they were whispering among themselves and saying things loud enough for me to hear, I turned to them and said, *'Jó napot!'* – 'Good afternoon!' in Hungarian.

And they immediately went quiet.

What you say and how you say it has way more power than you think it does. Those guys in Hungary were probably saying, 'Look at that idiot in a dress.' 'Hey, Fred, he looks like your sister.' Just the stupid things that men say. And then you shout 'Good afternoon!' in their language, and there is no response as they weren't expecting it.

I often now use politeness to stop people shouting hellish, negative things at me.

While I was touring America in 2015 I performed in a town that had clearly suffered under the economic subprime economic meltdown. Our hotel was on a street that had some nice shops in one direction and more boarded-up shops in the other direction. Rachael Downing, a fine artist as well as makeup artist, who is often my makeup artist on tour, came up with the idea that every morning we should find a really good local place to have breakfast so that we could get to know a little bit about the town we were visiting. I was totally into this as you often don't meet enough local people. That morning, in this town in particular, we started walking down the street in the other direction, where there were about five guys sitting on the road, drinking out of bottles wrapped up in brown paper bags (standard street drinking for most states in America).

There I was, walking along in my heels and makeup – not distinctly girly but in heels and makeup – and I walked past them and I realized that I should say something to them to defuse the possible negativity. So I said, 'Hello! How are you? Lovely weather we're having!' They weren't expecting that and replied, 'What . . . How many?' And I moved on, but they were obviously thrown that I would start the chitchat.

I think this should be called non-victim behavior. A surprise offer of bright cheeriness and self-confidence on people who were probably about to say negative things to you, in order to make you a non-victim and just a member of society. Because all people seem to say in response to these bright, cheery things is, 'Ahhhh . . . Yes, the weather . . . not bad.' They are so busy thinking of what they were about to say to you that it throws them off if you start the conversation first.

It's only taken me fifty years to work that out, but there you go. Please try this, if you wish.

I still get hassled and abused like I did that day in Highbury Fields, but now I'm more used to dealing with it. And I've worked out another coping mechanism for when people are whispering and giggling and pointing at me.

In the old days we had cigarettes, so if you wanted to hang out somewhere looking relaxed, you could just light a cigarette and lean against a lamppost and smoke it. You could lean against a wall in a station, or sit in a chair or on a bench. You could hang out anywhere with a cigarette. Now most of us have given up cigarettes, but we've got our mobile phones, which we can use much in the same way: we stand somewhere or sit somewhere while doing almost anything – reading a book, sending an e-mail, checking our texts – on our smartphones.

Something happened during the same recent tour in America I just mentioned. A group of us had gone on a day off to a restaurant for dinner, and as we were going in, another large group turned up at the same time. The other group was of young men in their late teens or early twenties, and one of them held the door open for us. As I walked past them, I could feel and hear their whispering and giggling.

But instead of coming in after us, they let the door close behind us and stood outside instead. I suppose so they could whisper and giggle in peace. So, realizing this, I immediately turned around and went back outside, but instead of directly confronting them, I just stood near them and texted on my phone.

Now, if you are in a whispering and giggling mood, it becomes quite tricky if the subject of your whispering and giggling is standing right next to you. So, then, what you do, if you are in a group, is you tend to move away so that you can whisper and giggle with a certain amount of spare distance.

But I gradually edged my way over to them, still checking on my phone. This made it impossible for them to get enough of a comfortable distance to properly whisper and giggle. It seems people need a certain amount of space between themselves and the person they're mocking.

Then something kind of fun happened: they started to peel off and walk away. The group of about eight went off in ones and twos until there was only one guy left. They were actually retreating. What made me sure about this was the last guy, who shouted to the others, 'Hey! Where are you going? I thought we were going to eat!'

That guy was obviously made of stronger character material, someone who had just come to the restaurant to eat, and thought the giggling was pointless, didn't even pick up on it, and couldn't understand why they would come to a restaurant to eat and then all start walking home.

Again, this isn't a perfect science, but I've found that when people are giggling at you, if you go and stand right next to them, they seem to find giggling much more difficult.

I should add that I don't think this technique works with overtly aggressive people. So use your best judgment.

In 2016 I reported someone to the police for shouting homophobic abuse at me near my home in London, and a case was made and passed on to the Crown Prosecution Service. It went to a magistrate's court and the man in question was found guilty on two counts. So one always has to be wary, and standing up in court and putting over your side of the story can often be a tough thing to do. I'd rather not do this. I'd rather we all just have respect for each other on the streets, but some people just don't.

Going out the door in Islington in 1985 for the first time was the hardest thing – maybe that I've ever done.

That door was like an *Alice in Wonderland* door – but instead of leading to a magical world, it led to a different world, a new world, a world I could begin to try to change in my own personal way, carving out for myself a small slice of freedom of expression.

And that is actually what has happened.

Coming Out To Your Father

My dad and I seem to be 75 per cent similar.

He gradually developed a plan throughout his life.

He worked his way from a working-class background to live a middle-income (middle-class?) life, committing to a job for thirty-five years to retire at only fifty-six with a great pension. Dad hacked his way up the ladder at BP, not through the standard route, really. Whatever it is that is the normal route up the corporate ladder, he went up a different ladder, one that the high fliers would never use.

Some people don't question things in their work – systems, procedures, what's the best way to get things done. But Dad is someone who did question things, and I question them, too. At some point I noticed that we had this similarity, a stubbornness; a logical, commonsensical approach to life; a refusal to do tasks that seem stupid or just don't work – because they're not creating anything useful. He didn't go to university, and I dropped out of university without taking my accounting exams. Later on, I found out that he was supposed to take accounting exams and had decided not to either.

I've always felt lucky to have Dad as my dad, but never more than the day I came out to him as a transvestite.

I'd come out when I was twenty-three, but I put off telling him for the next six years, mainly because some people told me that my dad might not be able to handle the news. I felt pretty sure that wasn't true, but I couldn't ask him whether or not he could handle it. It was a risk, and one I knew I had to take before I talked about it openly onstage.

I told him on a Saturday in 1991, after a football match.

Dad had, at that time, two season tickets to watch the Crystal Palace Football Club and he was going to see the match that particular Saturday. Sometimes he would go with my brother, Mark, sometimes with me, sometimes with someone else. That day I had planned to go with him and I'd decided I'd tell him there.

But then, when I got there, I thought, *This is a football match! I can't tell him at a football match! What if I told him and we lost the football match? That wouldn't be good!*

At the end of the game, when everyone was streaming out of the stadium, I changed my mind again. Now I thought: *I can't tell him I'm a transvestite in the street! What if his response was a very loud 'You're a transvestite?' Then all these football fans might give me a very hard time.*

So I suggested that we go somewhere to eat, and we ended up at a classic old British café where they serve a menu of sausage, bacon, eggs, and chips all day, a café that just happened to have a main front room but also a back room that was perfectly designed for telling your dad you're a transvestite, in case any readers are looking for a place like that.

In the back room of the restaurant there were three tables. By that point, I was very nervous, and picking a table felt rather like *Goldilocks and the Three Bears* – none of them seemed exactly right. One table was occupied, but since we had to sit somewhere we sat down at the middle table – as it looked like the occupied table near it was soon to finish up and leave. Within about five minutes, they had. The coast was clear and I thought:

There's no one else in the back room. Tell him right now before someone else comes in.

So, I did.

I told him that I was TV – a transvestite.

To the best of my recollection, my dad said, 'Okay.' And then, something like: 'It's all right.'

It was a great relief. I'd had it all worked out – just like every kid does who has to tell their parents about their gender issues – preparing myself for what I would do if he'd said, 'I'll never talk to you again.'

Years later, when we made the *Believe* documentary, he said that he 'wasn't best pleased,' which is a very British way of saying, 'It's not really at the top of my hit parade.'

After I came out to him, he wrote me a letter in which he said, *I'm okay with this, and if your mother was still alive, I think she'd be okay with this, too.*

And that was amazing. Hearing that my mother would have accepted who I was, just as he did.

As time went on, he was supportive of me, especially when I'd say things like, 'I'm just a weirdo,' which was my way of preventing anyone else from saying it first. When I said that he'd say, 'You shouldn't say that.'

Which was kind of nice to hear.

As grateful as I was to have a supportive and accepting father, I knew that when it came to my gender issues, he couldn't really help me. No one could. I would be on my own with that for the rest of my life, and, like every other unusual path in life that I have followed, I knew I would have to find my way myself.

The Streets of London

When I came back up to the Edinburgh Fringe in 1985, I returned as a street performer.*

I had seen street performers in Edinburgh when I was there as a sketch performer, not achieving my comedy goals. A street band called Pookiesnackenburger and a comedy sketch group called Cliffhanger performed huge and highly popular street shows at the Edinburgh Fringe every day at one p.m. Their joint show – *Lunchtime at Mr Cairo's* – had blown us away. Our own group, Sheffield University Fringe (later SUF Theatre Company), had energy and invention, but we weren't really that good and we definitely weren't successful. These guys were amazing, and they were doing shows together there on the streets in Edinburgh, and separately down in London and in Brighton, where they were based. Luke Cresswell and Steve McNicholas from Pookiesnackenburger eventually set up *Stomp*, an amazing show of street percussion and movement, which now performs all over the world. I saw an earlier version, and then I saw a version fifteen or twenty years later, and it had got even better.

When my plan to get noticed by television people at the

---

*Street performer, not busker. Buskers tend to be musicians and have audiences that continually pass by. We street performers gather an audience and do a show to them, with a beginning, a middle, and an end.

Edinburgh Fringe failed, I'd come to London in 1984 and done nothing professionally for an entire year. I knew I needed to think up a new plan. At some point I decided that I should start doing street performing. I thought maybe I'd get some success that way.

This wasn't a detailed plan. But it was the best new strategy I could think of at the time.

The alternative comedy scene had started in London's Soho, but I hadn't really picked up on it. Nobody I knew was aware it was happening. Street performing seemed to be a way to get performing work without needing to find an agent or book a theatre.

Again, I was being inspired by the Nuffield syllabus: if you have a theory (that you might have some talent) and you want to prove that this is the case, then come up with a series of experiments (a series of performances) to show that it is true.

I'd already taken three shows up to Edinburgh and felt I should be able to make a show work on the street. Unfortunately I discovered that street performing is terribly difficult and I was terrible at it. But once I started I felt I had to keep going.

Apart from Pookiesnackenburger and Cliffhanger, there weren't that many well-known street performers. But there was also the fabulous poet/comedian John Hegley and the street band the Popticians. Problem was, it was difficult to become well-known as a street performer because you had no posters, and no publicity, and no well-known venue to be seen at. The beauty of street performing was that you just turned up and started performing on a piece of street where there was no car traffic but lots of human traffic. One group, the Vicious Boys (Angelo Abela and Andy Smart), had won the 1984 *Time Out* Street Entertainer Award (which my comedy partner, Rob Ballard, and I hadn't known existed until then). Their winning idea was brilliant.

The Vicious Boys mimed out a comedic version of various films. They would mention a film and then they'd mime out a small comedic scene in front of audiences at Covent Garden in London (or wherever). Because it was mimed, they would get huge crowds: people could see them, so they didn't need to hear them. When I saw them performing their routines on television or in a comedy club (they were that successful – they were not only on television but they had also performed in New York), I thought, *Wow, if they found that idea, there must be another idea one can do like that on the street.*

But there wasn't. They came up with the best comedy idea going. I tried for four years to come up with an idea like that. I couldn't find one.*

Rob Ballard and I started performing at Covent Garden toward the summer of 1985. We had met at Sheffield University. He was in a band and I was busy setting up revue shows. He had a lot of energy and drive and together we had set up Alternative Productions, essentially to get cheaper printing done through the student union. Grad-

---

* Until after I stopped street performing full-time, and then I came up with a beautiful street show where a small kid with a rubber ball in his hand would be floated around an audience (like a lead singer, crowd surfing at a rock concert) until a point when he had to just bounce the rubber ball and knock over some tin cans. Reactions we got to this show were immense, even though it doesn't really have anything to it – but if and when the ball knocked over the tin cans, the crowds went wild. I've performed it with other street-performer friends only five times.

ually he had moved out of being in a band and suddenly I found he had a great natural talent to perform comedy as well. Together we went on to set up the Official Touring Company of Alpha Centauri, performing comedy shows with two other students: Helen Caldwell and Neil Gore – including a very low-budget version of *Ben-Hur*, which we performed in Sheffield and Edinburgh. We four, I had thought, might go on to turn professional and do our own show on TV, but that was not to be. Helen and Neil chose different directions and the four of us became two, as 'Official Touring,' and then just 'The Officials,' when Rob and I came down to London and became a double act.

Our first show at Covent Garden was a load of 'failed tricks' – a toy beaver leaping through a heap of newspaper because it was attached to a piece of elastic, a water-evaporation trick where all the water disappeared into my Wellington boots, a cornflakes-disappearing trick where you just ate all the cornflakes, and a fake knife-throwing act. That's what the show ended up being for the first year as we tried to come up with something better. It was rather all over the place, as we were just piecing these 'failed tricks' together.

At a certain point Rob decided to go off and take a break, and so I said, 'Don't worry, I'll rewrite it and make the show better.' But when he came back, we realized that my rewrite had made the show worse. I had, by that point, written sketches for several shows and taken three to the Edinburgh Fringe, so I thought I should be able to write comedy material for a street-performing show. But I could not. It is a very difficult medium to write for. Part of the problem is the attention span of the audience. Which is very, very short. Adults become like children and children become like animals. There are so many other things to do at a 'street venue'* that these all compete with your performance. I found that in order to get any attention as a comedic street performer, you had to say and do extreme and outrageous things.

For instance, if a kid was playing around in front of your show – not paying attention and playing around with your props – the audience found it really funny if you said, 'Right – now we're going to put this kid in a box and stick knives through the box.' Of course you wouldn't do this; you wouldn't do anything to the kid, but the audience would laugh like crazy. I realized that the comedy that works on the street is like a *Tom and Jerry* cartoon or 'Itchy & Scratchy' from *The Simpsons*. You had to do things in a much more loud and outrageous way just to hold people's attention on the street.

Another thing that makes street performing so difficult is that you have to find and build an audience, when often there is no one standing near you to begin with. This is *incredibly* hard to do. It is one of the hardest things I've ever done. Learning how to hold an audience so that they'll

---

* Any piece of street where successful street performers work becomes a 'street venue.' The trouble is, the 'venue' just looks like a piece of street. When booking street performers, particularly around the UK, some bookers would just say, 'There is a street. Go and perform in it.' Initially we didn't have the language to say, 'Yeah, it's a street, but it's a terrible street venue.' The problem was a lack of human traffic (people walking about) and the sounds of honking cars. There are many things that make a good performing venue, and it's easier to tell a good performing venue indoors. Outdoors it's a science that most people don't understand. So often you were asked to perform in completely terrible street venues. You therefore failed, and the booker would think you were a bad performer when in fact you had been trying to perform in a bad street venue.

watch what you're doing on the streets when they can just walk off, have a cup of tea, see a film, or go shopping – seems almost impossible. The trick is to perform physical-situation comedy – developing a story that hopefully includes some danger or jeopardy in it. And it's useful to have a volunteer from the audience because then people get invested in your show, because the volunteer is one of them, and they'll want to stick around to the end of it to see how the volunteer does. But that is not what I had learned with indoor sketch comedy, so I had to relearn half of what I'd learned when I started street performing.

When Rob and I went back up to the Edinburgh Fringe in August 1985, we did not do well. I thought it would be much easier this time because we didn't have to bring costumes and props, but our show just wasn't very good, so a lot of people ignored us. We were new to street performing and it was much harder than we had thought.

One of the reasons people ignored us was that they often did not notice we were actually performing. When you do a street show, you set yourself up and put your props out – things like a squeaky toy or a bucket or juggling clubs or whatever. It's good to have a lot of props in street performing. Without a lot of props, you're just standing there wearing clothes on a street while everyone else is just walking around wearing clothes on a street. But if you're standing there wearing rather unusual clothes on a street, surrounded by a lot of props on the ground, then it looks like you are maybe about to perform a show.

I remember performing our show with Rob at the 1985 Edinburgh Fringe on one occasion. We had managed to create a small audience. We were performing away, but then eight or ten people just started casually walking through our performance area, ignoring us totally and oblivious to the fact that we were in the middle of a show. These people were just people on holiday, sauntering through the Edinburgh Festival, but they walked right across the centre of our show. If you don't have enough excitement going on, it's just an ordinary street and people will walk right through it. This was a horrible thing to have happen because it completely denied that we were doing anything interesting at all (we probably weren't). The equivalent would be an actor onstage in a theatre with a live audience and then having a party of people being shown through the theatre and just walking across the stage, ignoring the actors.

But in the end, Covent Garden made me. Covent Garden accidentally broke me down and built me back up. I have heard that drama schools will do this to you, and that the armed forces will, too. I accidentally creatively did that to myself. I accidentally broke myself and eventually rebuilt myself by continuing to keep at it until, slowly, I learned how to perform on the street and I developed a brand-new confidence. I didn't know it would get better, but I just kept going anyway. It wasn't really determination – I simply had no better plan. So I just carried on trying to be a basic street performer until one day I started to improve. One thing I didn't do was give up and go back to accounting – so that part of it was just grim determination.

I gradually got a sense of becoming a better performer, but I was still very much in a hurry. I still felt I had to get things done quickly. After I discovered Monty Python in my teenage years, I decided that I wanted to be part of a comedy TV show by the time I was twenty-five. Most of Monty Python was doing that by the time they were roughly that age. I was already twenty-three in 1985, having dropped out of university at nineteen, but things were not stacking up right. By the spring of 1986, we knew we had to change our show, because our show was sort of rubbish. People thought it was rubbish and we thought it was rubbish. At its best, with our knockabout comedy show, the reaction would be 'It's rubbish, but they are fun and crazy.' At its worst, people would say, 'It's rubbish and they're rubbish.'

The Vicious Boys used to do their sketches to huge audiences. Annoyingly huge audiences (we wished we had had them). And at the end of each sketch, they'd say a very short 'thank-you,' which was a bit like the Beatles bowing after the end of each number in the early 1960s. The thank-you would signal that it was time for the audience to go crazy because this double act had done a lot of funny things and now it was over. Basically – please applaud now.

I realized that we needed to do something like that.

Since we couldn't copy their thank-you, we decided to say – 'Go wild!' A rather lame thing to say, but that's the only thing we could think of (our comedy brains lacked confidence and inventiveness at that point). And that was the point: when we started street performing, it was so difficult we were clutching at straws.

On the street, there were a number of performance ideas that were commonly used – possibly invented by a few different people, though most performers would use them. As a sketch comedian, I had prided myself on being able to come up with interesting lines, but I couldn't do it on the street. I just couldn't come up with funny lines that worked. As time went on, I got a little better at it but not much.

Now, 'arranging' your street audience was a craft you had to master and it could be very, very difficult. The audience of forty to fifty people on a good day (five to ten people on a bad day) would form a straggly edge around us. But this was very important. Getting this right is almost a science. When there is a tidy curving front line to your audience, people will walk up from behind and say, 'What's going on there?' And then you will start to get a bigger and bigger audience. A straggly edge of people in front of you was not good. Often we would actually 'arrange,' or 'wrangle' (an American word, but I think a good one here) people into line:

'You – walk forward, please. You, bloke with the hair – just stand there. Family on the right – you go there.' But people often wouldn't move. And if you came toward them to encourage them to come forward they would actually move away. So there was a fine line between 'wrangling' people and freaking them out.[*]

There was one very small piece of pure street performing I invented that I still think is wonderfully fun. It sort of indicated where my stand-up was to go in the future.

---

[*] Now, if you're a brilliant performer this doesn't matter: the audience will stand and they will watch you because you're brilliant. But most of us were not so brilliant, especially not initially. Then one day, Rob and I had an idea: We decided to buy about one hundred meters of yachting rope at the boat shop at the top of Neal Street in Covent Garden. Then we'd go out at the beginning of our shows and wrap the cord around people who were initially watching us on the West Piazza of Covent Garden – as if they had now become posts. Unfortunately, they really hated this and would just remove the rope and run off. So that idea lasted only a few weeks.

Rob and I had bought a lot of animal tea cozies. If you don't know what a tea cozy is, a tea cozy is sort of a duvet for a teapot that keeps the teapot warm (if you don't know what a duvet is, it's like a tea cozy for humans). The tea cozies we had bought were a hippo, two penguins (one big, one small), a duck, and a pig. I would stand in front of my audience in my early solo years, 1987–1989, and I would say to them, 'This hippopotamus has got fantastic powers. It's actually a boomerang hippo. No matter where I throw this hippo, it will always come back to me.' Then I'd repeat the lines: 'No matter where I throw this hippo, it will always come back.'

I would say that line a few times and imply to the audience that it was a boomerang hippo. Then I would throw the hippo tea cozy over the heads of the audience so it landed behind them. It would just fly over and land about two or three meters behind the audience of my show. Everyone would just stare at me and I would repeat, 'As I've said, this is a magical hippo. Wherever I throw it, it always comes back.' I'd just keep saying that until somebody went behind us, picked up the hippo, and threw it back.

I would be ecstatic when they did. 'You see? It always comes back!'

That silly trick never failed. Some member of the public would figure it out eventually. So yes, it came back, and I loved the fact that it always would.

By 1986, Rob and I were getting a bit more confident as street performers, and the new show that we'd developed was actually exciting. For once, the audiences (and even the other performers) weren't embarrassed to be seen watching us or talking to us when we were hanging out in Covent Garden. The new street show was a sword-fighting show and had been inspired by the fact that Rob and I had performed *The Three Musketeers* at Sheffield University in 1983 (I was directing, he was playing Porthos). We had been inspired to learn sword fighting from watching Richard Lester's 1973 version of *The Three Musketeers*. William Hobbs had done all the fight direction and we had bought his book. We absolutely loved the film and the fantastic fight arranging and inventive swordplay that he had directed. I was later very pleased to meet him once at Pineapple Studios, in London, when he was working with Joseph Fiennes.

Back at Covent Garden, we bought fencing épées and with them performed a sword-fighting show on the street. The public liked it and other performers seemed to respect it – at least a little more than what we had done before. It was a bit edgy and it was definitely different. And it was a rather new idea, which seemed (for me) almost impossible to come up with in street performing. We kept trying to create a narrative within the show, but in the end, the show was mainly about how to dispatch someone with a sword when you're happy, unhappy, sad, drunk, or insane. Death of all kinds by sword fighting. The final 'scene' we did in slow-motion. This made things safer, but also quite graphic, and as I've said, loud or extreme seems to work very well on the streets. (If you've seen the film *300*, we would have been very influenced by that, except we did it first.) We'd start the slow-motion section by hacking at each other, slowly, with two swords. This built up to an ending where

Rob would charge toward me, brandishing his sword in a slow-motion final attack. But as he got close, I would actually throw my sword through the air toward him, aiming (for safety) to get it under his arm so that it looked like it had gone through him. This is quite a tricky thing to do, but I actually got rather skilled at throwing the sword through the air in a safe way. I basically angled the sword diagonally downward so that it flew through the air, not horizontally, but almost vertically. As I said, we were trying to be safe. Rob was very game for it and we got quite expert at it, so it all worked out.

Now other performers started talking to us. There was a lot of talent at The Garden (as we called it). And I had a lot of fun watching and later performing improvised shows with inspired performers like John Fealey, Alex Dandridge, Vince Henderson, Stewart Harvey-Wilson, and many others, from all around the world.

The *Time Out* Street Entertainer Award for 1986 was coming up. Suddenly, with our new act, we thought, *Oh my god, we've got this exciting show, maybe we can win it.*

To win it, though, you had to first win your section — comedy or juggling or magic or music or whatever – but then, having won your section, you also had to win the grand finale.

I felt this was it. *We have a good show, we're actually being funny, it is new and inventive. We're gonna win the whole thing and go to New York and we'll be in a television show and things will take off.*

What actually happened was we didn't even win our section.

Now the winners of each section were invited back to a

winners' marquee behind Saint Paul's Church at Covent Garden. They'd set up a big stage in front of the main West Piazza for the grand finale. Under the portico of St Paul's Church is where the street performers hung out (then and now), and it's also the exact place where Eliza Doolittle sold flowers to Henry Higgins in *My Fair Lady*.* At the back of the church was a very quiet and peaceful little garden where they'd set up the winners' marquee. Normally we could all go into that garden, but we couldn't now because it was only for the winners of the sections.

We were not one of these. Again, we were just the losers.

That's when I came up with a pithy line that I liked: 'Maybe it's just not our millennium.'

This was long before all the millennium craziness of 2000, but I quite liked the sardonic nature of building on 'Maybe it's just not our year, maybe it's just not our decade.' I'd really thought this was when it was going to happen, when we'd finally be able to get something going.

But once again, it apparently was not our time. They had roped off the entrance to the Saint Paul's Church garden, one of those ropes you can click open and closed like in front of a nightclub, and I remember looking at it and thinking, *Is this ever going to get better?*

That said, even though we were still losing the big competitions, I was still developing a new confidence as a performer.

*

---

* Watch that film again. Even though it's filmed on a set, it's a pretty good representation of the columns in front of the church where we sat, day after day, hanging out watching shows. (This is St Paul's, the actor's church – not St Paul's the cathedral.)

By the spring of 1988, Rob mentioned to me that he was going on holiday with his wife, Barbara. Since we were a double act, when either of us went on a break or took a holiday, it meant the other couldn't work. Rob was good at taking holidays – and I mean that seriously. He would take a break and go off and he and Barbara would enjoy themselves. I was not (and still am not) so good at doing that. Anyway, his being away meant I couldn't work, so I thought, *Oh, what the hell. I'm going to go and do a solo show.*

Now I had spent all my life up to that point being quite sure that I was not a solo performer. The idea had never come seriously into my head. I loved Monty Python, and I'd always thought I wanted to do something like that: comedy within a group. And then suddenly, out of nowhere, I started doing a solo show. The psychological difference between the two is huge.

I'd noticed that escapology shows at Covent Garden (people escaping from ropes and chains and padlocks) were quite entertaining and they didn't seem that hard to do. Serious escapology is a highly skilled art and it is very hard to do. But if you get two volunteers from a street audience and ask them to tie you up with ropes and chains, they generally tend not to tie you up that tightly because they're not usually experts on the art and science of ropes and chains. If they were in the Mafia or police, perhaps they would be better at it. But most people don't know how to do it, so if you're escaping there's almost always an amount of slack that you can use to shimmy out of your restraints.

Street performer Paul Keane is known as Captain Keano. Paul is an amazing performer and character: generous and funny and dark and twisted and brilliantly acrobatic and confusing and many other things. Paul had two or three different shows that he could perform, one of which was an escapology show. All of a sudden, I had decided to do a solo street show, and I knew Paul had ropes and chains that he wasn't using (since he hadn't done his escapology show recently). So that Friday, in about March or April of 1987, I said to him, 'Paul, can I borrow your ropes and chains?' And he very easily said, 'Yeah. No problem.'

That Saturday I went out for my first-ever solo show. I set out some animal tea cozies and then I got out two volunteers and asked them to tie me up with the ropes and chains. Once they had tied me up, I asked another volunteer to count down from two minutes. I told the man on the stopwatch to shout out 'Ten elephants' after ten seconds and 'Twenty elephants' after twenty seconds – all the way up to two minutes. It wasn't terribly inventive, but I got a small audience, people stuck around and watched. I tried to be funny and interesting and silly and in the last thirty seconds we switched from counting up to a countdown. I managed to get out in time. I think I earned about ten pounds.

And that was it. I had got the bug for performing solo. Two weeks later, Rob and I amicably split up. Another performer friend of ours from Sheffield University, Richard Parry, had just arrived at Covent Garden wanting to perform, but he didn't know what to do. As he'd been in our *Three Musketeers* production (he'd played Aramis), he knew how to sword fight. I suggested, 'Why don't you sword fight with Rob and I'll go solo.' Which seemed a way for me to

RIGHT: With Sarah Townsend in the 1990s in Sussex, visiting my Dad.

BELOW: Christmas in Bexhill, sitting next to Sam, the coolest (and most relaxed) dog ever.

Around the time of my show *Unrepeatable*, in 1994.
By now I was beginning to look vaguely together.

I played Westbeth Theatre for four months in early 1998. David Bowie and Iman turned up.

Me as a Bad Fairy for the Monty Python BBC anniversary in 1999. Probably the most girly I've ever got.

Me with my heroes – the Pythons, in 1999. Terry Jones, John Cleese, Michael Palin, and Terry Gilliam (Eric Idle should have also been there, so I was a spare Gumby).

In a limo in New York, the *Circle* tour 2000.

During a fitting for the jacket/coat I wore for the *Sexie* tour, 2003.

The University of East Anglia gave me an honorary doctorate in Letters, July 2003. Thank you.

Backstage during the *Stripped* tour.

Radio City Music Hall is the London Palladium of New York.
Great to play it and great to sell it out.

I love playing the piano. I always jump on a piano and play, if I see one.

The *Stripped* tour, Christmas 2009, touring arenas in Sweden. A long way since holidaying in Sweden back in 1965.

I got rid of my fear of flying by becoming a pilot.

The *Stripped* tour set being constructed.

The skilled crew who constructed the *Sexie* tour in many arenas.

Billy Crystal, Robin Williams, and Garry Shandling – the comedy greats. Plus some other bloke on the right.

A great honour to meet Nelson Mandela in 2010. His charm and vitality were still very evident at age 92.

Great to be running marathons near Cape Town and throughout South Africa, meeting the local people on the way.

ABOVE: Me in front of a statue of Nelson Mandela outside the prison from which he was finally released.

LEFT: Getting my breath back, after finishing 27 marathons in 27 days, at the foot of the huge statue of Nelson Mandela in Pretoria in 2016.

I am very lucky to be performing comedy and making filmed drama all around the world. My thanks to all of you who come and enjoy it.

go solo without causing an upset. So suddenly, only two weeks later, I was a solo performer, even though, all my life, I'd never planned to be. But after an amazingly short time I found it really suited me.

I continued with my nascent escapology routine. I slowly started to develop confidence as a solo performer and loved the freedom it was giving me to perform as much or as little as I wanted. My show wasn't that interesting or inventive – I was just getting tied up in ropes and chains and then trying to make a whole jokey-fun atmosphere as I headed toward the high point of my escaping just in time.

Paul Keane also said something else to me, a piece of wisdom I have never forgotten. After a few months of solo performing, I had just done a street show where I'd been tied up with ropes and chains, but this time very expertly. I really couldn't move. There was no slack in the ropes and chains; the guy had taken his time over it. After about ten minutes of struggling, I had to turn to the audience and say, 'Could somebody get the keys to the padlocks out of my bag because I can't get out of this.' It was embarrassing but not too bad, as my general performance ability was now quite strong and I hoped it was just a one-off. Paul had seen this and he said to me, 'You've got to believe you can get out, otherwise you won't be able to get out.'

It was quite a logical thought, but I hadn't thought about it before. Then some months later I did another show where I was tied up very tightly, and I decided to take his advice and believe that I would get out. It took me about fourteen minutes to get out (it should normally take thirty seconds to a minute), but I did eventually. I realized that belief is a key ingredient in trying to do things that are difficult. I had to believe that I could be a good street performer before I could become one. And then I had to believe that I could be a good stand-up, and a good actor, and that I could run good marathons. So his words that day have really stuck with me.

In the end, on the street, I finished up escaping from manacles (iron handcuffs) whilst balancing on a five-foot unicycle. This I called *my big bullshit show* because it took a certain amount of training, but you didn't have to be a genius to do it. I did feel that when I was balancing on that five-foot unicycle in manacles and saying to the audience that I was going to get out, even on a tough day when the weather was bad and the wind was blowing, a certain-size audience would always stick around to see if I succeeded, or if I died.

Not died comedically but actually died.

That show even got me my first gig in America, in 1988. A photograph, taken by Alex Dandridge, of me wrapped up in chains with a cigar in my mouth and a pair of red sunglasses on my head was what did it. I looked like a crazy tank commander. This photograph got me a gig at the Memphis in May International Festival in Memphis, Tennessee.* So my first-ever gig in America was, slightly bizarrely, at eleven thirty p.m., in a car park outside a restaurant (Boscos Squared) in Overton Square.

---

* The Memphis in May International Festival had decided they wanted street performers to perform at Overton Square, Memphis. They celebrated a different country every year, and in 1988 Great Britain was that country. Someone told the people from the Memphis festival to check with the administration at Covent Garden for good street performers, and my new photo had just been added to the mix. And because the photo was so interesting, I got the gig.

By the time I'd got to Memphis I'd never actually performed this new manacles-and-unicycle show, which I was initially doing in rather a dangerous way: I had my hands manacled behind my back, then I would be helped up on to my unicycle, and then I would balance on top of the unicycle while trying to get out of the manacles.

My first performance in America was to U.S. Marines! They were part of a military band that was just relaxing and drinking in the car park outside the restaurant. Once on the unicycle, I stayed up for forty or fifty seconds but then I fell off. I had been doing a countdown to see if I could get out in under a minute, but after only about forty-five seconds I fell off and it looked like the show was over. If I had asked for some money then, the marines would have logically said, 'Well, you didn't do it, so no money.' So instead I quickly said, 'Stop the clock!' and then I made my case for why they should give me the last fifteen seconds. 'Look, okay, I've fallen off, but if I get back on, we can just continue on from there for the last few seconds.'

There was a sort of logic to that and they'd all had a bit to drink, so they seemed to agree. Someone helped me back up on the unicycle, they restarted the clock, and this time I got out of the manacles in under fifteen seconds. When I collected the money afterward I counted about twenty-five dollars. Which was fantastic, because we weren't getting paid to perform at the festival – just airfare and expenses – so I had a great breakfast the next morning at the Holiday Inn.

On my way back home I adjusted my return ticket to Britain and flew via New York and spent a few days at the

Hotel Chelsea. I was a bit intimidated by Manhattan; it had such a history, but I badly wanted to visit it. I'd heard that Manhattan never sleeps, that it's open twenty-four hours a day – 24/7 – so I decided, 'I'm going to choose a shop, any shop, and come back at three in the morning.' So I chose a shop, came back at three a.m., but it was closed! So the lyrics should be: 'I want to wake up in a city of which a certain per cent never sleeps.'

I performed at Washington Square Park when I was there: I wheeled my unicycle out of the Hotel Chelsea down Fifth Avenue to the fountain in the park, where people were performing, and even doing stand-up comedy through beatboxes and small amplifiers. After waiting around for a bit, I did one show in the middle of the fountain (which was never working back then – I don't know if it is now). It was good just to say that I'd performed in New York. A great feeling!

In the end, when it comes to the Edinburgh Fringe, I performed there twelve times over thirteen years. It took a long time for it to get any easier, but in 1990 I was voted Best Newcomer for the Perrier Comedy Award, and in 1991, I got nominated for it. In 1992 I was not allowed to compete for the Perrier Award (apparently I was doing too well or something like that – I never quite understood why). And in 1993 I played my final Edinburgh Fringe at the George Square Theatre, a five-hundred-seat theatre on the University of Edinburgh campus. A long way from the twelve noon show in an eighty-seater in Brodie's Close back in 1981. Those were my wilderness years, but they had trained me well.

*

So going solo in 1987 was a key turning point for me. The whole of the 1980s was a time for me when nothing worked, but in the end, I learned stamina. And maybe stamina is what you need above all in this life. With hindsight, I would probably choose to have those wilderness years all over again.

PART THREE
Finally the Beginning

Stand-up and Be Counted

Sometime in late 1987, a few people said to me, 'You should do stand-up.' I suppose because I was very chatty and talkative in my street show. I remember another performer, Steve Rawlings, always encouraged me to do it. Steve was someone who had single-mindedly put his own juggling and balancing act together, and it was quite different from what other people were doing. He was very good at getting ahead and making things happen for himself.

Now, if you were a street performer on the cabaret circuit (which became the comedy circuit in the 1990s), you were considered a specialty act. A 'spec act.'*

I remember the respect that was given to the stand-ups who were performing on the cabaret circuit, especially the well-known ones. This is when Rob and I were occasionally performing on the circuit, in the late 1980s. Compared to the lack of respect we got for doing a 'failed tricks' specialty act, the respect that stand-ups received was totally different. As a specialty act, you were considered the 'palate cleanser.' You were the ginger in the sushi of this evening of tastes. They almost never closed a show with a specialty act. You'd have to be pretty bloody amazing. You'd have to kill yourself in the show every

---

*Pronounced *spesh* (short for 'specialty').

night, explode your stomach with a grenade or something, to be the closing specialty act.

And in late 1987, after I'd become a solo street performer, I started thinking, *Yes, I've got to do stand-up.* Even though doing stand-up had never appealed to me, mainly because I just didn't think I could do it.

But somehow now I could. I had become a solo performer, I was developing my own voice (by 'voice' I mean the style of one's delivery and the content of one's material), and I was beginning to understand that voice and confidence go together.

I had started to develop my own voice when I was working with Rob in our double act. At the beginning of each show, we had to entice people in to watch – I was down stage right (at the front and on the right) of the space we were performing on (most often the West Piazza of Covent Garden), and Rob was always down stage left. So I would talk to the people in front of me, front and right, and he would talk to the people in front of him, front and left, to encourage them to come forward and commit to watching our show. To pull them in, I'd do my own little show. Not that it was a show; it was more my own little bit of chitchat. I'd try to get the people on the piazza in front of me relaxed and engaged, and in the process, I remember realizing:

I'm developing my own 'voice.'

If you act or perform characters, then you never have to develop your own voice. Having played characters myself, I feel that you often have a certain extra confidence that comes from committing to the character and enjoying living (and, to an extent, hiding) inside them. But if you have played characters and then you start talking or per-forming to an audience in your own voice, your 'voice' can often lack a certain energy or dynamism.

I know that used to be true for me, and I know very good performers who have less energy and presence in their own voice and are actually less confident of how they sound that way. They may not be aware of it, but because I have de-veloped both things, I can instantly see it and I can feel it. And an audience instinctively feels it, too.

Before I started developing it, I had felt I needed to put that on a shopping list: *Develop your own voice.*

You have to have your own voice as a solo, non-character stand-up.

After I became a solo street performer, I had developed the ability to build up an edge (an audience) from just two people. Because I had a lot of confidence by then, I would crouch down in front of them and actually explain to them my audience-gathering technique. I would just say to them, 'So, I'm now going to talk really quietly to you and then other people are going to come up behind you because they'll wonder what we're doing, and then we'll build an audience. So from now, if you could possibly just laugh hysterically at anything I say, that would be great. If you could give me a round of applause when I ask for it, too, that would be even better.' I was confident and chatty with them, so when I did that, they tended to play along. In my final year at The Garden, I was going out and starting shows by just talking to an imaginary crowd. I'd go out and stand there and just start talking to no one in particular: 'Hello! Welcome to my show!' – as if there was a massive invisible audience there. I suppose I looked curious and confident and people would gradually stop and pay attention. When they did stop, I'd say, 'It's good to have some visible people here as well as the invisible people watching today.' Then I'd pull those visible people forward and start building a small crowd up from there. And that's how I ended up developing my audience. From nothing.

Later, when I did street shows at the Edinburgh Fringe, I remember standing in front of the steps of the area called the Mound in Edinburgh, by the big art galleries. The show that I did there, which lasted for over an hour, was just me endlessly chitchatting and mucking about with people. By that time my confidence was flying high. I felt I could do that, even though I didn't have the stand-up ability yet.

Doing stand-up would mean taking the voice I had developed on the street (which was just me turned on rather brightly) indoors and talking about ideas and developing scenes, instead of using my voice to explain a physical comedy show. There was almost no change here except that I didn't have to narrate the structure of the show itself, the way I did on the street: 'I need two volunteers. I'd like you to manacle my hands. Please help me get up on the unicycle. Now, can one of you do the timing as I try to get out of it?' None of that had to be done anymore.

Indoors, you just stand there and say, 'Chickens. What's going on with chickens?' Indoors, it's all about ideas and you can talk about chickens for ten minutes (if you really want to).

*

I admired great comic voices when I heard them: Billy Connolly was a comedian I loved for his great storytelling and his ease talking to huge audiences. Richard Pryor was another comedian I admired for his incredible character work and voices: he could play different people by just turning his body slightly and changing the character he was playing. And I loved Steve Martin's stand-up for his surreal silliness, which was bonkers and I identified with it. There was also Robin Williams, Woody Allen, Lenny Bruce, Garry Shandling, and many, many others. I remember listening to every stand-up comedy tape and album I could get my hands on, in awe of them all, soaking in every bit. But above all, Monty Python was my biggest influence. They are, from beginning to end, my comedy gods.

Eventually, in late 1987, I thought, *I think I can do this. I think I can learn how to do stand-up comedy. I've got my voice now, so I can talk about things. I just need to learn how to develop stand-up riffs and then act them out like the great stand-ups do.*

The only problem was: I couldn't work out how to write a piece of stand-up. I just could not do it.

I thought, *Well, I have to learn stand-up because it's the best way to move forwards. I don't want to be the greatest street performer in the world. I've got to go and do stand-up because indoors is a better place for me than on the street. Indoors you can develop the comedy of words and ideas. Outdoors you need to master physical situation comedy and one-liners.*

I knew that when I got into the zone (a comedy place you go to when you're flying high and making everyone laugh) I could ad-lib a kind of stand-up comedy, but I could not write it. I would sit down and try to write words and comedy riffs, but I felt my brain was going faster than my fingers and I couldn't write out anything funny.

So I started attending a stand-up workshop at Jacksons Lane Community Centre in Highgate, North London, in about November of 1987. This is a wonderful community arts centre that has various classes and a performance space. In the stand-up workshop we all had to write a bit of stand-up each week and perform it. Which was scary. I didn't really want to do that, even though I knew that was the whole reason I was there. I'd had a few good attempts and got one or two laughs, but nothing much. Then there came a point, after not really progressing much, when I remembered an old comedy sketch that I'd written that maybe I could adapt for stand-up. I'd originally written it for a television sketch show, in early 1987, for new writers and performers called *Comedy Wavelength*, which was the breakout show for the very funny and surreal Paul Merton. Paul was supposed to be the warm-up act (the person who keeps the audience happy but doesn't appear in the TV show), but his stand-up was so funny and our programme was so not funny that he became the host of the show and took off after that. The producer of this programme had seen Rob and me doing our knockabout double act and he'd said to us, 'You're obviously writers. Come and write for this new sketch show.' I remember thinking, *You feel we're good comedy sketch writers from watching our knockabout physical comedy? That doesn't make any sense to me.* But I wasn't going to question it, because it was finally an actual TV show on Channel 4, and in early 1987 I still really wanted to be in a comedy show on television. As it turned out, I didn't get to do any acting in the show because the producer didn't see me as a performer, only as a writer. This blew my mind into a bag because one thing that I was sure of was that I was a performer and *maybe* I was a writer as well. To have a TV producer tell me the complete opposite made me actually feel physically ill. It meant my whole analysis of who I was or what I could do seemed completely back to front.*

But anyway, all that happened in the end was that two sketches I wrote made it into the TV pilot. One of the sketches I later thought I could turn into stand-up. It was an interview with an addict – but he was addicted to breakfast cereal. It went something like this:

'Yeah, I used to do a lot of Frosties and things. Once, I ate two packets of Frosties in one day and I was coughing up blood. I used to put porridge on a piece of tinfoil and inhale the fumes. I called that "chasing the Scotsman."'

It was an interview with an addict, but I just took out the interviewer part of the sketch and made all the lines mine, turning it into a breakfast cereal addict's confession straight to the audience.

I performed it to the stand-up workshop and it worked! People seemed to laugh for real.

Which made me think: *Well, I can't write stand-up, but I can write two-hander sketches. I wrote loads of sketches between 1981 and 1983. So I will just write lots of two-hander sketches, where someone is interviewing another person, and then I'll cut out the interviewer. Then I'll say all those lines from a personal perspective, and that will be my stand-up.*

---

*Having used analysis to explain my sexuality, I was now using it to explain my creative abilities.

Weirdly, as soon as I had used this technique once, I never needed to use it again. Suddenly the single-hander jokes and funny lines just started appearing on the page or out of my mouth without me having to create, and then delete, the 'interviewer.'

Before this I had had another *belief* problem in my head. I didn't believe I could write stand-up. Therefore I couldn't write stand-up. Paul Keane was right. If you didn't believe you could do something, you wouldn't be able to do it. I was stuck inside of a negative belief system and not a positive belief system.

Once I'd figured out that trick to help me write stand-up, my next problem was getting any gigs – specifically, finding a lot of 'open spots' (five minutes unpaid onstage) at comedy venues. You had to discover the home number of the person who was running the individual venue and beg them, 'Please, can I have an open spot?' In 1988, they would say, 'Okay, I'll give you one that's two or three months ahead.' Nowadays, they probably book a year or so ahead, which must feel like an eternity for those comedians. I bought a diary and started shoving those small gigs in. And that's how I started attacking the stand-up comedy circuit. This was my third medium of comedy. That's not usual. Normally you do one, maybe two. That was training you couldn't buy.

The first stand-up gig I ever did was in fact at Jacksons Lane Community Centre in March of 1988. I was trying to start a relationship with a woman who had just come out of another relationship, and we had just had one of those 'Should we go out?' conversations. I had tried to make the relationship go somewhere and it had not really gone any-where, so that afternoon, when I was supposed to be rehearsing for the gig, I instead had a rather emotional conversation with a person who was just not that into a relationship. It was in this frame of mind that I went into my first show.

Having that afternoon's discussion still in the forefront of my mind, I thought, *Okay, I don't know what I'm doing here. So what I'll do is I'll drink an entire pint of lager and then I'll just wing it.* I don't normally do that (drink an entire pint of beer), but I drank it and then went onstage, hoping it would make me looser and maybe connect with the funny in me. This was obviously Dutch courage.* So I stood up there for five minutes and said whatever I said. I got the words out, and while I didn't do much more than that, at least I'd done my first proper stand-up gig.

I'd done it. I'd taken the first step in stand-up and sur-vived. I had the first brick in the first layer of confidence to build on.

The second show I ever did was at a place called Bunjies, a vegetarian restaurant where Bob Dylan was reputed to have played, very near the Ivy restaurant in London. I said a new joke that day which I quite liked even though it could never be extended further:

'I went fly-fishing yesterday – I caught two flies.'

This was the sort of joke that I liked, but it was only a one-liner that took ten seconds to say, so I knew I would

---

* From Wikipedia: 'Dutch courage refers to courage gained from intoxication with alcohol. The popular story dates the etymology of the term to English soldiers fighting in the Thirty Years' War.'

need a lot more. Later I worked out how to develop seams of comedy (like seams of gold).

After that, I just did as many gigs as I could. I was on a mission by then. As this was my third medium of comedy, I was going to fight like crazy to make this one work.

Patrick Marber, who became a playwright and film writer, was a stand-up comedian before that. We were both at the Jacksons Lane stand-up workshop at the same time. We get along very well now, but back then, I think he found me rather annoying because I kept going on and on about what I knew – or what I felt I knew – about performing. Having done four years of street performing, I'd felt I had a lot of performance knowledge I could impart – I even had ex-perience dealing with hecklers. What I did not have was any experience performing actual stand-up material (verbal jokes and comedic ideas). At one point in the workshop, everyone was being asked to do impressions of the other people in the group and he was asked to do me. His im-pression of me was something like, '*Blah blah blah . . . street. Blah blah blah . . . performing. Blah blah blah. . . . This is how you do this.*' It was a kind of laconic 'god, this guy is a pain in the ass' type of impression, but it probably was pretty accurate, as I really was on a mission and I felt I'd learned a lot about performance.

I just pushed and pushed and pushed. Like the time I went to do an open spot at a club, but when I got there I was told that the club had closed down. I thought, *Screw that!* So I quickly bought a copy of *Time Out* magazine, which listed all the gigs in London, and I found that there was another club just nearby. As I said, normally you have to book three months ahead, but I just went straight round there on the off chance they would let me do a spot. And they said, 'Actually, the open spot hasn't shown up, so you can be their replacement.'

It was that kind of doggedness – going for it, going for it, going for it – that made things happen. But in the end, I just had to hammer my way up this final ladder, up through bigger and bigger clubs, until I finally took off.

The Comedy Store, the most prestigious club in London (and not linked to the one in LA), had, back then, an eight p.m. show and a midnight show, Friday and Saturday. The open spots were always during the Friday shows, which started at midnight. If you were funny enough and could handle that audience – the Friday midnight shows were very shouty and drunk – the Comedy Store would (maybe) book you for some future gigs. But the new acts went on after the headlining acts, which meant that sometimes you wouldn't get onstage until two or three in the morning.

I went on two or three times after one particular comedian, who would tear the place apart, and I just kept dying. Now, when you start to fail onstage, you can become overwhelmed with fear, and when the fear happens, you start speeding up your normal speaking pace. When you do this, you begin to blow your timing and you also start leaving bits out – like punch lines! The punch line is a very bad thing to miss because that's the whole bloody point of your job. About the third time I went on at three in the morning at the Comedy Store, after the main comedians had just blown everyone away (been really funny), I went on and started flailing again. First joke, no reaction.

Second joke, no reaction. Third joke, no reaction. But this time I forced myself not to speed up. But it still didn't help much. I still bombed. But I felt it was a death with honour.

After that I thought, *Okay, I've done death with honour at the Comedy Store, but that's it. I am not coming back to the Comedy Store until I am really nailing (succeeding at) all the other London clubs.*

So I stayed away from the Comedy Story for about a year and a half, and then I came back and said, 'I think I am ready. Can I do an open spot?' They said, 'Well, we've got a competition happening for up-and-coming comedians. Why don't you come along and do that instead?'

I was pretty confident in my stand-up by then, because once you have learned to perform in three different mediums of comedy, and you're doing well in all the other stand-up clubs in London, your confidence is going to be fairly bloody high. The night of the gig, I had just come back from Spain. Everyone at the Comedy Store was discussing what order we should all go on. No one wanted to go on first because the audience wouldn't be warmed up. So I volunteered to go on first, because I felt I could handle it. Then I decided I would just improvise my five-minute slot by talking about going through customs coming back from a short holiday in Spain. So, in the end, the gig went okay but not brilliantly. But I didn't mind because they did say they would book me in for the future.

I was just continuing my theory about the benefit of making things hard for yourself. The idea is, if you make it hard for yourself, then that will be good training for when things do actually get hard. So ad-libbing my set, going on first – adding those extra layers of difficulty – seemed to pay off. Not in the short term, but in the long term.

Before they got famous in Britain, the Beatles played residency gigs (playing many nights over a period of a few months and performing long sets) in Hamburg, Germany. Hamburg, a port city, had an exotic sex-show scene, and there was a demand for musicians to come in and play between the acts of women in various stages of undress. So the Beatles started doing up to eight-hour shows and that's probably where they really honed their sound, after which they became unstoppable.*

For me, the London comedy circuit was my Hamburg.

London had accidentally developed a massive comedy scene. Today there are still something like sixty to eighty different comedy clubs in London. Whilst both New York and LA have, I believe, about ten or fifteen clubs. This isn't because we're better at comedy – it's just how it turned out. A lot of London comedy clubs are run by individuals and enthusiasts who love comedy, while the clubs in America are more likely to be franchises: places with bars that are open all week. A lot of our clubs are just open one night a week. Sometimes it's a function room in a pub that has a comedy night, because from Chaucer to Dickens we have

---

* I once asked Paul McCartney, 'How did you learn to play the piano? Did your dad teach you? Because he played, didn't he?' And he said, 'No, I was in Hamburg and my guitar broke. There was a piano there on the stage, so I just got on it and started hammering away.' I don't think most people know this.

I made a point of playing Hamburg (in German) when I was playing a two-month residency in Berlin in February 2014. Hamburg was a great gig. I just loved the fact that Hamburg, with all its troubled World War II history, helped the Beatles become the Beatles. I think that's rather wonderful.

a long history of people traveling around to inns with function rooms in the back. Instead of turning those function rooms into storerooms or apartments or other things to earn money, the pub owners (often big breweries), for whatever reasons, have kept them as function rooms, which can be used as small venues for weekly comedy nights.

The best comedians in my day were doing four shows on Fridays and four shows on Saturdays – because there were (and still are) so many clubs that we could get a lot of practice. We were trying to get good, and to get reviewed by Malcolm Hay, the then critic of *Time Out London*. We wanted him to give us a good, positive adjective. And he didn't use that many positive adjectives. If you were an 'effective' comedian, it meant you had been around for a while and you got the job done. If you got 'funny,' that was good. 'Very funny' was amazing.

I remember one time, I was playing the Comedy Store. By this time I was good enough to get booked on a regular basis there. Then another comedian came into the Store and said to the rest of us comedians backstage, 'I can't do a gig in the Chuckle Club. Does anyone want to do it?' The Chuckle Club was run by a man who went by the name of Eugene Cheese. I said, 'I'd do it for you, mate, but I can't because Eugene Cheese doesn't like my stuff.'* When he told me Mr Cheese's son was running the club while his dad was on holiday so it wouldn't matter, I agreed.

After playing my eight p.m. gig at the Comedy Store, I

---

* In the early part of my stand-up career I'd played a five-minute slot and a ten-minute slot at a couple of clubs run by Mr Cheese. It was in my early days when I was struggling, and he didn't think I was strong enough, so after that I didn't get any bookings.

went off to do this extra gig at this other club. Now, when playing the clubs, I was thinking in my strategic way to get my comedy career moving forwards. I had a map of London and I had different-colour pins to indicate different goals achieved: whether I had played at a club, done good at a club, or 'killed' at a club. I knew that if I did a good gig at the Chuckle Club, word would get back to Mr Cheese and then maybe I would start getting booked there regularly. So I decided to try and 'rip the roof off' the place.

That was something I was able to do by that point. I knew how to storm a show. I couldn't guarantee it, but I would try and get in the zone.

Quite simply, I would do my set and toward the end I would gradually get faster in pace, till by the end of the show I was just delivering the jokes so thick and fast that the audience could hardly breathe. You go, *Bam, bam, bam, bam, bam, bam,* and then you say *Thank you – good night,* and just walk off the stage. Many experienced stand-ups work out how to do that. So that night I went for it, managed to rip the roof off the club, and Mr Cheese's son said, 'Will you come back?' And I said, 'Yeah, but your dad doesn't like my stuff, so it's not going to work.' He said he'd talk to him, and so I did come back, and I ripped the roof off a second time. After that, he booked me regularly and we got on fine.

When things started working for me on the circuit, I knew other comedians were thinking, *Hey, what's going on here? Why is your career moving at such a speed?* But that speed was just an illusion. It was 1990 now – nine years since my first show in Edinburgh, in 1981. I'd desperately wanted a big career break at nineteen or twenty or twenty-one or twenty-two – people get discovered at those early ages, even younger – but I was not one of them. I was still trying to find my voice, get my act together – literally and figuratively. The ten or eleven years of nothing happening had wound the spring very tight, so I was moving very fast.

I played the comedy circuit up to the end of 1991. But then I decided I had to leave. I had to start playing theatres. In 1992 the *Observer* planned to do an in-depth piece about me. I thought: *I'm just going to announce that I'm transvestite. Once it's announced, I can't back out of it and I'll just have to see whether my career gets destroyed or not.*

At the time of the interview, my comedy was in a good place, which is why they were doing the article about me: they were interested in my career. I had hacked and climbed my way to a point where a big newspaper was finally going to write about me, and I knew that once I said, 'I am transvestite,' it would be out there, and once it was out there, I couldn't put it back in the box.

I did not want it to be in the box any longer. I did not like the feeling of living a lie.

As my career had slowly taken off, I knew the subject of my being transvestite would have to be dealt with in some way. I'd told my closest friends and then my father, but until the opportunity of this article presented itself, I hadn't quite figured out how or when to make a more public announcement. And it hadn't seemed necessary: I hardly thought anyone would care enough about me for this to be news. But I knew that if I became any more successful it would indeed be news, and I felt, even then, that it was better to

286

be the one to tell my story than to have others tell it for me and get it wrong.

I had one joke about being TV that I had been carrying around for about four or five years. It was this:

'If you're a comedian, it's good to have something to rail against.

'So if you're from a working-class background, you can say, "Oh, the rich people! They're always in control."

'If you're a woman, you can say, "Oh, men! They're always getting paid more."

'If you're from an ethnic background, you can say, "Oh, white people. They're always making it hard for every ethnic group."

'But if you're a white, male, middle-class stand-up, you have no one to rail against. So thank god I'm a transvestite!'

It was one joke, just sitting there, and I'd always thought, *This is the first joke I'm going to say when I talk about it onstage.*

When I finally told the joke it got a laugh, but people didn't actually believe that I was a transvestite. They thought I was joking!

So I told the journalist from the *Observer* that I was TV, and she wrote the article. I was relieved and also a bit worried about how the news would be received.* I'd got used to the experience of 'coming out' to the people I knew well and the eventual relief of it. But I found in the early days that it was a very clunky thing to put into a conversation. If you meet someone and you look like me – more blokey

---

* I was actually very nervous. This was the early 1990s in Britain. I was well aware of the stakes. There was a distinct possibility that it could have killed my career there and then, just as it was about to take off.

than girly – and you say to someone you meet, 'Hi there. Nice weather. You know, I'm a transvestite?' It's a bit awkward. It doesn't really fit into a conversation.

I remember dropping it into one conversation with some other stand-ups one night, but they ignored it. I think they thought they'd misheard me. We were all going to a gig in Canterbury, and as we were driving along, the subject of the conversation turned to sexuality. I thought, *I'll just throw it in.* So I said, 'Well, I'm a transvestite and I've noticed this, that, and the other.' And then there was silence, and then more silence, until somebody said, 'How long 'til we get to Canterbury?' And the conversation just carried on. I assumed they must have been silently thinking, *Did I hear that? Did he just say he's transvestite?* But nobody said anything, and at some point we all got out of the car and went inside to do the gig. Business as usual.

Shortly after the article came out, I did my first-ever gig wearing makeup, heels, and a skirt. It was 1991, in a basement of a pub that could have been the Camden Head (or maybe another pub near Islington Green), just north of King's Cross, in London. I performed at the New Material Night. If you were part of the group of stand-ups who performed at this New Material Night, you were considered one of the up-and-coming comics, and all our names were put in the listings. Lots of comedy fans would come along to watch because the tickets weren't expensive. Afterward, we would all have a big meal upstairs at the Pizza Express nearby. To be part of this group was a great honour for any comedian.

I had friends, but I'd never been part of any social scene

at boarding school, at university, or in my career. I was always tracking my own path. Keeping to myself wasn't a deliberate thing. I suppose it's just how I'm wired.

That night at the Meccano Club, my new material directly addressed the fact that I was in girl mode.

I knew that if I did material about being transgender/transvestite, the audience should be able to go there. *He's wearing lipstick, he's wearing heels, he's talking about being transvestite (transgender), I get it.* But then I thought: *What happens if I start talking about the evil monsters on* Doctor Who – *the Daleks?* I realized that if they see a guy in lipstick and he's talking about Daleks and they're still laughing, then I have a career. If not, I don't have a career. It was as simple as that. It was real roll-of-the-dice stuff – a key moment for me.

So I talked about being a transvestite ('Thank god I'm a transvestite'), and that worked. But then I went with the Daleks stuff ('They travel around on wheels – surely if you just run upstairs you'll be safe'). And to my great amazement, that worked, too. I still had a career.

Later on, people sometimes said, 'Oh, that transvestite stuff got you ahead because it was a gimmick that got you noticed.' But actually – my stand-up was already taking off before I informed the press. Now being TV may have caused more attention to be focused on me, but comedy audiences don't pay to watch an unfunny person wearing a dress. It's not like being a transvestite or transgender comedian was all the rage. It certainly wasn't then and still isn't now. While there were a few gay comedians on the circuit, there weren't any transvestite or transgender comics, so it was definitely not an area of comedy that was looking to be started. Most of the comics I worked with were supportive – we were all a pretty cool non-sexist, non-racist bunch, so I didn't expect anyone would be overtly negative.

My goal had been to be accepted first as a comedian. Then, I thought, if I had the guts to reveal it, I could introduce my sexuality. Without first establishing myself as a comedian, I was afraid I'd be seen simply as a comic who performed in 'drag' – which I feel is another word for 'costume.' I pushed back against that idea because what I was trying to say was this:

The clothes I perform in are (essentially) the same clothes that I arrive and walk off in. Sometimes I arrive in girl mode, perform in boy mode, and then leave in girl mode.

And I think people understand that now. Though some people still say, 'You have a drag character.' But how I dress and what I look like is not a character. It's me. I'm just talking. And sometimes I just happen to be wearing lipstick.

So I did that first set, which was five minutes, and then I did another, longer set, sixty minutes at a gig advertised in my name, to see if that worked. I performed my full comedy set, and my audience seemed to like it. I was hugely relieved. I could be open about my sexuality and still have a career. In January to March of 1993, I finally performed in London's West End. I would do entire nights in girl mode, and then entire nights in boy mode, and I kept changing it around. I was trying to get a look together, which was tricky. I had to experiment, to see what I could come up with. I'm happy to report that it all got easier as time went on.

Sarah

I met Sarah Townsend in 1989 in London at an Edinburgh Fringe meeting. It was my eighth Fringe festival, but it was the first time I was going to perform stand-up. Sarah had set up and was running a venue, Greyfriars Kirk House, and was looking to encourage acts to book there; I was looking for a venue to do my show for three weeks. I decided I would like to perform at her venue.

The first time I realized how much Sarah did at the festival was on the festival's last day. During the festival, she and her business partner, Sophie, were running the venue and dealing with all the acts that were performing there. But she was also directing the play *Epicæne*, by Ben Johnson, in a different venue at the same time – an incredible amount of extra creative work to take on. I have never heard of anyone doing both things at once. She had no backup and no financing. She was doing it all on willpower and determination. That really blew me away.

She was the first person I had ever seen with as much drive and energy as I had.

The day after the festival finished, as we had already started a loose relationship, we slept (just slept) overnight in the venue on the floor in sleeping bags. Which was not necessarily allowed under the terms of the contract with the kirk.* The next morning a man from the kirk let himself in and was very grumpy that people were asleep on the floor.

It wasn't until that morning that I saw all the scaffolding and the lights – all the equipment that had been used to turn the Kirk House into two theatres, everything that had been put together and then taken apart, that I finally understood all that went into the work she had done. Here was someone with a huge amount of energy and determination, someone who was building her life and everything in it completely on her own. She'd grown up in Derry/Londonderry, and everything that she'd made happen was by being single-minded. My dad had a well-paying job, and if things went wrong I could turn to him, and I did turn to him in the early days, simply for an advance of cash to keep me going. She didn't have that financial backup. She'd grown up in Northern Ireland at the height of The Troubles and had experienced tear gas in the streets, bombings, evacuations, and army patrols for many years.

Our relationship started then. It was an off-and-on relationship. She did her creative things and I did mine, and we had each other in between. Gradually she turned her attention to music as well as directing. She's more naturally artistic than I am, and maybe I'm more naturally commercial. I would probably sell more rubbishy stuff for cash than she would. I got to learn taste and design from her. If you can find the perfect intersection of work that's both artistic and commercial, that's the most beautiful place to be.

---

* Scottish for 'church.' When in Edinburgh, do check out Greyfriars Kirk. It is an amazing church/kirk. Greyfriars Kirk House is still there, just down Candlemaker Row from the kirk.

Both of us liked producing projects and making things happen. And that's what we wanted to do in the future.

As my career was beginning to take off, there was more and more scrutiny of me and my shows – not just of the material I was doing but of how the show looked, how I looked, what I wore.

I would hugely benefit from her advice and design in these areas. At that early point, no one was directing my shows: they were just sort of rambling stand-up pieces that existed without direction. Looking back, I think some of the shows were probably too improvised – especially *Live at the Ambassadors*. Sarah took it upon herself to analyze all my material and, among other things, she analyzed my tendency to repeat certain subjects that I like. I asked her to direct the recording of the show *Stripped*. Then I asked her to do my next show, *Force Majeure*, as well.

In analyzing the early shows, we found that improvisation when doing a recording doesn't work very well. It's also very difficult to film and edit convincingly. Improvising stand-up can be really fun and exciting and in-the-moment, but when you record it, it loses maybe a third of its power. Part of that's because no one really believes you have improvised the good stuff. If you're in the room, watching it happen, you absolutely believe it because you see all the not-really-good stuff as well. But if you record the show, you'll edit out the weaker bits so all that's left are the stronger bits. And as good as those stronger bits may be, they're still not as good as a well-scripted show.

So from *Stripped* and particularly *Force Majeure*, we tried to work out an actual script and she gave me direction over what was working and what wasn't. Trying to hone and tighten the comedy and work on a more scripted show was something that I felt I needed to do as my shows had progressed, but it was hard, since that's not how I have got used to working.

The method I use to develop new material is what I call 'verbal sculpting.' I develop the shows on stage in front of a live audience. A lot of people write their stuff down and then perform it, but I still have great difficulty writing stand-up. So I don't write it down. It's the oral tradition of storytelling. Human beings have been doing it for thousands of years. Instead, I develop pieces of material and then, between those pieces, I can break off and go in a different direction. It's a bit like a jazz musician saying, 'I'm going to go off on a solo here.' But I haven't got a band, it's just me. All my material was improv at one point, which is why it feels like I'm making it all up. I'm not, but it is conversational. My material is loose so I can improvise off on a tangent or add a new piece in whenever I want to. Even though I have a very bad processing speed (because of my dyslexia), I apparently have a large 'mental map.'

These days when I start a new show, I begin with a whole bunch of ideas that I have written down in the Notes app on my iPhone. Then I do a series of work-in-progress gigs to try out these ideas and see if I can get them into shape. I use the audience as a script editor. Their reactions to my ideas proves whether they work or not. I think this is about the laziest and also the hardest way of working. Bizarrely both at the same time. It is hard because you have to stand in front of an audience that has paid money to see you perform comedy, but you are just going to muck around with ideas and see if you *can* be funny.[*]

That's quite a tricky thing to do. And it's only because I have done it before that I believe I can do it again.

And it's also somewhat lazy because you don't actually have to work through the original idea before you get to the stage. That's what one would normally do. I think it would be great if I could develop or write pieces of stand-up material beforehand, but that's just never been how I've worked (in stand-up). There is no real way to rehearse comedy without an audience. This verbal-sculpting technique I developed is what I've used since the beginning and I believe a number of other comedians use it, too. It's nothing particularly special. Back then I would do it without the work-in-progress shows. This meant that I was constantly adjusting my show – putting in new material and editing out older material. Unfortunately, using this method, I was reported to a television watchdog programme in the UK, in the early 2000s, and accused of using old material while advertising my shows as new shows. I was completely thrown by this and I tried to explain that this was what I had always done: I had always started a new tour with the old show while constantly changing and adding material to it. This basically meant that the beginning of a new tour would have the same show as the end of the last tour, but I would gradually change the show over the course of the entire tour until it was a new show. Then I would record it.

[*] Usually the work-in-progress shows have a cheaper ticket price.

But the idea of being angry at a comedian for doing older material did seem a little strange because bands do it all the time. The Rolling Stones are still performing live, a huge (and excellent) back catalogue, and no one complains about that.

But back to Sarah.

In addition to the tightening and honing of my material, Sarah created theme music and a lot of the visual aspects of my shows, from *Live at the Ambassadors* onward. A lot of stand-ups aren't worried what their set looks like or about the design of the show, or the posters or advertising. I assume they feel stand-up is about the connection between an audience and what the comedian is saying onstage, so the rest of it doesn't really matter. But with Sarah's instinctive eye, I wanted to push things in that area. She was in charge of the look for the photo shoot for the *Stripped* poster and DVD. What she went after was a look which she described as edgy, rock-and-roll, *Performance*-era Mick Jagger with tailcoat, jewelry, and walking cane. And she came up with the whole *Avengers/The Man from U.N.C.L.E./* 6os look for *Force Majeure*. The photos from these shows have become a huge part of my identity out there.

She influenced what I wore onstage from early on. I knew that if I was going to go around wearing a bit of makeup and some heels, I'd better get a look together, because the 'frumpy transvestite' look – or frumpy anything look – isn't going to be on top of the hit parade for people buying tickets. No one says, 'Let's go see that frumpy guy doing his frumpy show.' That's just not going to happen.

Sartorially I was really all over the shop. Sarah changed that. She suggested that I should channel the danger and androgyny of the music she loved – David Bowie, Iggy Pop, and Lou Reed – to give me a cooler, more glamorous image that would work for a transgender person. So instead of the basic bloke-in-a-dress look, I moved into more black eyeliner, dark painted nails, PVC trousers, and frock coats. It really started to come together by the time of *Definite Article*, in 1995, and it made a huge difference to the perception people had of me, and even what I had of me.

If you're a young girl or a young woman and you're developing a look, a style, you will try things out and your friends will go, 'Oh, that doesn't work.' Or, 'Yeah, that works. That suits you.' Trying to figure out what suits you – when you have a blokey boy body and you're a male tomboy trying on skirts and heels and makeup – is hard. I got it wrong a lot and probably still do, though it's easier now; it's got better. But back then I was trying things out on the street and on photo shoots and trying to see what I could do with my size and weight and shape. Eventually I worked out that I should wear the clothes and the looks that women had borrowed from men – jeans, boots, jackets, kilts, short hair – and that worked for me. I just keep borrowing back things that have been borrowed, in a good way, by women.

Sarah had been creatively involved in all the shows (except *Sexie*, due to other commitments) since *Live at the Ambassadors*, in 1993. But in the early 2000s, I asked her to officially direct a show. She asked if she could film a documentary about me instead. I'd already thought that it would be good to do a film about my weird life, despite the fact that wanting to make a documentary about yourself means your ego has obviously run amok.* In my defense, the reason I agreed was: I felt I was doing things in a slightly different way from the norm and I thought maybe that difference would (or might) be interesting or helpful to people who were having trouble believing in themselves enough to get their things going. I knew that having someone you're in a relationship with do a documentary on you would be hard – but I also knew I could trust her and that because we were so close she would challenge me and make me answer questions that I would normally avoid.

The problem was that I wouldn't, or couldn't, open up about what I was thinking and feeling. Probably years of covering things over (about being transgender), making light of things, and not being emotional enough and almost never crying had made it difficult for me to go deep. In the end it reached the point where Sarah was ready to forget about making the documentary, before something cracked and I did actually open up. Those moments are illuminating to me – particularly toward the end of the film, when I talk about my mother.

In the end, Sarah got the Emmy nomination for Best Documentary for *Believe*. I think it's a really good piece of work that will hopefully stand the test of time: a story that shows that if you struggle hard enough and believe enough in yourself, you can make things happen.

---

*Not to mention when you decide to write a book about yourself.

Although me and Sarah are no longer together, we have learned a great deal from each other. Nineteen eighty-nine seems like a long time ago, and at times both of us working creatively and having a relationship at the same time was very hard.

We are still a great creative team, however, and I continue to rely on her to give me an honest opinion on my work.

Into the Wild West End

It took ten or eleven years for me to make something that worked. The 80s were terrible for me. I simply could not get anything going. Mrs Thatcher was in power in the UK during that time, and almost from the moment she arrived on the scene until the moment she left, my career was no good.*

One thing I did learn in the 1980s was stamina. The great director Ridley Scott said that making films is really about stamina,† which is illuminating, especially since he said it after he was already hugely established. And it's also true in other areas. Stamina is the big thing you have to learn if you want to achieve success in any kind of career, especially creative careers.

It is extremely difficult to keep creativity flowing. I've known a number of very talented and creative comedians and I assumed we would all jockey for position and gradually move up together. But at a certain point, some of these comedians felt 'No, this is not for me.' And because they have decided it's not for them, then it *is* not for them. That is a very subtle point, but it's something I think is

---

* I don't think the two things are really connected, but it just seems to be true. Or it seemed to run parallel. The moment she left office, my career started picking up.

† 'I think the first requirement of a director, now that I've done a few films and maybe over two thousand commercials, is stamina. Because without the stamina, it's a bit like being a long-distance runner – you don't complete the course.' – Ridley Scott

absolutely true. It goes back to what Paul Keane told me
when I started to perform by myself on the street:

If you think you can't do a thing, you will not be able to
do it. If you think you can do something, then you have a
chance of achieving it. Believing doesn't mean you will instantly be able to, but you've got to believe that you can,
otherwise you definitely won't be able to do it. I've seen a
number of people who I thought could do something brilliant and creative but they didn't seem to believe in
themselves and therefore didn't, or couldn't, do it.

By the end of 1991, I realized I had to come off the London comedy circuit. It was difficult to leave it once you
were in it because the London comedy circuit was established, and if you were good enough it could sort of
guarantee you a living. If you left the circuit to go and play
theatres on your own, you were out into the unknown. No
one usually went off and started playing theatres on their
own without a hit TV series. I knew really talented comedians who'd played the circuit, achieved that ambition, and
then got stuck on the circuit. When they tried to get off it
and tour outside London, the gigs would run out and they
would lose momentum and have to go back on the circuit.
If you weren't moving into your own television series,
what were you doing? How were you earning your money?
It was like a rocket coming back to Earth. We all knew that
these comedians had left (because they were so good) but
that, unfortunately, some of them would come back to
play the circuit again. If you were performing outside the
London circuit, your career was without a safety net. To

play the circuit was still difficult, but if you were good enough and established, you could keep playing it.

Again, like other times in my life, there was no obvious path to follow – no map or blueprint for what I needed to do next. But analytically and also on a gut level, I felt the next move was to take the risk and start touring theatres around the country – and see if I had the momentum to make it to the West End.

London's West End is the equivalent of New York's Broadway. As far as I know, before 1993 all the comedians or comedy acts that had played the West End had had a hit television show. At the end of 1991, I was booked for a full weekend at the Comedy Store in London, the weekend before Christmas. It was the top time to play there, when the management knew it would be packed and they wanted the best comedians available. I was lucky enough to be one of those chosen (I'd fought hard for it by that point). When the last show was over, the person who booked the acts, Kim Kinney, asked me, 'Can I book you for some more gigs in the new year?'

For the first time in all the years when I'd been desperate to play the London Comedy Store, I said: 'Thank you, but I've got to leave the circuit.'

He probably thought I was crazy because he knew as well as I did that leaving usually doesn't work. But I'd already booked a short run at the Bloomsbury Theatre, a 500-seater in central London. The key thing for me to test was to see if I could come off performing with a roster of comics at an established club and now play solo, under my own name. Just me on the poster, in a theatre, and sell enough tickets.

That short run at the Bloomsbury Theatre in January 1992 worked: I sold out three shows and added an extra show.

Two months later, in March, I did one show at the Hackney Empire, a 1,200-seat theatre in North London. That worked, too. So I thought, *Let's jump again.* In May, I played the Wimbledon Theatre, a 1,600-seater in Southwest London. Then for July I booked the Shaw Theatre on Euston Road, Central London, which was a bit outside London's 'theatre land,' but it was a 440-seater and I wanted to play a number of gigs there. If things went well at the Shaw, my plan was not to play in London for six months (just perform outside London), wait until January, and then try to play the West End.

The two weeks at the Shaw Theatre went pretty well. And that's when Pete Harris and I started hunting around for a West End theatre to play. Pete and I had set up H&I Management in order to be the management company that would help me move forward. Pete had a lot of energy and was very enterprising, and we both believed in the idea that going for the West End without a hit TV series could work. He felt the Ambassadors Theatre would be the best one to play. It is one of the smallest West End theatres, with only around 450 seats. The idea now was to take it for a month, starting in January 1993, and try to sell tickets. If we sold enough seats, we'd take it for a second month.

Things didn't work perfectly. The first month started okay but sold a bit slowly. But by the end of the month, when it looked like I was finishing, it began to pick up. Then we decided to add a second month. That sold moderately at first, and then again sold out toward the end of the second month. As the second month sold in a similar way to the first, we decided to go for broke and add a third month. The reviews were good, it was seen as a success, and after receiving a number of offers to do a video of the show, I asked another comedian, John Gordillo, if he would shoot our own video, which later became *Live at the Ambassadors*. We paid for it ourselves and then auctioned the distribution off to PolyGram.

John Gordillo is a very funny and talented comedian but also has a keen interest in films. He had a massive library of VHS videos bigger than anyone else's I'd ever seen. As I knew he loved film, I just thought I'd ask him if he would do the video for *Live at the Ambassadors*. He did a great job having to deal with my improvising a lot, which is never easy. But what we were doing was outside the norm, because normally you have to get a 'big' production company to come and do it for you. But we wanted to do it ourselves. John also directed *Unrepeatable*, the second video, at the Albery Theatre (now the Noël Coward Theatre). These two were my first-ever videos and I think John did a great job on both, especially as he was being thrown into the deep end.

The reason we did our own video is because I'd learned that you should never try to sell your copyright. It seems a weird piece of information to throw in here, but it is an issue bound to arise in the story of any creative person. The story of how I learned this is:

Back in the mid-eighties when I was going nowhere and decided to join the Association of Independent Producers in Britain, I used to buy *Screen International*, which is the UK version of the American trade magazine *Variety*. In *Screen International*, I read a story about Kirk Kerkorian, the Las Vegas financier who had recently bought MGM. And after he bought MGM, he sold off the studio buildings and kept only the back catalogue of MGM films. I remember thinking at the time, *My god, you're crazy! You sold the buildings where they made these fantastic films and you kept the fading old prints? What's that all about?* I thought about this for a while and slowly I realized that film studio stages are just big empty aircraft hangars that you can shoot a film in – they don't contain anything intrinsic. The back catalogue, on the other hand, is not only the films – the original prints – but also future rights on remakes, spin-offs, video and DVD sales, downloads, and whatever will be invented in the future.

Once I understood that the corporate suits wanted the copyright, I wanted the copyright, too, and by the time people came to me with money to make in videos in 1993, I was thinking, *Are you trying to buy my copyright? Sign it over to you in perpetuity? Well, I'm not going to do that.* Now, it's hard to hold on to copyrights, because you have to make the recordings yourself and then secure distribution for them – but that's what the game is all about. So, like Charlie Chaplin, Lucille Ball and Desi Arnaz, Billy Connolly, and probably a small handful of other comedy copyright owners (but not that many), I own my copyrights. I've owned mine since 1993.

After the Ambassador Theatre in 1993 came the Albery Theatre in 1994 (where *Unrepeatable* was filmed); then the Shaftesbury Theatre in 1996 (where *Definite Article* was filmed); and then Hammersmith Apollo in 1997 (where

Glorious was filmed). In 1998, *Dress to Kill* was filmed in San Francisco, but by then the American part of my story had already started.

So when I was twenty-five, the direction for my career suddenly became shaped by my *Field of Dreams* rule:

'If you build it, they will come' – 'it' being quality and imaginative shows.

Previously, that had not been my thinking. Quality was not high on my list of priorities. Speed was. But who the hell cares if you get somewhere very fast? The only person who cares is you. If you could get somewhere faster, then you'd just have a lot of money, a big house, a big car, and a big cat. The individual is the only one who wants to get somewhere very quickly. It's what you want when you're young. The idea that you get into comedy and then you have to wait for ten years for anything to happen? If I had known that in the beginning, would I have done it? I'm not sure. At nineteen I had thought that I would begin to cut through in a few years, but that was not the case. At twenty-five I was racing to get somewhere quick and getting nowhere. So I turned the plan completely upside down:

Don't get somewhere as fast as possible. Get somewhere as good as possible.

No one ever says, 'This piece of creative work is crap, but they made it in a couple of weeks, so let's go and check it out.' Contrariwise, no one ever says, 'Now, this piece of creative work took ten years to make and a lot of care and attention – so it's brilliant but I'm not going to check it out because it took so long to make.'

There is something fun about a fast trajectory, someone's career taking off very quickly. It's all about wind in their sails. But in the end, you want your work to last. And to do that, the work has to be good.

When I now think back to where I started – *Fringe Flung Lunch* at the Edinburgh Fringe in 1981; my first Edinburgh Fringe as a street performer in 1985; my first solo show in ropes and chains on a unicycle at Covent Garden in 1987; my first stand-up piece about being addicted to breakfast cereal, in 1988; my first West End show at the Ambassador in 1993 – I see that it's been a bit of a journey. It may not sound that long, but it was twelve years, and to me it felt like a bloody eternity.

Surely it would have been easier if I'd gone to Cambridge University and made it into the Footlights. I wouldn't have had to build everything myself, from scratch. I might have been successful quicker, and I might have made more things in those ten lean years. But in the end, I believe there was something in those wilderness years that was very important for me to experience.

There was something I had to learn. It was stamina. And it was also the idea of quality over speed. But definitely: the stamina, determination, and desire for quality that I'd built up during this time helped me at every stage from now on. But right now they were going to help me play – America.

Across the Magical Ocean

I have a theory that the Atlantic Ocean is a magical ocean. The Pacific is not a magical ocean because it's too big.

When American people, American stars, or American films come over to Britain, we tend to go, 'Wow. Oh my god. I can't believe it. You've come across the Atlantic!' We heard there was another country over there but we didn't actually believe it.

On the London comedy circuit in the 80s, if someone turned up and said, 'I'm a comedian from America,' we would almost say, 'Well, just jump onstage. Show us how it's done.' There was a feeling that modern stand-up comedy came more from a post–Lenny Bruce America than from us. It works the other way around, too: in America, there is sometimes a sense that if we are from Britain or Europe, we are maybe more cultured. There is a sense that we all live in castles, that we're all related to monarchy, that we're all the children of Shakespeare. Conversely we feel that all Americans are rich, have many cars, live on mountains, go to the moon, and are all film stars.

Neither is essentially true, but there's some truth to all these feelings.

As my comedy career was growing, I felt that I had to (and really wanted to) go to America. Particularly, New York City and Hollywood. Even though I knew that Hollywood had a lot of very commercial and not necessarily artistic things there, there was still a buzz about it that I had had in my head all my life and an admiration for those who were doing really good work there. I was intrigued by people like Bill Murray, Steve Martin, Eddie Murphy, Robin Williams, and Garry Shandling, among many others: comedians turned actors who had been able to broaden and expand their stand-up into film and television work. I wasn't going to be bamboozled by the place, sucked in by it, fooled by it. But I did feel I needed to go there and figure out its secrets, to learn and understand how it worked.

After thinking about how to break into America, I came to the conclusion that I had to go and try and win over New York. I had already played some shows in Canada and America, but no one was really paying much attention. I knew other comedians or comic actors had gone over to America – some had done films, some had done comedy clubs – but my gut instinct was to bring my stage show to New York.

I felt I should play a small theatre for a number of months. I had to just play New York and play New York and play New York until New York said, 'Okay, you're good enough.' Particularly until the *New York Times* gave me a good review. That would be key.

New York was, and is, the tastemaker for America (and, maybe, for Canada, too).

It was 1996. But I knew no one who really had a method or strategy for getting into America. A lot of comedians had crashed and burned trying to break into America. Some had succeeded – Monty Python was picked up by PBS in

Dallas, of all places, and had then gone on to be a huge cult hit. But I don't think they had actually planned that. I believed I had a chance because if Americans – not all Americans, but groovy Americans – liked Monty Python, then surely they'd dig my stuff because my comedy was hugely influenced by that style of silly but intelligent.

I said to myself, 'I'm going to try to get America.'* I didn't have any proof that I could do this, but then I hadn't had any proof that I could get my stand-up to take off in the UK. I had one indication: Mr Al Pacino had come to see *Definite Article* in 1995 at the Shaftesbury Theatre in London, and when he came backstage afterward I asked him if he thought the show would work in America. And he said, 'Sure.' I knew he wasn't necessarily a comedy expert, but it did give me a boost of confidence.†

So in October of 1996, at PS 122 in New York City, I did my first American theatre gig, in their eighty-seat auditorium. And a very interesting thing happened on the first night. At the end of the show, my comedy managers, Caroline Chignell and Peter Bennett-Jones; the New York promoter Peter Holmes à Court; my excellent tour manager Mick Perrin, and I went to have a meal and we immediately started discussing the idea of touring America. In that moment, after this first show, everyone suddenly seemed completely confident that performing my stand-up, all across America, would work.

---

* I was channeling sitting on my bed in Sorby Hall back at Sheffield University in 1981.

† Apparently, I was told, he sat in the theatre smoking a cigar and the fire officers were telling each other that they had to go and tell him to stop smoking. But none of them had the guts to tell him, so he was allowed to carry on.

Until we did the first show, we really had no idea. So that change in confidence was a wonderful feeling.

And this is interesting because there was no information and no model that we were following. That's what I find the greatest challenge: doing difficult but positive things that have no model to follow – doing the Nuffield syllabus. There's no route, no ladder, no guidelines, no book you can read. You have to work it out for yourself.

It was the NASA Apollo space missions without any of the danger or finance or expertise or rockets. When I was lucky enough to meet Nelson Mandela in February 2010, Neil Armstrong was walking out when I was walking in. That's a pretty good queue to be in.

No one was lining up to put me on in New York. Later on, no one was lining up to put me on in Paris, either, but I ended up playing Paris and many, many cities all over the world despite that. For me, it gets interesting when people say, 'That can't be done.' Which is often what people say when I announce what I want to do next. It's not that I always try to do things that haven't been done before – it's just that a number of things I want to do are not on an established list of career goals and so I've got to work out how to do them on my own.*

I played at PS 122 in the East Village in New York for four weeks, and the show sold out very quickly. The only

---

* At the time of writing, I am just arranging to perform in Kathmandu. I met a kid in New York City when I was there in 2010 performing David Mamet's *Race*. He said to me, 'Aren't you that comedian?' And I said, 'Yes. Who are you?' He said, 'I'm a student from Kathmandu.' I said, 'Crazy. Could I go and do a show there? Do the kids speak enough English to understand me?' He said maybe so, so I told him I would go. I shook his hand and that was a deal. I have just played there now, in 2017, so I apologize for it having taken me so long.

problem was I discovered that the people coming to see the show were almost all British or Irish people who knew of my comedy and who were either on holiday or who lived in New York. I knew that I had to get actual American people to come and see the show and hopefully like it. Then they could go and tell other Americans. I needed American-to-American word of mouth. I felt that was very important. There was (and maybe still is) a feeling among American audiences that British humour was different. And there was also a feeling among British audiences that American humour was different. I ended up trying to prove that there wasn't an American sense of humour or a British sense of humour. (In fact, any national sense of humour.) I believe that humour is broadly the same around the world. There are mainstream comedians and alternative comedians in every country – and it's just that the references, as you move from country to country, will be different. If you are surreal in America and surreal in Britain, or in Ireland or anywhere else, your style of comedy will speak to the same kind of people as long as your cultural references are universal enough. Monty Python had already proved this.

I was lucky enough to play Lenny Bruce in the stage version of the Dustin Hoffman film *Lenny*, in 1999 in the West End, directed by Peter Hall. It was a wonderful opportunity to play Lenny Bruce because I don't think many actual comedians have had the chance to play him onstage. Which includes acting out his life as well as doing his stand-up material. I was also allowed to have access to other documents and material that he had written that most don't get to see. It was a very tough acting job and I actually got ill doing it over the three-month run in the West End. His stand-up was different from mine, but in some ways it overlapped. He had certain pieces that were somewhat surreal and crossed over to an area that I loved to live in. His early material was really very mainstream, but his later material was still really edgy in 1999 (even now). But it was an amazing experience.

Now, before I performed in *Lenny*, I didn't know that much about Lenny Bruce. It's very hard to get into his material if you are British, but even if you are growing up in America right now and you listen to his material, you could find it difficult to understand because he's referencing people and news items from the 1950s – Eisenhower, Vice President Nixon, the Kennedy assassination, Sophie Tucker. The Lenny Bruce experience made me realize that I needed to try and create material that would stick around after I might have disappeared from this world. Because how can you laugh at material that references things that now are less known or have been forgotten? In my show *Force Majeure*, I do material about human sacrifice, and medieval kings in Britain. These kings are old and gone, but if you introduce them you can say, 'Okay, Richard the Lionheart was an English king who actually spoke French. He spoke almost no English.' Some people might have learned about Richard the Lionheart in a history class, and people may not have heard of him. But if you tell your audience who he is and when he lived, your material should work in every country in the world and hopefully in any decade or century of the world. You're just introducing characters to a story.

In 1997, I returned to PS 122 in New York and played

their 120-seater this time, for three weeks. In 1998, I moved
to the Westbeth Theatre, then on Bank Street in the West
Village, which was run by Arnold Engelman, who became
my American promoter to this day. I remember talking to
Arnold and saying, 'Can we hold some tickets back on the
door every night so that if there's any word of mouth from
Americans to Americans, they'll be able to buy some tickets
even if a bunch of Europeans have already bought most
of them?'* Arnold's first love is the theatre, but he was very
quick to pick up the world of comedy, as soon as it walked
up to him. At the time of writing, we have just played *Force
Majeure* in Hawaii – the fiftieth state – having already played
all of the other forty-nine of the United States, and Madison
Square Garden and the Hollywood Bowl.

So I pushed very hard and played the Westbeth for four
months, from March through early July. Playing for four
months was an endurance test that I think we passed, since
lots of people came to see the show, even though sales went
up and down. David Bowie even came to see the show. I
was rather stunned by this because I didn't think I would
necessarily be his cup of tea. We met after the show and it
was great just to hang out for a short while. On a later tour,
somebody came up to me after my show and said, 'You
know, David Bowie is doing a bit of your stand-up. You
know that thing you do onstage when you say that some-

*This situation does happen: Performers from other countries will come and play in your country,
and you may not know they're performing because the citizens from this performer's home
country who are living in or visiting your country will buy all the tickets. So you won't even know
that they've sold out a big theatre or arena. In Britain, we get performers coming from India who
play stadiums, selling tens of thousands of tickets, and your average person in Britain wouldn't
even know that they'd been there.

thing is true, then you say, "No, it isn't" – "Yes, it is" – "No, it isn't'" – referring to a bit where I would confirm something, then deny it, then confirm it, then deny it, until it got quite silly. When I found out that David Bowie was doing that onstage, I thought it was pretty cool. Later I went to see his show at Wembley Arena in London, and when I met him afterward, he said, 'I'm doing that thing you do onstage.' Again my mind was slightly blown away.

Back at the Westbeth, since I was a performer wearing makeup (I was performing in girl mode at that point) there was an idea that I was a type of 'alternative-sexuality performer' and that sexuality would be a big part of my comedy. Actually, sexuality or age or lifestyle doesn't determine whether someone will like my comedy: The only thing that matters is whether or not they are into surreal comedy. That was, and still is, the common denominator, and it applies to all audiences that like my comedy, from all around the world.

By the end of those four months at the Westbeth Theatre, I'd come up with a new show: *Dress to Kill*. Because I'd still been performing my show *Glorious* at PS 122 in October of 1997, I felt I couldn't come back in March of 1998 with a brand-new show. It was too quick. So what I decided to do was begin my run at the Westbeth with all my early material that had worked well but that hadn't been seen in America. So I started my *Dress to Kill* show with that earlier material (which was actually recorded as a separate show on audio cassette tape) but then I gradually changed the material over the four months to do the new material that became *Dress to Kill*.

In May or June of 1998, Tracey Ullman saw the show and came backstage afterward. She was very friendly and chatty. She asked if anyone from HBO had come to the show (as they did lots of comedy, one-hour specials). I said no. But I think she went away and put in a positive word for me, as she had her own show on HBO. Once I'd finished at the Westbeth, Arnold and my comedy manager, Caroline Chignell, and I started discussing the idea of playing the West Coast – San Francisco and LA. At a similar time, a wonderful message came in from Robin Williams and his wife Marsha, saying, 'Would you like to do the show on Broadway? If so, we would be happy to be involved.' I said, 'Actually, I don't want to do Broadway at the moment, but I would like to play the West Coast. Could we do something together in San Francisco and LA?'

I'd met Robin Williams the previous year between the stand-up shows I was doing in London, when we were both shooting the film *The Secret Agent*. I knew he was filming in London in a scene that I wasn't in, so I decided to go and visit him and say hello. I walked up to him and said, 'Mr Robin Williams.' And he looked back at me and said, 'Mr Eddie Izzard.' And that really did blow me away. Robin's material had been discussed at the stand-up workshop at the Jacksons Lane Community Centre back in the winter of 1987–88, and just to be working with him about five years later was amazing. Later I handed him a copy of my first video, *Live at the Ambassadors*, and said, 'Would you look at my video?' It was such a crappy thing to do, but I couldn't help myself. He went and watched some of it straightaway. I knew this because about an hour later I was watching him act on set and, between takes, he made a joke to me that referenced my material. Again, this was all quite surreal to me. I asked him if he thought my comedy would work in America. He said, 'Yeah. With the smart people.'

But then, in September of 1998, with Robin Williams's name endorsing my show posters, I played two theatres in San Francisco that were right next to each other. For four weeks I played a downstairs theatre called the Cable Car, and then for an extra week I played the theatre right next to it that was called the Stage Door. On opening night Robin and Marsha invited loads of people, including Sean Penn and Robin Wright and the mayor of San Francisco, and it was quite a thing. After the four weeks at the Cable Car, I filmed *Dress to Kill* at The Stage Door theatre.

Then we went to the Tiffany Theater on Sunset Boulevard in Los Angeles for three weeks, until the end of 1998. Again, Robin invited loads of people to the opening night, and Eric Idle bought a whole night of tickets, as well. What they both did really helped me 'arrive' in LA. You'd think that having lots of named people turning up and seeing the show, all invited on these specific opening nights, would make one rather worried or anxious. It did, but by that time I'd done so many gigs that I thought, *Let's just ignore the stress and try and enjoy the performance.*

Sometimes at the Tiffany in Los Angeles, I found people weren't really laughing that much. I think maybe some people were 'people watching' rather than watching comedy. Also I think some people were wondering whether it was cool to laugh at this material – whether everyone thought this show was the next best thing or just a bit too different.

317

Sometimes during the show I would stop and say, 'That was a joke there. I'll point them out as they go by.' This was rather different from San Francisco and New York, where people had laughed in a very relaxed way.

Three nights before the LA show ended, Chris Albrecht of HBO came to see it and a week later said they wanted to film it. I told him we'd already filmed it ourselves and he said, 'Okay, we'll air it.' And they did. HBO aired *Dress to Kill* in 1999, and while I think the viewing figures weren't quite what they'd hoped, it became a big underground hit.

Dress to Kill won two Emmys, one for writing and one for performing. I was filming *All the Queen's Men* with Matt LeBlanc in the Austrian Alps at the time of the awards ceremony, and I remember saying to the director, Stefan Ruzowitzky, 'I'm nominated for two Emmys, can I go to Los Angeles? Can I take a couple of days off so I can get there and get back?' And they said, 'I'm afraid you're needed here.' And I said, 'Please, I don't think you really need me,' because I wasn't the lead and I don't think I had much to do in the scenes I did have. And he and the producers just said, 'Sorry, you can't go.' And to be fair – those are the rules in film. They own your time.

On the night of the Emmys, I was up all night listening to events on my phone (there was a live Internet feed but of only the red carpet portion of the show). I was talking on the phone to my US publicist, Tresa Redburn, who was watching everything unfold through a live feed on a big screen. Suddenly she said, 'Oh wow, you've won the Best Writing Emmy!' I went, 'Really? That's amazing.' And then it came to the next award and she said, 'You've won two!

You've won Best Performing as well!' It was a great honour, but I was a continent away.

The next morning, Stefan came down and casually said to me, 'How did it go?' I said, 'I won two of them,' and he said, 'Oh god.' I don't think they expected me to win anything. But they immediately started planning a party for me, which was a nice ending. We had the party in the Alps, and eventually Tresa very kindly brought the Emmys over to Austria and Matt LeBlanc 'awarded' them to me at a small ceremony that was set up. Which was cool. So that was my introduction to Hollywood awards ceremonies – in the Austrian Alps.

The Tiffany Theater, Sunset Boulevard, people throwing parties, living there, renting a place, staying at the Chateau Marmont Hotel: it was all bonkers. I've now got more used to it and have spent a lot of time in Los Angeles. Also, there are so many places in LA that have been featured as locations in films and now I know these places and roads and buildings. I find that quite trippy. Just about all of LA has at some point been used in a film. People think of Hollywood as a very separate place from LA, which it is mentally, but not geographically. The relationship between the two is unusual. There is really no specific 'Hollywood.' The Hollywood studios are spread out all over Los Angeles, sometimes miles from each other.

Since Northern Ireland, when I used to watch the American imports *I Love Lucy* and *Bewitched* on TV, I wanted to know what Hollywood was like. So I was pleased to go there and work there, even though I never want to be locked into the proverbial Hotel California.

Also, LA is a very atypical city. To me, Downtown LA should be the pumping central heart of that city, but for years it was a place where not much dynamic activity was happening. If you do decide to walk all around or in many places in LA, you could actually be stopped by the police for doing so, because everyone else is in cars. As if that's a law. New York, London, Paris, or Berlin – these are emotionally more my kinds of cities. Places where you can walk around, jump on the Underground, a bus, a cab, and say to friends, 'Hey, we're all meeting in the center.' 'Hey, we're all going to the West End.' 'We're walking to another restaurant.'

But I do love knowing LA. I found it intimidating when I first got there, but now I like knowing the city. I like flying in and then saying to the cab driver, 'Yeah, let's go via Fairfax using surface routes, or, if the traffic is clear, you can take the 405, or the 105 then the 110' – because now I know there are a few ways. And that feels good.

In 1999, I did my first Hollywood film: *Mystery Men*, with Ben Stiller and Geoffrey Rush. My initial strategy was not to do comedy films because I thought it would be harder to be accepted in dramatic films if I was doing lots of comedy. But my agents thought I should do this one (as I'd just arrived), and before I knew it I'd said yes, not even thinking about the fact that I was doing a comedy – the thing I'd said I wasn't going to do. I came on board saying to the director that I would be happy to play my character, Tony P., as long as I could 'rewrite him a bit.' Unfortunately, I think everyone had said that about their own

characters. Later I was told, 'You can rewrite your character as long as you don't change any scenes and that any
changes you make don't affect anyone else's lines.' So you
could add a word here and there but that was about it. I
was treated very nicely. I wasn't as nervous as I would have
been if it had been my first-ever film. So even though this
was my first Hollywood film, I had already acted in a
number of films by the time I did it.

Later, I acted in *The Riches*, a wonderful television drama
series. It was filmed in Hollywood, in 2007–2008. I'd gone
to a meeting at a production company about a different
project entirely but ended up hearing about the develop-
ment of *The Riches* from someone I'd met at the front door
when I came into the building: Michael Rosenberg. He just
happened to be there, smoking a cigarette. He said he
wasn't coming to my meeting because he'd heard I didn't
do television. I said it was just a block on comedy on television. So he came to the meeting and during it, he told
me, 'We're doing a show about a grifter/con artist family
who take over a house and another family's identity.' I said,
'Well, I'd like to do that.' And that small pitch turned into
The Riches.

I was built into the project, created by Dmitry Lipkin,
from the beginning, and I became part of the group that
pitched it to different studios, which was a fantastic process
to go through – scary as hell, but you can't know how to do
it until you've done it. John Landgraf, head of FX, said yes
in the room (which was great to experience). We went with
him because of his passion. I was also part of the group

that was auditioning people for other roles, reading in my role against theirs, but it always felt slightly fraudulent that I hadn't been auditioned myself. It felt unusual not to be scrambling to try to get into something – especially a drama.

We did two seasons, shooting forty-five minutes of edited drama in only seven filming days, which is very fast. Normally, eight filming days is the minimum – often longer. But since I'd never had any formal acting training, it was a brilliant learning experience: a film school, TV school, and acting school all rolled into one for me. Having been a kid street performing just a decade before, *The Riches* was the thing that dramatically got me grounded acting-wise.

Television is quite a verbal medium, so you have to learn to 'inhale' lots of dialogue. I remember filming one night, in the second season, when I had to learn an entire scene that I hadn't expected to shoot. We were going to shoot it at one in the morning and there were two guest actors in the scene who already had their lines down. They started shooting the scene doing their coverage (filming close-ups) on the two guest actors. I knew when the cameras turned around and pointed at me I would have to know that script, and I knew that if I panicked, I wouldn't be able to learn it in time. When you're panicking, your brain won't let anything go in because it's very busy 'doing panic.' But I knew that if I could just keep my heartbeat low and keep focused, I could actually do it. So I calmly 'inhaled' all the dialogue I needed to learn and by the time cameras turned around, I was ready. The whole series was a kind of baptism by fire – a huge, incredible learning curve.

A number of people say to me, 'Is it hard to work with

other actors when you've done so much performing onstage on your own?' I don't find that it's hard, because I've always wanted to do this. I liked acting in plays when I was younger. And even though I took off by doing stand-up comedy, my first love was, and is, acting. But now that I can do stand-up comedy, I want to keep doing that as well. What I really love doing is filmed drama, be it for television or cinema. The care and attention that goes into the acting and the lighting of the scenes is something I love. To look back at a scene that is beautifully lit in a great location with wonderful acting, and then to be part of that scene, is just incredible. When comedies are filmed, usually there is much less finesse going into the acting, lighting, and composition of the scenes.

The Riches was a wonderful series and a fantastic group of professionals to work with. We had very passionate fans but not quite a big enough army of them. The numbers weren't quite right, so we got only two seasons. I remember I went to see the numbers guy at FX and I came out more confused than when I'd gone in. They break the numbers down into so many different packets that it's hard to understand what it all means.

After *The Riches*, I was cast in *United States of Tara* for Showtime. By that point, with my dramatic acting, I had learned to relax more. I felt that I had 'graduated' from filmed acting school by the end of season two of *The Riches*, and by *United States of Tara* I was beginning to let go and see where I could get to.

In stand-up comedy, you know immediately that if the

audience is laughing at what you're saying, you're probably in 'the zone.' You don't have to go back and look at the take to see if you're in the zone because you're getting a huge reaction from a live audience. But filmed drama is different – there's no audience there. You just have to feel it. Which initially I found very hard. Sometimes I found that I was doing a scene and thinking, *That felt good*, and then later, when I saw it edited together, I'd feel, *Oh, that was awful. What was I thinking?* But sometimes I would think, *Oh, that felt like good work*, and then when I watched it, it was actually good. The ability to tabulate my mind, so I could tell if I was doing good work, I found very tricky. By this I mean to have your instincts well honed so that when you feel you've done a good scene, you've done a good scene, and when you feel you've done a bad scene, you have done a bad scene. Maybe (probably) other actors just go in and can sense this straight off, but I couldn't. My sense of *I'm doing good* or *I'm not doing good* is so much better now than it was back then. What's really nice is when you do a take and you look up and the director turns to you and says, 'That one' – and you've already thought, *That one,* in your head, too. Because then you know that your gut instinct and the reality are matching up. This is when you can begin to do good work.

I've also learned a lot from the people I've had the fortune to act with. Other actors won't pull you aside and tell you what to do, but just by observing you can learn a lot. Acting up against other great actors has been brilliant training for me. More than anything I learned about being relaxed and in the moment from them. I wasn't very good when I started being a film actor. It took me some time to get my feet. But that's the way it always is with me.

I think back to when I was seven years old and knew I wanted to act, and to when I was fifteen years old and broke into Pinewood Studios. Sometimes it's hard to believe that I've finally got to a place where I'm doing dramatic work with fine actors and going, 'God, that was good, being in that scene.' I do love that.

In plays on Broadway and the West End, there was a problem that you act the same story again, night after night, for a minimum of three months. But I've discovered that you actually have a 'corridor of emotion' that you can move about in. This is how I describe it. A corridor of emotion. I think if you're doing a play night after night, you can change how you're playing it in a way that doesn't actually upset the script. You can just move the emotion around a certain bandwidth and see what changes. The corridor of emotion doesn't work with film because you will shoot that scene and try to do your best interpretation of it with every 'take,' and then only one take will actually make the final cut of the scene. In the cast commentary from the *The Lord of the Rings* DVD, the great actor Ian Holm was described by his co-star Ian McKellen as making every take of every scene a slightly different interpretation of Bilbo Baggins: 'This is why he always looks so fresh, because he presents the whole kaleidoscope of the character and lets the director choose what he wants.' Which is a bit like the corridor. But the corridor of emotion is designed more for a live performance you do night after night because, I've found you can get locked into a single interpretation of your live acting performance and it becomes locked in concrete, and then I feel you start to fall out of the play. It's like a prayer that's repeated so often, like the Lord's Prayer in Christian religion – *Our father, who art in heaven* – that you stop thinking about what it actually means when you say it.

With live comedy and plays, you can get it so locked down in the repetition of a performance that you lose the life of it. But if you can move it around emotionally, if you can punch a thought or lay back on a thought, then you can get a totally different feel. But it's still the line. What you've done is shifted the emotion in it, which I think keeps it alive for the other person you're acting against because they don't quite know how you're going to act it each night. And I do find that fascinating. I do like being alive and present in the moment. I think it's the centre of acting, stand-up, music, and all living performance.

(No More) Fear of Flying

I remember watching Neil Armstrong step out on to the moon on July 20, 1969. I was seven, and we (me, my brother, Mark, my father, and the Atherton family – kids Ian and Paul, and their mum and dad) were staying at their house at 6 Grailands, Bishop's Stortford. We were seeing Neil Armstrong take the first-ever moonwalk in history on our televisions. I've never forgotten that moment. It cemented my fascination with all things space related, which began with the free spaceships I used to get in my breakfast cereal.

My early obsession with NASA and space and the moon made me briefly consider a career as an astronaut, but due to my fantastic ability to throw up inside any moving vehicle, and especially inside all aircraft, I quickly became certain I would not actually become an astronaut.

Throwing up is one of the worst feelings a human body can have (I think). There are probably worse feelings, but as a highly experienced practitioner of motion sickness, I actively try to not have the feeling ever come back to me again. This doesn't seem possible, though. I just had a feeling of nausea today, as a matter of fact, trying to read from an iPad in the back of a car. I took my first flight when I was three months old (from 'Adan to London). One of my first memories is getting sick on an airplane – actively filling that sick bag that you get with flying. Which meant that every time I flew again I would feel scared about being sick, which would make me feel sick as well. I even stopped eating before any kind of travel-related motion so I couldn't be sick, but I think not having anything in my stomach also made me feel sick, which made me sick.

Then, in my thirties, I thought: *I should learn to fly*.

That's a bit of a leap, and it wasn't my next step after having the thought, but in the end that is what I did. A positive, though radical, step: get rid of your fear of getting sick while flying – knock it on the head – by learning how to fly.

I should add that the idea of learning to fly a Spitfire was also very appealing. A Spitfire is a beautifully designed classic WWII fighter airplane, featured heavily in the Battle of Britain. It is a plane beloved by many in the UK (and Commonwealth) because of its amazingly shaped elliptical wings and the sound of its Rolls-Royce Merlin engine.

Having learned how to fly, I can tell you that learning how to fly is a very good way of getting rid of the fear of flying. Apparently there's an actual term for this – *immersion therapy* – which has you confront your fears head-on, just like this, but I had no idea what immersion therapy was or that it even existed. For me, learning to fly was yet another version of the Nuffield syllabus. On my very first lesson, we flew, for a very short time, like a Spitfire.

It seems Spitfires had a technique they had to use for losing height rapidly. They would drop, say, the left wing and then kick their tail rudder round to the right. This would make them slide down out of the sky at a very fast speed, without going into a spin. The instructor told me about this and then showed it in action. Fantastic to experience.

328

Now, I learned to fly in the late 90s, when I was traveling to gigs all around the world. By then, most passenger flights were in jets or turbo propeller airplanes, which fly fast enough and high enough over the weather for a smoother ride. There is still turbulence, but it's not as bad as the old days. Which I know because I was flying in the old days.

The technique used to teach flying is to pair you up in a flying school with one particular flying instructor. I think the theory behind the method has to do with consistency: if one has a single instructor, one can get used to them and feel more relaxed while learning.

But I wanted to learn to fly as fast as possible. In hindsight, this is not the best way to learn anything, especially flying. Who gives a monkey's if someone has learned to fly in a short span of time? People care only if you can fly an airplane well. I've also realized this is exactly the conclusion I came to in my creative career.

I took flying lessons at Denham Aerodrome, to the west of London, but since I kept turning up on different dates to see if there was anyone free to give me an hour in a Piper PA-28, I had many different instructors. Probably way more instructors than is usual when learning how to fly. In the end I think I had about ten or fifteen instructors, and they all signed my certificate when I passed. That was nice.

I was in my late thirties, and most of the instructors were in their early twenties. I found that being taught by someone nearly twenty years my junior was quite a leveler: to accept that I didn't know enough about flying (of course I didn't; I hadn't taken any lessons) so someone fifteen years younger than I will have to tell me what to do as if they were fifteen years older than me. But I actually found it quite liberating, because it shows you can learn from anyone – which, of course, you can – as long as you can wind your ego down to accept their knowledge.

After a number of flying lessons and after logging an amount of flying hours, you are required to take a written ground exam before you can fly solo. Once you pass the exam, you're legally entitled to fly solo. The most difficult part of flying is landing, and to get a lot of practice landings in, you fly circuits – taking off, turning to the right or left, flying down one side of the airfield, then across the back, and then doing the 'final approach' to the runway before doing a 'touch-and-go' landing. This is when you actually land the plane but, once down, you immediately go 'full throttle' and gun the plane down the runway to take off again immediately. In this way, you can get as many practice landings in during each lesson as possible. But you do all that with a flying instructor sitting next to you. Flying solo means you fly one circuit completely on your own, with no one else in the plane, and land at the end of it. Quite a thing to do for the first time, all on your own.

There's still more to learn after completing your first solo flight – another five written exams – and you have to fly solo cross-country to three towns or cities in a big geographical triangle, returning to the initial aerodrome. You also have to complete a Practice Forced Landing (PFL), which is the equivalent of the emergency stop in the car when the driving instructor says, 'I am going to hit the dashboard.'

In the air, of course, you can't come to a standstill because you are in the air, so instead you practise doing emergency landings.

The PFL test happens something like this: You'll be flying along at around one or two thousand feet in the air and then the instructor will just pull your throttle (engine power) down to zero. The trick is learning how to 'trim' the plane to glide altitude so that you can glide down and stay in the air for as long as possible. You don't want to go down like a brick out of the sky, so you need to learn to adjust the plane to glide as well as the plane can. Once you're trimmed for glide altitude, you have to very quickly choose a field, line up into the wind, and bring the plane down over whatever fence or hedge is around the field, ready to land your plane. You don't actually put the plane down when you're learning how to fly, because you would be landing in someone's field, and you might ruin the field (and your plane), and the farmer who owned it would be very pissed off since it might cost a lot of money to repair the field. But for the PFL, you just have to get as close as possible to the field you'd want to land in so the instructor is convinced that you would have been able to put the plane down successfully if you had to.

I was pretty good at PFLs, until the actual day of the test. On that day, it took me several times to get it right – by which I mean I got it wrong several times – until finally, at the end of the test, the flight instructor gave me one last chance, this time, back at the Denham Aerodrome, where we'd started from. The previous two times I had tried the PFL I had been too low, and the flight instructor had ordered me to go full throttle and climb into the sky again. This time I wanted to be sure I wasn't too low. Unfortunately this meant I was too high. Suddenly I realized I had to use the Spitfire technique I had seen on my first lesson. So I dropped one wing, kicked the tail rudder around, and slid down out of the sky. I couldn't quite believe it but it worked and I managed to do an actual PFL and land back on the airfield. After this, the flying instructor said, 'Well, that was rather agricultural (like you landed a tractor). But you landed it successfully, so I will give it to you.' A good result.

Once I learned to fly, I had this crazy idea again that maybe I could learn to be an astronaut – inspired by all those American and Russian space missions from the 60s and 70s. On the International Space Station (the ISS), the main languages spoken are English and Russian, and since I wanted to learn Russian, I just thought, *I could go up there and do a gig in both languages*. This may just be wishful thinking but I do like the vibe of the ISS.

When I ran my marathons in South Africa, the British astronaut Tim Peake phoned me from the ISS to say hello and tell me that he was watching the route of my marathons from outer space, which is amazing. I never imagined, as I was fishing toy spaceships out of boxes of breakfast cereal that one day, I'd be talking to an astronaut who was looking down on a tiny running me, while he orbited the Earth. But it happened.

So I qualified as a pilot in the late 1990s, but I haven't really used that ability much since then. I still want to learn to fly a Spitfire, but I'd have to do a lot more training to be able to pilot one of those. In regard to motion sickness, particularly in airplanes, I am now much better at coping with it. I do feel fear is a big problem for a number of fliers, and now when I get into turbulence, I just think of it as the air equivalent of a bumpy road. When we come in to land, I am also much more relaxed. When I hear the under-carriage coming out and locking into place, I know that that is what it is. Before, I had no idea what these incredibly loud mechanical noises were. Bizarrely, no one ever tells you on an airplane. I also know that when you have trimmed the airplane and you are on full flaps coming in to land, the only way you adjust the height of the plane is by adjusting the throttle. This means that you will from time to time hear the engine noise increase as you're coming in to land. This can be rather worrying because it sounds like the engines are straining. In fact they are just turning faster, which is simply the technique to keep the airplane at the right height as you fly down the glide path and come in to land. It is standard procedure, but it does sound rather alarming if you don't know what it is.

As someone who was scared of flying but is now a pilot, I think the captain of the plane should add a short explan-ation of these two 'landing sounds' when doing their final talk. This could be really helpful to calm some passengers and I see no downside to saying something like, 'You will soon hear two useful sounds: the undercarriage deploying and the throttle adjusting – both very positive sounds.' And then give a short explanation of what is about to happen.

I think the flying machines and underwater machines and space machines from my favourite UK childhood tele-vision series *Thunderbirds* were my first gadgets.

Thunderbirds, which was produced in Britain but had a story set in America, got me hooked on the idea of space travel. I totally identified with American space adventures. I would have identified with Russian space adventures as well, but Soviet Russia didn't put out a lot of press, whereas NASA in America put out a load of press. I thought NASA was 'our' space programme. I thought 'we' were going to the moon. And essentially, 'we' (the West?) were. NASA was obviously paid for by the American government and was trying to actively win a space race against Soviet Russia and therefore they utilized publicity as much as they could to put forward the positive story about their race for the moon. But going into space *was* always a great adventure. It would have been entirely wonderful if Soviet Russia had decided they were going to publicize their space missions as well. If we'd been bombarded in Britain by both sides, I would have probably known as much about the Russian cosmonauts as I did about the American astronauts. But the reality was that in the 60s, I was getting most of my space information from America and breakfast cereal.

As recently as ten years ago, I bought a *Thunderbirds* toy for my niece, which was a little bit bonkers, as it was forty years later, but I think she liked it. My brother had been showing her and her sister the DVDs, and the toy had moving bits that pull out and push in that you can change around. Moving bits are always the key.

I think I like (or people like) gadgets and technology because they give you power. Some people don't like technology. Some people are afraid of technology. But I've found that people usually have selective techno-fear. As soon as they find that a machine is useful – 'Ooh, I can send e-mails across the world or take photos or videos with this iPhone' – they stop rejecting it and embrace it. Usefulness overcomes phobia.

I think gadgets are used by young people to instinctively increase their power. If you think about the essence of being an adult – you have the power, the control, the freedom to say, 'I will do this now, I will go there now.' And I think young people want to do that but are told they're not allowed to. Technology gives them the ability to access huge virtual power and a deal more actual power.

I started thinking about this when I was playing a computer game with my two nieces a few years ago and everyone playing was in control of their own avatar, their character. Even though I was very good at *Asteroids* back in the early 80s, I couldn't play the game that I was playing with my nieces very well.* They had been playing the game probably for months, and so they were very good at it. At one point, my youngest niece said, 'Don't worry. I can see you're struggling, but I'll put you in my backpack.'

And then she picked up my character, put it in her backpack, and just carried me along for the rest of the game. Psychologically, I found this rather annoying: I was powerless and essentially useless and she was carrying me all over this imaginary world with casual ease.

She had the power.

---

* I was a 'king' of *Asteroids* back in the day. I once played one game for about an hour and a half and would occasionally get scores of more than a million. To put this in perspective, the first time you played a game you would be lucky if you got a score of a couple of thousand. *Asteroids* gave me the virtual power to kill many big rocks.

People want to be wizards. If someone came to you and said, 'Wanna be a wizard?' you'd probably say, 'Is there a catch? How much does it cost?' And if they said, 'Two pounds fifty a month – wizard, full powers,' you'd probably say, 'Yeah. I'll be a wizard.' You'd also check out what their powers are, and all the different wizard packages available. I think we all suffer from wizard envy.

Back in the 60s, when I was four, or five, or six, all I was able to do in my world of gadgets and technology was maybe to switch on the television.

I do remember when you switched on a 1960s television, nothing would happen for some time. You would just stare at a dark screen and then after a while, people would start talking from out of that dark screen. You would *hear* the television first, and voices would indicate that something was happening on the telly, but there would be only a white dot in the centre of the television while it warmed up. Eventually the white dot would open up and you would be able to see what they were talking about.

Back then, Dad had a car (a cream-coloured VW), we had a television, my brother had a bicycle, and I had my bicycle, which was probably the most important gadget of my early childhood.

Then there were model trains. I loved train sets. My brother, Mark, and I recently donated our childhood train set to the Bexhill Museum, in East Sussex. Bexhill was where we lived as children from 1969 to the late 1980s, and it's where my father still lives. The train set was started by our father, in early 1960, so clearly he liked train sets, too. Me and Mark helped build the countryside and hills and tunnels and bushes, on to a chicken wire frame, covered in plaster-of-Paris, when we lived at 74 Cranston Avenue in Bexhill, all to add to the realism of our little train world, which we loved playing with. If you ever go to Bexhill Museum, you'll see some of our original trains, coaches, and buildings with a lot of other detail added to it by the Bexhill Model Railway Club.

The modern era of gadgets came to me in 1974. That's when my father flew to Dallas for business and came back with a Texas Instruments Prinztronic Countdown calculator. I still have this calculator and it actually still works.* It could do only addition, subtraction, multiplication, division, and percentages, but it was still more advanced than anything around. I think I was one of the few kids at school who had a calculator in 1974.

The other amazing thing about this calculator was that I didn't even ask for it – normally I was begging for presents and toys, as I was a rather greedy child. The kind of greedy child who would almost scream at his grandparents the minute they arrived for a visit:

'*WHAT HAVE YOU BROUGHT US? WHAT PRESENTS HAVE YOU GOT?*'

Back then, I thought, *If you don't have presents, what the hell is this all about?*

---

*While doing revisions for this book, I was home, at my dad's house, for Christmas in 2016 and I realized the original calculator was in my drawer, so I took it out, put some batteries in it, and turned it on. I tried some sums and they all added up, just like the last time I used it, back in the late 70s.

I was just so acquisitional. I've since heard of a saying: *Whoever dies with the most toys wins.*

Back then I thought so.

But in 1974 I was twelve, and it was fantastic to get this calculator. It was like having a piece of gold. I calculated everything I could on this gadget, which, if anyone remembers having their first calculator, isn't that much, because there really isn't that much you can do with it. You can't actually think of enough things to work out on a calculator when you're just a kid at school. Now if you have an iPhone and you have the calculator app on it, how often do you use it? Imagine that was the only thing you had – your whole iPhone was just a calculator. Occasionally you use the calculator and it's useful, but you're not using it forty times a day unless it's your job to add things up.

So I had this calculator and I wasn't allowed to use it in class or during exams, because that would be cheating. I had to continue to add and subtract and multiply and divide without using the calculator, which was exactly what the calculator was meant to do: help lazy students with mathematics.

Bizarrely, I had a similar problem later in life. When I learned to fly, they were coming up with lots of GPS devices that could help you with all the complex navigational calculations you need to do to fly everywhere, but the instructors would say, 'Well, if you do that, you won't actually learn to do the mathematics and the geometry that you need to do.' Again, the GPS navigation device was a calculator I wasn't supposed to use.

It was the same thing when I went to Eastbourne College

in September of 1975, at the age of thirteen: You were not allowed to use calculators. But in the first week, the mathematics teacher held up a thing that he'd taken out of a long, gray plastic container and said, in a very dramatic tone:

'This is a slide rule! With it, you can calculate things. A slide rule is something you need. A slide rule you have to have. A slide rule is *very* necessary. It can save your life.'

He continued: 'Slide rule – learn it, find it, love it, marry it, this is it. If you're in a dark alleyway, and someone's about to attack you, you need a slide rule to be able to work out how long it's going to take you to heal from your injuries. You have to pay extra for it, but get one of these because without it, you're dead in the water. You will drown in a sea of badly added-up numbers.'

And we were going, 'Okay, okay, we'll get it, we'll get it.'

So we all bought this plastic slide rule.

The following year, in September of 1976, the same teacher stood up and said:

'This slide rule is a piece of crap. Hit it with a hammer, throw it out the window, flush it down the toilet. It's useless. Buy a calculator – they're so much easier.'

For some reason, there had been a slight time delay – calculators had existed for almost two years but hadn't been allowed in schools. This is a kind of heresy – techno-heresy. Having a gadget for two years and not using it and then finally using it, even though it was a two-year-old gadget? Heresy. Pull out a two-year-old device now – an old iPhone or iPod or flip phone – and you could get shot for being so behind the times.

Marathon Man

Most of us think that while we are here on Earth if we eat cake and watch television, that's fine. That's what we're supposed to do. But that's not what our bodies are built for. I believe we can all do more than we think we can do. This is the conclusion I have come to, having done a bit more than I thought I could do.

In 2009, I already knew that I wanted do something challenging. I was at a point in my life when I wanted to do something a bit different. Initially I was already planning to do a long run, but then I hooked up with the UK charity Sport Relief, which had developed the unusual idea of asking people who are not very sporty to take on unusual sporting challenges.

I decided my challenge would be to run around the United Kingdom. All the way around. I would run back-to-back marathons for six days a week with the seventh day off to rest.

Quite unintentionally biblical.

I liked the idea of running marathons. There's determination, fortitude, and a great deal of bloody-mindedness involved in running a marathon. It is the easiest way to be in your own action movie.*

---

*The story of running marathons, though, is slightly less dramatic than a movie because you do the same thing every day.

Of course, I had no business running marathons – I wasn't trained, I wasn't particularly fit, and I had absolutely no experience in running anything that long, let alone running multiple marathons. But I was determined to do it anyway.

My plan was to set off in July of 2009 and run from capital to capital throughout the UK: from the capital of England to the capital of Wales, to the capital of Northern Ireland, to the capital of Scotland. So, from London to Cardiff to Belfast to Edinburgh, then back to London. I wanted to carry the flag of each country or province I was running in to make a statement of positivity with them. I also found it was useful to have the flag to wave at cars and large vehicles so that they wouldn't hit me. And there was a crazy additional idea to have an ice-cream van follow us and give out ice cream to people and kids we met along the way, in return for donations. The ice-cream van played the theme to *Chariots of Fire* to keep me inspired and to attract people to get ice creams. The people who donated this vehicle to help us were fantastic people. I thank them for their imagination.

I thought this whole thing was an adventurous plan, but I think the good people at Sport Relief felt I was a bit bonkers: not just because of the flags and the ice-cream van, but because I had not run for years and had never been a distance runner. And, given my schedule, I did not have much time to train for the challenge: I would have only six weeks to work with a trainer, Greg Whyte, who also probably thought I was crazy to think I could run over 1,100 miles in just under eight weeks.

I was a bit bonkers. But good bonkers. There is a difference.

The great thing about working with Sport Relief is that you can raise money, have an adventure, and put out a little human political message. The first message I wanted to share was that we are all different, but we are all the same. I ran with the four different flags of the different parts of the United Kingdom. I even invented a flag for Northern Ireland, which, if anyone knows the politics of Northern Ireland, is a very tricky thing to do. I came up with the bottle-green colour of the Northern Ireland football team, with the white dove of peace in the top-right corner. In the end, no one really hassled me for it, because they didn't recognize it as a flag that had anything to do with Northern Ireland. In any event, it was a reminder for me of the great home we'd had there when Mum was alive.

At the beginning of the challenge I was a complete mess. I suspected this would happen, but I kept at it and eventually figured out that it takes about ten marathons to train your body to run multiple marathons. After about the tenth marathon your mind and body sync up and they get you match-fit. The brain goes, 'Okay, let's do this. We're doing this one-marathon-a-day thing.' It also switches on faster body-healing abilities.

At one point, in the Lake District, some ultramarathon runners found me on my route and joined me to run for the day. I said to them that I initially had thought that endurance running was 70 per cent mental and only 30 per cent physical. I said that I had now come to the conclusion that it was 80 per cent mental and only 20 per cent physical.

They said to me, 'Actually the joke we have is, it's 90 per cent mental and the other 10 per cent . . . is in your head.' A nice joke, and when I thought about it, I agreed. It's the brain and our determination that decide what we will and won't do.

Ten marathons got me from London to the town of Brecon in Wales. After that it got mentally easier. By the twenty-third marathon or so I got to Scotland, which is at the top of the UK, if you're looking at a map. At that point, more than halfway through the forty-three marathons, I figured people would say, 'Oh look! He's run to the top of the UK, and it's all downhill from there.' Which is obviously nuts, but for some reason it made sense. What I was doing and the fact that I was actually doing it had finally become a reality to me – and maybe to the public as well.

Now all I had to do, then, was finish it off. Just twenty more marathons.

It wasn't easy. I started it on a wing and a prayer. My legs often felt like lead; my feet had blisters that re-blistered themselves. Blisters on top of blisters. Every morning I'd get up at six thirty, get into a hot bath as quickly as possible, eat porridge, have a leg massage, bandage my feet, and be out and ready to run by nine a.m. At the start of every day, I'd always think: *Okay, I'm going to get into the running zone today.* But after a few miles (particularly in the early days) I'd think it was bloody awful and wonder why I was doing it. Each night when I'd finished, I'd take a quick warm shower, then a fifteen-minute ice bath for muscle repair, which was an incredibly painful thing to endure. Then I'd eat as much as I could, watch a little TV, and go to bed usually with the help of a sleeping pill, since I was told that overtraining often interferes with your sleep.

I remember some interesting people running with me during that challenge, including an ex-marine who ran twenty-two miles with me. We talked about his background and what he'd been through, and as we talked, the distance seemed to disappear. I also met up with old performer friends when I had a day off in Edinburgh and decided to run up the famous landmark Arthur's Seat. Most of the time, though, I liked to run completely alone. But I was helped all along the way by Sarah Johnson, my tour manager, and Jo Denby, my sports therapist, who followed in the support van, mending me and keeping me going when things got tough. There was also the ice-cream van and at least two vans of documentary makers who were filming the challenge for BBC Three following as well. People often ask what I thought about when I was running: I took in the surroundings, huge vistas looking out over the landscape of England, Scotland, Northern Ireland, or Scotland. Running up to the top of Arthur's Seat in Edinburgh was one of the most memorable views of the adventure – you could see Scotland for miles – as was the Brecon Beacons in Wales. Or looking back toward Newtownards from the hills to the west of Belfast; and an incredible sunset when I got to Nottingham, after almost a complete day of rain.

I thought that I would slim down during that challenge but interestingly I didn't. I think it's because I was eating a high-carb, low-fat diet. At that time, people thought that was best. Things were changing around then, and the thinking became almost the exact opposite – that one should have a high-fat, low-carb diet when doing an endurance run. Now, you can eat butter again.

Completing this UK challenge – running forty-three marathons in fifty-one days – was one of the hardest things I'd ever done. But still not quite as hard as leaving my flat that first time in a skirt and heels. It was also one of the most rewarding things I've ever done. I helped raise £1.8 million – roughly $2.7 million – and we gave away ice-cream cones to lots of small children along the way, who had no idea why they were getting them.

I believe we should be running or exercising as adults as much as we were doing as kids. If natural animals stay fit all their lives, I think we should, too. I've now run more than seventy marathons for charity, and if I can do this sort of thing, anyone can.

We are all natural animals who came out of the trees two million years ago. We learned to walk erect, and then we gradually headed toward farming and then settlement building and civilization. But we are still all natural animals. Most of us don't think we are, or at least have forgotten that we are. In the wild, animals hunt or are hunted, so they all have supple and fit bodies that can stalk at a slow speed and then chase at a high speed (or just run and dodge like crazy). And they do that throughout their lives. They play when they're young, and they hunt (or escape) when they're older. Animals are always match-fit.

As kids, we play and we run about a lot. When we're adults, we think we shouldn't do this. We think it might be bad for us. Our knees. Our backs. As we get older, if we use some part of our body and it begins to hurt, we think,

Oh, that's wrong, I should not push on that, I should back off from it. But I think if something hurts when you are exercising, stopping may not be the answer. It could well hurt because you are not using it enough and if you got fit and used that part of the body regularly, then maybe it wouldn't hurt. The problem is, most people find something hurting and then give up all activity on that part of the body, deciding that they are maybe too old to do anything now. I think this thinking is back to front.

In February of 2016, I ran twenty-seven marathons in twenty-seven days in South Africa, in honour of Nelson Mandela and the twenty-seven years he spent in prison and to again raise money for the UK Sport Relief charity. The route I ran retraced his life geographically, starting in Mvezo, in Eastern Cape, where he was born, through to Robben Island, near Cape Town, where he was in prison, and ending up in Pretoria, on the steps of the Union Buildings, where he was sworn in as president. The route was 1,138 kilometers (707 miles), and because the weather was so hot there when I ran, it was an absolutely grueling experience. One day it got up to forty-one degrees centigrade (one hundred and six degrees Fahrenheit).

In 2012, I'd attempted the same challenge, but on the third day (marathon three), I'd started peeing brown and at the end of the fourth day I ended up in hospital, where I was diagnosed with rhabdomyolysis, a condition that causes the muscle tissue to break down and release muscle fibre into the bloodstream. Apparently, a prescription drug for slightly high cholesterol that I'd been taking did not agree with the severe terrain, humidity, and altitude I had encountered. Untreated rhabdomyolysis can lead to kidney damage or death, so on the advice of the doctors, I was forced to stop and give up on the challenge. It was a terrible disappointment to have to stop. It felt humiliating to not be able to continue, failing to make good on a promise I'd made. I took it quite hard and vowed to return and try again.

After a few times trying to go back, I finally returned in 2016, but this time, again after only four days, I had to stop and go to the same hospital I'd been to in 2012 in Queenstown, Eastern Cape. Over the next two days, I ended up changing my mind-set five times about whether or not I could keep going. As ultra running succeeds on the strength of your mind, changing your mind-set five times is incredibly hard to do.

I was running marathon four, not peeing brown, and feeling like I was doing better than I was doing four years ago. My sports doctor and friend, Dr Gary, had tested my blood a third of the way through the fourth marathon to see how everything was doing. At the end of that marathon, I felt okay. The Olympic-level sports therapist, Tim Cruse-Drew, had just tested my urine and it had tested clear. There was no blood in my urine, so we were very happy. About ten seconds later, Dr Gary phoned us and said the blood work was worrying. He wanted me to not run on day five and get another blood test.

On day five I felt bizarrely good, mainly because I wasn't actually running (it's always nice to get a day off), and my blood was tested in the Queenstown hospital. Then we had lunch, and at the end of lunch, Dr Gary phoned and said the blood work was looking better and allowed me to do a walking marathon on day six.

I thought, *Walk a marathon: That's fine. I'm back on. I'm not out of the challenge.*

The next day, I was very positive. The sun was shining, it was a brilliant African morning, we started at dawn. I was listening to Mozart's Clarinet Concerto in A major, which is a piece I used to play on the clarinet, and is in the film *Out of Africa* – it's the piece that Robert Redford plays to Meryl Streep and all the monkeys come and listen. So I was marching, marching, marching, but as we got through the halfway point of the marathon, the heat started getting really high – around thirty-five degrees centigrade (ninety-five degrees Fahrenheit).

By two-thirds of the marathon I was struggling, which was when my medical team – Tim, my physio, and Tony Wolfe, our medic – told the BBC Three producers who were filming the challenge that there was going to be a change in plans. They decided I needed to see a kidney expert, a nephrologist, at the big hospital in East London, to get my blood tested again.* I was not happy about this. I wanted to go on. But they thought I needed checking. So I stopped.

This was my fourth mind-set change.

The nephrologist at the hospital soon discovered that I was some bonkers person from the UK doing this crazy running challenge, and that it was a salute to Nelson Mandela. So he began to warm to the idea. 'I was about to go

---

*I'd never even heard of the word *nephrologist*.

348

home,' he said, 'but I'll stick around until your blood work is ready.' When he came back with the results, he said, 'It's okay. You can continue the run. But it's your hydration that's the problem, not your kidneys. You've got to keep the hydration up.' He had already set up a three-litre fluid drip, and he said, 'All this has to go into you before you can go, but you will be peeing all night.' In the end, I didn't pee at all, which I think proved that I had a hydration problem.

But this meant that the run was back on. It was my fifth mind-set change. I was definitely running twenty-seven marathons. Then I was not running any marathons. Then I was definitely running them. Then I was not running them and then I was back on – running the twenty-seven marathons. And that was over only two days – so it was really tough. Everything that happened in my life up to that point meant that I was focused on one idea: 'Let's bloody do it.' But those two days were a masterclass in motivation.

Part of what made it difficult was that by that point I had done four and two-thirds marathons in six days, which is a messy piece of mathematics to have in your head. The next day, I ran a marathon, which meant that I had done five and two-thirds marathons in seven days. I thought, *This is too confusing*. I felt I couldn't punch the sky and say easily, 'Hey, I've done five and two-thirds marathons in seven days!' It just felt confusing. The mathematics were really bugging me. Probably most people would not even consider this, but for me it was a psychological problem.

On the ninth day, having done six and two-thirds marathons in eight days, I decided – today I am going to do a marathon and a third so that at least I can be only a day behind schedule and clean up the mathematics in my head. Again, you can think this is bonkers, but for my mind it was necessary.

We were in Hogsback, in Eastern Cape, that day, which is very wild and beautiful. J. R. R. Tolkien is believed to have been inspired by stories of the amazing landscape of Hogsback – or maybe Hogsback was inspired by the amazing stories of J. R. R. Tolkien. There are mountains, and there are waterfalls, just like in the world of *Lord of the Rings*, and it's a great area except that it is home to a number of snakey snakes.

The camera team wanted to know about the snakes because they're dangerous and obviously you're looking for drama when you're shooting this kind of thing. Having been asked this by our producers, Nils, our South African guide, and his partner, who were showing us around, were talking a lot about the local snakes. Now, this was fine, except I didn't want to be running near snakes if they really were going to be an issue. I think I'm very much like Indiana Jones in this way (he hated snakes). I just didn't want to have to look out for them. I was trying to get through my marathons, trying to catch up on this extra third so that I could get to have completed eight marathons in nine days, and unless the snakes were going to be pace setters, I didn't want to have to think about them.

Apparently a puff adder bites so fast that if it were to bite a balloon it would have to bite the balloon twice before it exploded. Why a puff adder would be attacking a balloon I really don't know. Nils probably thought I was overly worried about the snakes, but the problem was that I just didn't know what level of worry to have about snakes and I didn't have any spare energy to put into that. So yes, I was worried about the snakes because I didn't know if their attack rate was one person a year or seven people a day.

I should mention that Nils also said they had no anti-venom. He also told me that if you do get bitten by a snake, the best thing to do is crawl to the side of the road and just wait for someone to come, because you've got to get your heartbeat down low enough so that your blood doesn't get pumped fast throughout your body: if it pumps fast it will spread the venom faster and kill you quicker. So the trick, ladies and gentlemen, to surviving a snakebite when you haven't got any anti-venom is to get yourself slowly back to a road and then wait for a car, otherwise you're a goner.

But should I have been worried about the snakes? I just didn't know how many snakes per kilometer there were. Do they climb up the trees? Surely I wasn't just being paranoid. In the end, I didn't see any snakes, but I'm sure there were between a hundred or a hundred and fifty of them just hiding behind trees and laughing at me in their snakey way.

We finished the first forty-two kilometers, the day's marathon, done by lunchtime. And later that day we drove to a town called Somerset East and we went up on to a high trail road to run the extra third of a marathon – fourteen kilometers. There was a beautiful sunset when we finished and that was a total of fifty-six kilometers (thirty-five miles) and the end of marathon eight on day nine. The mathematics were now good and I knew what the hell I was doing, so I was happy. It finally looked like the twenty-seven marathons might be possible.

In the end, after twenty-seven days, I completed the twenty-seven marathons, which was even more challenging because of the final day, when I had to do two marathons. Tim prepared me for that final day during my last four or five marathons, doing time trials within a marathon (running bits of the marathon at different speeds in order to test my ability to do a double marathon on the last day). This was very tricky to do – training me to get my speed up to a steady 7.5 kilometers per hour so that I'd be able to finish ninety kilometers in twelve hours (which was my cut-off point).

Tim and Dr Gary weren't sure I could do this. I said I would give it a damn good try. Not only would I be running two marathons – eighty-four kilometers (fifty-two miles) – in one day, but I'd also decided, as an additional tribute to South Africa, to do my final day like a Comrades Marathon, a ninety-kilometer run that takes place annually in South Africa. The Comrades Marathon is about six kilometers longer than two marathons put together, and it must be completed in under twelve hours.

Having made it pretty hard for myself, I somehow managed to do it all in under twelve hours. It was sheer bloody-mindedness that got me through – a lot of swearing and tension and looking at my watch obsessively to make sure I was keeping my speed up. I ran the first eighty-four kilometers in eleven hours and five minutes and managed to finish my twenty-seven marathons about three minutes before the live feed back to the UK was cut off. This probably raised an extra £500,000, as people could see the finish actually happening. But after finishing the eighty-four kilometres and doing some interviews and taking photographs, with my body seizing up after eleven hours of running, I still had the six kilometers to run to make it ninety kilometers.

I looked at Tim and he said, 'Well it's up to you.' Part of me was thinking, *Maybe I'll just knock it on the head – twenty-seven marathons in twenty-seven days is pretty good.* But then I thought, *No, I've come too far not to do it.* And I had only fifty minutes left to get it done. So as the sun went down over Pretoria, we went out in a group of about six of us, running the six kilometers in forty-five minutes – leaving ten minutes to spare. Eleven hours and fifty minutes for ninety kilometers. And the next day I rested.

In the end, we helped raise more than £2.6 million, which is roughly $3.2 million (at the point of writing).* That's amazing to me. And it felt very good to achieve that goal, having failed to do it only four years before. If I want to do something that feels important and someone says to me, 'You can't do it,' I will push against that. Unless someone is telling me, 'You can't jump out of an airplane without a parachute and live,' then I would say, 'Okay. You're absolutely right. I definitely can't do that.' I'm not desperate to simply win a challenge – I want to build something, to stake my confidence, to try and succeed and increase my confidence by challenging myself to do more than I think I can.

---

*If I had done it on my own, the amounts raised would have been much smaller, and I put a lot of the fund-raising down to Kevin Cahill and all the people at Sport Relief with their expertise at getting the message out and the charity donations in.

Touring the World

Having toured the world I can well see why one can find it pleasurable to be on a plane or a boat or a train and staying in hotels all around the world rather than being at home having to deal with a lot of day-to-day problems. At this stage of my life I am probably away more than I am home, having played forty-three countries so far, including all fifty states of the United States of America. I find going on tour, or going off working on location for a film, something I really look forward to. Traveling broadens the mind, while making more everyday problems seem far away (because they physically are).

When I was about fourteen, I said to my father, 'I am going to cycle to Wales.' We lived in Bexhill, in the southeast of England, at the time, so what I was proposing was to cycle about 310 kilometers (roughly 190 miles) to Skewen, near Swansea, in South Wales, where we'd lived before. This was a little bit bonkers (again, good bonkers?), but it seemed like a good adventure for someone my age.

In my mind, the main idea of me traveling across a country, though, was less about adventure and more about losing weight. My plan was to cycle a long way and become good and healthy.

I told my dad, 'I won't take any money, then I won't eat any food, so it'll be a really healthy trip.'

He said this was not a good idea. 'Why don't you take *some* money and a map?' So he gave me £50 and a Little Chef map.

Little Chef is a chain of roadside restaurants all across the UK known for their sausage, egg, and chips meals. The Little Chef map was a decent map of the country, but since it marked every sausage-egg-and-chips place across the UK, it would ensure that I could (and in fact would) cycle from one Little Chef restaurant to the next to the next.

Of course, I didn't have to do that, but I just thought, *Well, I'm cycling a long way, so I'm allowed to have something to eat and then maybe a dessert.*

I thought that because I was exercising I could treat myself to a dessert in every single restaurant. So I would order pancakes and ice cream with maple syrup on it. Which is just death on a plate. I think I might have put on more weight with the Little Chef map than I would have if I'd stayed home.

I did get all the way to Wales, and I did get to say hello to some people I knew who were still living in Skewen. Then I cycled back. It was an adventurous if uneventful trip, but I was away from home. All I had to do was phone home every night. I had a tent, so most nights I would just cycle up to a farmhouse and say, 'Can I sleep in one of your fields?' And they would say yes. I didn't think they would, but they did. They were very nice.

Later I found out that my father had done something very similar when he was my age, though his cycling holiday had ended on a more drastic note: he ran out of money entirely and had to cover a hundred and fifty miles in a single day and night to get home, falling asleep on the bike several times.

The first time I sort of toured in a show was when, still at Eastbourne College, in the Easter term of 1980, teacher Andrew Boxer gave me the great role of Stepan Stepanovich in Anton Chekhov's farce *The Proposal*. With him directing, I'd already played two smaller key roles in Shakespeare's *The Comedy of Errors* and in *Cabaret*. In 'The Proposal,' there were just three of us – Claire Isitt, Johnny Ohlson, and me – and even though it was a small play, it was a hit at school. I loved this play because it was great fun to do and also because of being able to try a ridiculously long comedic pause that got a great reaction. Stepan Stepanovich is trying to propose to his next-door neighbor's young daughter, but he keeps getting into arguments about trivial things with the young woman he's trying to propose to. He gets so furious at one point that he storms off, complaining of palpitations and being near death. When he does this, his neighbor says, 'Come back, come back, you must come back!' Stepan says that he won't come back. 'Please,' the neighbor says, 'you must come back!' But Stepan repeats, 'I will not come back, I will not come back, there is no way I'm coming back.' At this point I paused – but I went for the longest pause that I felt was possible – maybe ten seconds – before shouting out: 'All right! I'm coming back!'

This got a huge reaction. It made me realize what you could do with a comedic pause (or a dramatic pause). We were good enough to go on to tour the show. And by 'tour,' I mean that a whole bunch of us got into a minibus and off we went, on the road to just one other school – called Ton-bridge. We did this one extra performance of the show – on 'tour' – and it also got a great reaction at Tonbridge. I do remember being on cloud nine. I knew that this was where I wanted to be. Above all, that show locked it in. I repeated the role again at Sheffield Uni, with Kaite O'Reilly and Richard Parry – and with an even longer pause.

When I started doing decent stand-up, it got fun. When you are first doing stand-up, it's tough and you're not very funny. People don't laugh and they don't like what you're doing. But as it gets better, it gets to a more interesting and even fun place. Touring around the circuit was tough but enjoyable. As long as I got there on time and did a good gig it all worked well. I had fun, the audience laughed, and I got paid. But the bar was set quite high then and I was competing with all the other really good stand-ups in the country as well. Once I got off the circuit in early 1992 and started touring on my own, it felt even better. Doing stand-up is rather solitary, but I felt I could deal with that and at every show, I feel I meet an audience of old friends (and some new ones) and we all have a laugh – and it's in a theatre as well.

So after all the years of things not working out, finally I felt I was on a roll. I played bigger and bigger theatres, up until 2003, when I started playing arenas. These can be between six-thousand-and fifteen-thousand-seaters. At this point you travel around in a big tour bus and there's probably another tour bus for the crew who put up all the equipment and staging before you get to the arena. But it's fun as long as you can deal with the pressure, to have all this rolling along.

In America, initially, we flew from city to city: America

is so big that that's usually what you need to do. But you can get some very nice tour buses with good bunks for people to sleep in and the main act gets a double bed in a room of their own at the back of the bus, which is kind of amazing. I didn't even know that tour buses existed to such a high standard.

The great thing about a bus is it reduces your stress points. With flying, you have about five stress points: the first one is getting into a taxi and going to the airport; the second one is checking in at the airport on time; the third is going through security; the fourth is getting onto the plane; and the fifth is getting from the airport to your next hotel.

Touring by bus means there are only two stress points: leaving the hotel and then getting to the gig, or leaving the gig and then getting to the hotel.

When we play arenas in America or Europe, there are three buses: one for myself and the backstage crew, and two other buses for the crew that is setting up the equipment at the arenas. Three buses for transporting people and five trucks transporting equipment is the most I think we've had. We have a skilled crew that can go into places where people haven't toured much before – smaller cities in Wyoming, North Dakota, South Dakota, Arkansas, and Mississippi – and they can put together a great setup. I like to put a lot of production value into my stand-up shows – some people think doing this is crazy, as a stand-up show can often consist of just the performer standing there in front of a black curtain, talking into a microphone, but I think audiences appreciate the production values put in.

The three crew buses and five trucks may seem a bit crazy as well, but as someone who was 'creatively born' on the streets of London, it impresses the hell out of me. It feels like we're a small army. You're going on a comedy mission where everything's gearing up, and the whole team has got to be creative, flexible, and have the ability to improvise.

I've said this before, but I feel this maxim is true. When it comes to human beings, we are all totally different, but we are all exactly the same. Even if you're visiting tribes in the rainforest of Cameroon in Central Africa, as I did for the BBC when tracking my DNA back two hundred thousand years. There you will discover that even if you think they are totally alien to us, you'll soon realize that they're the same as we are, even if they're doing things in slightly different ways.[*]

I suppose this is obvious if you think about it: Two hundred thousand years ago we were ten thousand people and now we're seven billion people. And that number is increasing at a fast rate. In fact, if you look at what makes us all similar instead of looking to find what makes us different, you'll see that there is one thing that is the same for all of humanity:

And that is love.

Parental love, romantic love, familial love: love matches up wherever you are. If you're a loving parent, a loving child, a loving partner with a partner who loves you back, then that is the same all around the world. And you know

---

[*] I don't usually hunt for rats, for instance, the way some tribes there do. But if that was all that was available, then I'm sure that rat pie would be yummy.

that if you went into a native tribe and you saw love there, you wouldn't say, 'Oh, your love is totally different.' It would be the same thing, and people would fight to defend the people who they loved.

Here's a story about how I came to feel like a European, as well as being proud of being British. This explains how I began to feel connected to the world around me, rather than separated from it, and what really inspired me to perform around the world, especially in different languages.*

Years ago, I was on holiday on one of the Greek islands. I was on a boat, out in that beautiful blue Mediterranean water, when the captain announced that the water was very warm and that we could all dive off and swim in it if

---

*I decided to do my stand-up comedy in other languages because I felt it was better to show the connections between the peoples of the world rather than the differences. At the time of this writing in 2016, political forces seem to be conspiring to pull the world into separate pieces again. Put up brick walls, encourage hatred between peoples and nations. The only end point in all of this is taking us back to the 1930s, and we know what happened back then.

So I initially thought, *If I could do my stand-up comedy in French, surely that would be a positive thing.* In the end, to do this was not that physically hard; it just took a hell of a lot of work and imagination. I got an A grade in my O-level French exam that I took when I was sixteen years old. That meant that I was pretty good at writing French but not very good at French conversation. I attempted my first show in French back in 1997 at La Flèche d'Or (the Golden Arrow) in Paris. This was a terrible show and it is in the *Believe* documentary. It was so difficult just to do five minutes in French and I was totally stressed out. But the next year I did one week in Paris, all in French, and in 2000 I did two weeks in French, at La Boule Noire, a club underneath La Cigale – a very famous Parisian theatre. I realized that the only way to get good at doing my show in French was just to do a hell of a lot of them. So I vowed to come back and do my show for three months in Paris. It took me until 2011 to make the time to do this, but in April of 2011 I played Paris at Le Théâtre de Dix Heures for three months. This show took me over the line. It made me a lot more confident in speaking French and then performing in French. In the end, that's all you need to do – lots and lots of shows. But I must admit that, until that point, no promoter really thought it was going to work.

In 2015, I did a tour of France, playing to over 5,200 people in the French language. This is a beautiful thing to do, two hundred years after the Battle of Waterloo, and I am very happy to have finally got to that point. I will continue to build from here.

we wanted to. Everyone seemed a bit confused – *Really? What? We just jump off the boat? In our clothes?* – and the boat seemed a little too high off the water for jumping in. But then one person jumped in. Then another person jumped in. And I jumped in, too. People from all over the world were jumping into the perfect blue water, swimming around together, shouting to each other in lots of different languages – Spanish and French and German and English and Greek and so many more – and I remember thinking to myself, *Wow, these are young Europeans, right here, right now. All having fun.*

I thought: *This is really good. I like this. This is worth fighting for.*

I also realized that back in the late 1930s, other Europeans might have done the same thing, but then they would have gone home, put on uniforms, and started killing each other in WWII. That thing that we used to do in Europe. So when I came home, I of course did absolutely nothing at all about it. Now many people wish to fight for a political issue. If your issue concerns climate change, you can join a climate change pressure group; if you're trying to save the whales, then you can join one of the pressure groups to help save the whales. But what could I do? I didn't know yet. Eventually it hit me: I could do performances in other languages. I could try to connect with as many people as possible, no matter what country they were from and what language they spoke, and show that we could all communicate all around the world because in the end, we're all human and we all have the capacity to love.

Love is universal and love is the same for all human

beings. We should all have the ability to love (do we?), and I really hope that love is stronger than hate, even though with Brexhate in Britain and Trump-hate in America in 2016, it does seem that hate this time has been more powerful than love, as it was back in the 30s.

But for me I decided, on that day, swimming around in that beautiful water in Greece, with people speaking all those languages, we are all worth fighting for. Running and hiding and separating, building walls, hating the Muslims, hating the Jews, hating immigrants – none of this builds a better world. The twenty-first century is a key century for us on this planet. Either we make a world, where all seven billion people have a fair chance in this century – or forget it. If we can't do this, I don't think we are going to make it as a species. Despair is the fuel of terrorism, and hope is the fuel of civilization, so we have to put more hope into the world than despair. Hatred and separation and building walls is not the way to progress. Going backwards is not the way to go forwards.

I consider myself a spiritual atheist. I don't believe in a god but I believe in us – human beings. And I believe there is more goodwill than ill will in the world. If you look at all the religions in the world, they have broadly two components: there are that religion's philosophies and rules for life (which you can agree with or disagree with – applying one's common sense), and then on top of them there is a mysticism. A mystical god that you can never see or meet. If you remove the mysticism, then there are just the philosophies and rules for life that you can agree with or disagree with. I encourage you to remove the mysticism and just apply common sense to the ideas. And there is a rule in every major religion, called the Golden Rule. Essentially: treat other people the way you'd like to be treated yourself. If we all did this, the whole world would work instantane- ously. Praying, meditation – fine. But just follow the Golden Rule and the whole world works. Making the world work could be that simple.

A Theory of the Universe

Normally, one should be a super-brained person, already proven in the area of universe theories, to have a theory of the universe. Well, I just thought I'd throw one in there.

If you are a professor of the Theory of the Universe department at the University of Cambridge/Oxford/Harvard/Yale, you're expected to come up with theories of the universe. If you work in a fish-and-chip shop, you're not. But it's a free world, if at times rather expensive. I should mention that the guy who came up with the idea of plate tectonics was not the head of the Plate Tectonics Department at the University of Big Pants. He was a German meteorologist, which is a scientist – but a sky scientist and not a ground scientist. But even so, he was much better qualified than I to come up with a theory to try to explain the universe (or the planet, or just stuff), although he died before everyone had accepted his huge shifting-plates theory.

Obviously, I am not one of these super-brained people. I've proven nothing in the area of universe theories, but I still have a theory of the universe. So I thought I'd tell you it anyway. And I should say that this theory could already be out there, if so – sorry.

I come to my theory as someone who is curious about all aspects of our world and universe. And as someone who has a relentless drive for 'universal logic.' To me, universal logic is the idea that there is a certain logic pertaining to all things in the universe. Okay. Now the theory itself:

Flash back five hundred years to the 1500s, the time of King Henry VIII of England, and we tell three people in a room to go off in three different directions. We tell them to get a compass, choose a direction, and hold that direction – to go around buildings and get on boats and climb over mountains. And we say to them back in the 1500s, 'If you do this for a long enough time, you'll come back to the same point.'

Five hundred years ago people would have said, 'You are mad, you are insane.' The religious people would have said, 'That is against God, you are a heretic, let's burn you right now.' The scientific people (or non-religious people) back then would have said, 'Well, that is a theory, but it doesn't make any logical sense. That goes against our sense of universal logic because how can you go along the flat Earth in one direction and then come back in the opposite direction? You would have to be living on a round ball.'

Five hundred years later, the present day, we now know that we are living on a round ball, but that couldn't be imagined or explained or even drawn back then. Now we can imagine it, explain it, and draw it – using gravity and lots of crayons. It's still a little difficult to explain, that people in the country exactly underneath where you are on the planet are actually walking around upside down (to us) and having no problems with it at all. Planes are taking off upside down, people are drinking coffees upside down, it's all going on upside down to you, but they think *you're* upside down. But because of Captain Gravity, it's all a happy-bunny scientific fact. And this scenario would happen on any ball planet anywhere. It will happen on the moon when we get our colonies there.

But from that starting point, if we take a similar three people and take them into outer space (outside our solar system) and then send *them* off saying, 'Go off in absolutely any direction, in any plane.' I think if they travel long enough, they'll also all come back to the same place.

That's what I think happens. This is me applying my own universal logic.

Can I do equations for it? No. Can I prove it? No. Can I get a compass and a ruler and show it? No. But if that's what's happening on a planet, I think that's what's happening in the universe.

This theory leans into the edge-of-the-universe problem. That there is no edge of the universe. There can't be an edge of the universe. That's always been a huge question: Where does the universe end?

Maybe it doesn't end. Maybe the whole universe wraps back on itself (just like our planet wraps around on itself).

That does get rid of an inconvenient problem (if not an inconvenient truth). There just cannot be a wall in space. You can't get to the edge of the universe and then find there's a squirrel there with a gun saying, 'Oh, don't come in here, we haven't worked this bit out yet.' It just can't be.

But if the universe wraps around on itself, no matter which direction you go in, that's more logical to me even though I can't draw it (I have tried to draw it, and it's lots and lots of circles going on and on and on in many different directions). But it does make sense to me that the universe folds back on itself in a curved way, because everything in the universe seems to be made up of curves.

All the planets are curved, all the trajectories are curved, the suns are curved, the solar systems are curved, the galaxies are curved. Every frigging thing is curved. The comets move in a curved trajectory. Space-time is curved. So I think everything in the universe curves and comes back on itself.

We no longer talk about the edge of the Earth, because we know the world isn't flat. Five hundred years ago they did talk about that. But today we never comment on the fact that there's no edge of the Earth. In fact, if you forget the magnetic poles, anywhere you are on the Earth is actually a centre of the Earth. One can say, 'I'm here in South Africa, and this for me, at this moment, is the centre of the Earth.' And if you live there, it will be. And so is Great Britain, and so is America, so is China, so is anywhere.

Now, a clever guy called Mr Hubble came up with a telescope, and he looked at all the galaxies with his big telescope and said, 'They're all moving away from us. The universe is expanding.'

If we apply my big, crazy theory here, we could say that if the Big Bang caused all the galaxies to move away from each other, maybe they're going around the back of the universe until they come back around and go into the Big Crunch (the opposite of the Big Bang). And if a Big Crunch condenses things and smashes things together, maybe that will cause another Big Bang. And maybe that's how it goes – Big Bang, Big Crunch, Big Bang, Big Crunch – like a heartbeat, that goes on and on, and that will go on and on forever.

Above all, in my theory of the universe, there is no god, no one controlling anything, no one planning anything. It just is.

Is this difficult for you? Well, people say that their god just 'is.' So we're in the same place.

Some people might say, 'God created it all.' But then did he just get up early in the morning and create himself before he went and created everything else? Using a boomerang magic wand.

'No, I don't want to let that go, I want cold, hard facts.'

Well, there are no cold, hard facts about gods, and we haven't got cold, hard facts about a lot of the universe. So maybe the Big Bang– Big Crunch– Big Bang heartbeat will make some sort of sense to you, some sort of universal logic, the way it does to me.

That is essentially a theory of the universe that seemed interesting to me.

People also talk about the Goldilocks Theory, which says that if the Earth were any closer to the sun we would burn up, and if it were any farther away from the sun we would freeze to death. Some people say this is proof that there is a god and that he/she/it has placed us here, in this perfect spot.

Or maybe this is just our planet's moment in the eons and eons of time that the Earth has been here and that it just happens to be we're having this existence right now. And therefore what we do on this planet, how we behave on this planet, is up to us. That no god is going to come down and help us, because if you look at the number of times that a god has come down and helped out human beings when there has been a tragedy or catastrophe – be it an earthquake, a tsunami, or a world war – the number of times that any god has come down to Earth and helped us is zero.

Absolutely zero.

There is no time that any god has ever come down and ever helped anyone – ever. No god has ever stood on the Earth and said, 'I'm here, I'm God – I've come with some angels and I've brought soup.'

People can say, 'Oh, we prayed and then this positive thing happened and that was because of God.'

But no. I don't believe so. World War II – that was the one perfect time for a god to come down and help us. That was the time when horrible, disgusting human behavior was happening, behavior that couldn't even be imagined was happening, and still a god didn't come down then. He didn't pop down, send a message via a bloke with wings to say, 'God here. Sorry, I hear there's some really evil stuff going on. But it's okay. I'm just going to take that Hitler guy out, because he's just a mass-murdering f@#khead.'

But that didn't happen. And it hasn't happened in the many, many awful times before or since. Which is why I feel, guys, that it's up to us. We're on our own. We have to sort the world out ourselves. Because if you look at the history of civilization, it has been human beings that have helped other human beings down through the ages – not gods helping human beings.

Some people say I am a nonbeliever. But I *am* a believer: I believe in humanity. I believe in people. I believe in our ability to make the world a better, more compassionate, and more civilized place. What I just don't believe in is the floaty guy in the sky.

Maybe I'm wrong. Maybe he's going to come down – or she's going to come down – and prove me wrong. I hope so. And if even one person – just one, out of the billions upon billions of people who have died in the history of the world – reached heaven and then got a message back from the clouds, saying, 'It's fine, it's here. There's a heaven, it's like a spa, they do massages,' then we would all change our minds.

Until then, I believe all we need when it comes to religion is this one simple ideal: treat other people as you would like to be treated yourself. Follow the Golden Rule.

The concept is in all of the major religions, and all major religions start from a good place, until some bastards come along and twist the meaning.

But if any god, from absolutely any religion, ever came down, then we would all be at their church/synagogue/mosque the next day, the next hour, and that church/synagogue/mosque would be packed. That religion will have won.

So anyway, our universe started roughly thirteen and a half billion years ago. If it started with a Big Bang, maybe it will all smash together again in a Big Crunch and restart again with another Big Bang.

A bit like a massive Etch-A-Sketch universe with somebody shaking it.

Only nobody's shaking it. Because there is no god.

If there were a god, surely they would have said the following sentence in a bible or any religious book: 'It's a round thing – that planet thing you're standing on is, in fact, a big round ball.'

And they would have said, 'There's lots of other worlds I've made, and some of them have hydrochloric acid as an atmosphere. Isn't that weird?'

And they would have said, 'My partner is called Shirley,' or, 'I'm not married,' or they would have written an autobiography, like I'm trying to do now.

They would have done these things.

Even if god were a huge turkey sandwich, it would have done these things.

So all in all, do pray for good things to happen in the world, but in the end I think it's up to us. Good luck to us.

The End of the Beginning

So we are at the end of the book now. It's time, I'm told, to wrap things up, draw some conclusions, tell some final truths, and say good-bye. I'm not very good at good-byes.

I try not to bother people. I'm sure that sounds weird, but it's true. I rarely phone people up to hang out. By calling them and asking them to go somewhere or do something or spend time with me, I feel I would be bothering them.

I find it easier to socialize with people I'm working with. Because in that way, everyone is getting something out of it. You're working together, but then you can back off and have your own time, where you don't have to be getting in each other's way. My dad and I are quite similar in this way – he didn't develop a huge social network, either, though he did have three marriages, and the nine years with my mother were, I know, very special to him.

There are people I've met that I haven't seen for ages, and I love spending evenings with them. But I don't over-push it. I under-push it, and maybe that's wrong. People have said to me, 'Come and hang out,' and sometimes I don't, and it's stupid of me. It's a failing of mine.

Maybe it all goes back to being young and not being in the most popular group in school. I didn't expect to be a part of that most popular group, but I suppose the feeling of being an outsider lingers. Even in my stand-up days there were two big social groupings and I wasn't part of either of them. But I was happy to float between the two.

I think I have always felt that I can exist on my own just fine. That maybe I had to. Losing your mum when you're six and going off to boarding school doesn't really give you a choice in that matter. Knowing you're transgender from an early age doesn't help, either. It just increases the divide: there's the world, and here I am, just a little bit different.

There's also the fact that I've always tried to do things with my life that impressed me and that I thought were interesting. I like to do things that make me personally go, 'I really don't know how I did that.' And I've always had a gut instinct that if you're part of a big social group and you say to them, 'Hey – I am going to run twenty-seven marathons in twenty-seven days,' they'll say, 'No, you're not, you big twit. No one does that.' My motto is: 'If you shoot for the stars, you could reach the moon.'

So I've kept a little bit of distance. I've never wanted to be talked out of my dreams. And you have to work hard to make your dreams come true.

Then there's the fact that friendships can end, and I don't like endings. Time moves on, proximity and distance change, and sometimes even really strong friendships don't last. That happens all the time, I suppose. A natural progression. Some people make friends and they are close for the whole of their lives and that's fantastic. But my experience has been different, perhaps because of the demands of my chosen career, the constant travel; perhaps because of the way my early life started, with Mum being taken away and everything before feeling suddenly lost: one minute my world as I knew it was there, and then it wasn't. Something about people coming and going in my life, the impermanence and uncertainty of people, has made me gravitate even more toward the security of never wanting to be surprised. Back in 1968 I was more surprised than I thought I ever could be and I never wanted that to happen again.

And then there is the question of relationships. There is always the question of relationships. I've spent so much time trying to get my career going that now, after so many years, really good dramatic roles are coming my way and the comedy career (touring the world in different languages) is off the charts, but I haven't got my personal life sorted out very well. I suppose that I do worry that if I spent more time on personal relationships and hanging out with friends that my career would start going backwards.

I guess I've always suspected, but don't think it's true, that you can do one or the other successfully, but doing both is very tricky. It's not so easy. It's a balancing trick. Like staying up on a unicycle and juggling cats. Trying to get it all working at the same time.

But I try not to regret anything. I feel that regret is a useless emotion. It's a useless space to be in because if we cannot change something, what's the point of wishing we could?

However, I do regret that my mother died. I regret that very strongly. But out of the things that I've personally done, I'm not really sure I have any regrets. Somebody actually asked me that question after a speech I gave: 'What do you feel you have done wrong in your life?' But I wasn't sure what exactly to say. There are a number of things that I have done in life and failed at, but you learn from the failures: you regroup, go back, and try again. And this is how you build your character. Do I regret anything? Because I went through street performing and sketch comedy and it was ten years before anything worked? I don't regret that, because it's made me tough as nails. I know I've got a ten-year stamina. I know things can be tough for ten years and I can still hang in there and come through. There are some plans I've got that haven't happened yet, but I'm still in there, encouraging them forward. The dramatic acting career is just beginning to really come through, and it's been over twenty years to get to this point.

But I'm happy playing the long game. Sometimes you have to wait a long bloody time for the long game to work, and most people don't even know if and when you're playing the long game. A good promoter friend of mine once commented on my career, saying roughly, 'You really climbed up that bloody mountain, didn't you?' I assume he had tracked what I was doing in my career over the years and had seen that I hadn't been helicoptered in to where I was. I'd hacked my way up the mountain. I feel I am still hacking my way up the mountain. Which is kind of a pain in the ass when you're doing it, especially when you're starting off. But in the end, if this is what you have to do, you do it. You can learn many things in life, but these could be the most important: stamina, patience, and determination. So do I regret leaving my degree in accounting? No. Do I regret doing those early, dodgy sketch shows or losing my confidence while street performing? No. Do I regret coming out? Absolutely not.

Because it has all led me here, to where I want to be. Performing comedy around the world, filming with really good actors, running multiple marathons, and being a political activist. But especially the film acting.

I've always loved acting. If everyone is trying to be invited to the party, then I definitely feel invited to the party when I'm filming on a production – a film or television drama. The amount of effort, the attention to detail, the amount of work, the skill, the number of people it takes to accomplish what you're trying to do – again, it's like a small military operation. But instead of fighting with guns and trying to push back an army, you're fighting with creativity and pushing back the boringness of everyday life to create moments of heightened emotion – of drama.

If you get it right, people will watch it at the theatrical release, and they'll watch it on their televisions and computer screens. If you get it really right, they will watch it forever. It will repeat and repeat for the rest of time. Films can live forever. People get excited when you come to town to do a play or perform stand-up, but when you come to shoot a film – that is the pinnacle. That's Mount Olympus with all the Greek gods on top – eating ice cream.

Instead of creating moments of heightened emotion and drama, writing this book has been an attempt to explain what actually has happened in my life. It's been a way for me to say, 'Would you like to have a chat where you never get a word in edgewise?' Hopefully it's explained the place where I've come from and indicates the direction that I'm going in. I do think that because my stand-up is rather rambling that most people thought I rambled to this place in life. It hasn't been a ramble. I always knew what direction I wanted to go in, it just took a hell of a long time to get it going.

I hope I haven't bothered you. I've tried not to. I hope you understand a little more about what I believe in.

Because believe me when I say – we can all do more than we think we can do. All I did was apply that to myself.

And if you believe in humanity, please do this, too.

Thank-you.

Acknowledgements

I'd also like to thank all the people who have helped me in many ways, for many years: Sarah Townsend at Ella Communications; Caroline (Chiggy) Chignell and Peter Bennett-Jones from PBJ Management; Nicky Van Gelder at Conway Van Gelder Grant; Max Burgos at APA; Arnold Engelman and Natalie Portelli at Westbeth Entertainment; Mick Perrin, Nick Handford, and Sarah Johnson at Mick Perrin Worldwide; Rachael Downing (makeup artist); Tanya Cookingham (makeup artist); Jennifer Meyerson (football trainer); Karon Maskill at Karon Maskill PR; Ina Treciokas at Slate PR; Kevin Cahill at Comic Relief and Sport Relief; sports therapists Tim Cruse-Drew and Jo Denby; Nick Catliff and all at Lion TV; Michael Harris, UK Business Affairs; and Scott Jeffers, USA Business Affairs.

Photo Credits

Pages 1–8: Courtesy Eddie Izzard

Page 9, top left and right: Courtesy Eddie Izzard; bottom: courtesy Steve Double

Page 10, top right: Courtesy Mick Perrin Worldwide; top left and bottom: courtesy BBC Picture Publicity

Page 11, top: Courtesy Eddie Izzard; bottom left: courtesy Mick Perrin Worldwide; bottom right: courtesy Eddie Izzard

Page 12, top: Courtesy Amanda Searle; bottom: courtesy Mick Perrin Worldwide

Page 13, top and middle: Courtesy Amanda Searle; bottom: courtesy Tanya Cookingham

Page 14, top and middle: Courtesy Mick Perrin Worldwide; bottom: courtesy Kevin Winter/Getty

Page 15, top: Courtesy Zelda la Grange; bottom five photos: courtesy Amanda Searle

Page 16: Courtesy Alfie Hitchcock